The
Resilient Child

Preparing Today's
Youth for
Tomorrow's World

The Resilient Child

Preparing Today's Youth for Tomorrow's World

Joanne M. Joseph

Foreword by
Dr. Irwin Redlener

PERSEUS PUBLISHING
Cambridge, Massachusetts

Library of Congress Cataloging-in-Publication Data

Joseph, Joanne M.
    The resilient child · preparing today's youth for tomorrow's world
/ Joanne M. Joseph ; foreword by Irwin Redlener.
        p.   cm.
    Includes bibliographical references and index.
    ISBN 0-306-44646-4
    1. Resilience (Personality trait) in children.   2. Self-esteem in
children.   3. Child rearing.   I. Title.
BF723.R46J67   1994
649'.1--dc20   94-2282
                                                                   CIP

10 9 8 7 6 5 4 3 2 1

ISBN 0-7382-0568-0

© 1994 Perseus Publisher
Published by Perseus Publishing
A Member of the Perseus Books Group

Printed in the United States of America

To my grandparents,
Attaf and Diab Joseph
and
Nementala and Jeannette Moses
for establishing the resilient standards in our family

To my parents,
Tom and Louise Joseph
for reinforcing those standards

To my husband,
Michael Moore
for helping me maintain the standards

Foreword

This is a book about self-esteem and resiliency in children. It is, therefore, also a book about our future.

Consider two questions:

1. What does a parent or a teacher *really* have to do with the future?
2. What difference does an individual child's well-being, or self-esteem, or ability to manage change and realize his or her innate potential actually make in the long-term stability and growth of our society?

The answers: everything, and all the difference in the world.

Ultimately, the "success" of our society—and perhaps the capacity of the human species to prevail on this planet—will depend on our ability to protect the future. Part of the challenge has to do with how we handle a host of environmental concerns. But the most important factors relate to how well we nurture and prepare each generation of children to function in an increasingly complex world.

Most informed people now recognize the necessity to preserve the environment and safeguard natural resources. We are aware that, at our current levels of consumption, nonreplenishable energy sources will eventually cease to be sufficiently available. We fear contamination of land and water with toxic wastes. Indeed, there is general agreement that protecting the *physical* environment must have our serious attention.

Yet there is also a case to be made that the future of our society will be at least as dependent on the productivity, creativity, and general well-being of *people* as it is upon the protection of the environment. If we are to survive and grow, *people* must face the challenges, adapt to new conditions, and deal with the consequences of forces within and external to our control.

Who will ensure that as many people as possible are prepared to assume the responsibilities of family, community, and the nation in the next generation? Society and government clearly have important roles here. Programs are created to support children; school systems are developed and enhanced to educate children; and laws are passed to protect children. Yet none of this matters if *individual* children are not given the opportunity to reach their full potential or not supported properly as they learn to effectively deal with challenges.

These principles apply to *any* child, regardless of family income or background. A child from a well-to-do family can be just as disempowered, just as vulnerable to adversity, just as unfulfilled as a child in poverty. The principles presented in this book are designed to enhance self-esteem and build confidence in all children (and all parents).

On the other hand, the severity of the challenges confronting impoverished families can be staggering. Since 1987 The Children's Health Fund has been operating mobile health programs for children otherwise unable to secure a regular source of appropriate medical attention. Most of these children are not properly immunized; many have untreated medical conditions that interfere with growth, development, or school work. Too many of these children have health problems that will block their ability to become fully effective and productive members of society.

There are several observations we have made. First, many of these children have problems that are manageable or correctable with the kind of basic medical attention to which most middle-class Americans are accustomed. Second, the parents of these children, including those trying to survive in the horrendous welfare hotels of our large cities, care deeply about the safety and the future of their children. I have seen parents under these circumstances, as well as parents in economically devastated parts of West Virginia, not eat for days on end in order to make sure there is enough food for their children.

Finally, in our work with families at the bottom rungs of America's economic ladder, we see children with enormous potential. Some will make it in spite of horrible living conditions, neighborhoods teeming with violence, and overcrowded, underfunded schools. These are survivors. They are children who have been raised by intuitively bright, highly courageous, and dedicated parents. These children have become, as Joanne Joseph would describe them: resilient. And indeed they are.

Yet what distresses us greatly are the many children we see who have great promise but little chance of fulfilling their inherent human potential. This is a tragedy for them, their families, and, ultimately, our society. For this reason, we have begun to expand our health services. We couple medical care with developmental assessment, parent training, educational placement, and other related services.

There is hope in all of this. The future of the country is, in fact, interlocked with the future of children. With great insight and clarity, this book lays out a unique prescription for making sure that each and every child in America reaches his or her maximum level of well-being, productivity, and creativity. Most importantly, this book is written precisely for people who can really make a difference: parents and teachers.

Every child is born with the capacity to dream. It might be said that this country was founded on the principle that dreams can be transformed into meaningful opportunities. For those adults who have the good fortune of being able to influence a child's ability to fulfill dreams, this book will serve as an enormously useful guide.

IRWIN REDLENER, M.D.
Associate Professor of Pediatrics,
Director, Community Pediatrics
Montefiore Medical Center-Albert Einstein College of Medicine;
President, The Children's Health Fund

Preface

If you were to describe the characteristics of an individual most likely to succeed, what would those characteristics be? Most people respond to this question with words and phrases such as goal-directed, self-motivated, self-directed, able to cope with life, self-confident, likable, cheerful, persistent, independent, creative, optimistic, good at communicating, and self-disciplined. I am sure you will agree that this is a lengthy list—but all of these traits can be summed up in two general characteristics: positive self-esteem and resilience.

Self-esteem, broadly defined, is a person's own attitude toward self. Successful persons perceive themselves as worthwhile, effective, and generally likable. This positive perspective is associated with achievement, leadership roles, and physical and mental health.

Resilience refers to the individual's ability to adjust and adapt to the changes, demands, and disappointments that come up in the course of life. Consider this example: John and Mark are informed by their parents that they will be moving. Upon hearing the news, John begins to wet his bed and pick fights with everyone around him. In contrast, Mark initially verbalizes sadness about leaving his friends and school but soon becomes excited about the prospect of making new friends and exploring new places. John is not coping well with the news of the move; Mark is.

John is already showing signs of distress; Mark appears resilient and ready for the challenge of the move.

Researchers in the field of stress tell us that good adaptive abilities make a person resilient to stress. A resilient individual is able to succeed in the face of change and adversity. The question is, What makes an individual successful and resilient? What contributes to positive self-esteem and good coping skills? Is a child born successful and resilient, or does the environment shape the adult personality?

The answer is not simple or straightforward. How a person functions is determined by the person's genetic makeup and by the kind of experiences he or she has during the formative childhood years. Families with more than one child are reminded frequently of the uniqueness of each of their children. One child is gifted musically, difficult to deal with, and high-strung while the other is mathematically inclined, social, and easygoing. Both children reside in the same environment, with the same opportunities, disadvantages, and caretakers. Why the difference? Well, behavioral geneticists who study the differences between individuals conclude that one's genetic makeup sets the outer limits for ability and aptitude. Genetics also explains some of the temperamental differences between individual personality types. In some cases it also predisposes or places individuals at risk for certain disorders. Genes, however, do not guarantee the development of the successful or resilient personality. Nor do they preclude the development of self-esteem or coping skills. Whether children realize their genetic potential, view themselves positively, and develop resilient coping skills depends on a host of factors that we personally have control over. A child who has a potential for math (or anything else) cannot develop this potential if he or she is not given the opportunity or encouragement to do so. Similarly, a child who is difficult is not necessarily destined to be an unhappy and nonproductive adult. Parents, teachers, and other significant individuals for the child do influence how the child develops. This influence comes in the form of teaching children attitudes and skills that promote the development of self-esteem and good coping skills.

Just how can a parent, teacher, or other person significantly affecting children go about this monumental task? The chapters that follow address this question by providing information, techniques, and suggestions for building self-esteem and good coping skills.

JOANNE M. JOSEPH

Acknowledgments

My sincere appreciation goes first to my husband, Michael Moore. This book would not have been possible without his technical expertise with word-processing systems and his never-ending patience and support. I also thank Dr. George Searles and Dr. Michael Spitzer for the editing support given during this project and Dr. Brian Bower, Dr. Geofrey Simon, Mrs. Lindsey Simon, Ms. Kathy Davis, Ms. Sharon Abelove, Ms. Ellen Short, Ms. Tracey Miller, Ms. Mary Paul, Ms. G. Shears, Ms. Marie Duink, Ms. Janice Kapps, Ms. Joan Kelley, Ms. Dawn Campion, Ms. D. Roberts, Ms. M. Dziura, Ms. Carol Gifford, Ms. P. Paruke, Ms. J. Chandler, Mr. A. Pollock, Ms. Janet Blando, Ms. T. Soren, Ms. J. Kearns, Ms. P. Gale, Ms. B. Manfredo, Ms. A. Dean, Ms. L. Simpson, Ms. Mary Wilcox, Dr. Maria Berne, Dr. Marsha Mirkin, Dr. Marybeth McCall, and Dr. Brad Bennett for the time they spent reading and commenting on early drafts of the manuscript. Last, I thank my children, Katie, Jessie, and Alex, for all the times they lighten my load with their humor, patience, and words of encouragement.

Contents

Chapter 4

PROMOTING SELF-ESTEEM AND RESILIENCE: THE
ROLE OF PARENTING 95

Chapter 5

STORIES: A NATURAL WAY TO TEACH RESILIENT
VALUES AND ATTITUDES 135

Chapter 1

Self-Esteem

Who comes to mind when you think of a successful person? I think of my immigrant grandparents, who despite overwhelming odds built businesses and established themselves in this country with little or no material resources. I think of a volunteer fire fighter who spends his days working at the factory and his spare time at the fire station. I think of my daughter's first-grade teacher, who viewed her role as more than just a job and put forth the extra effort to instill in her students a real love for learning. I think of a Down syndrome child who won an award in a local Special Olympics. I recall an oncology patient who refused to allow the cancer to interfere with her goals, graduating summa cum laude from college six months before dying at age 58. And, finally, I think of Thomas Jefferson, Marie Curie, Mother Teresa, and Eleanor Roosevelt.

What do all of these people have in common? Productivity: contributing in a tangible way to their own self-development and to the betterment of their communities and of society. Researchers who study productive personalities find that they share a number of specific qualities. Productive people generally have high self-esteem.[1] They are responsible, self-controlled, imaginative, re-

---

[1]There are some individuals who are productive but who have poor self-esteem. They are *driven* to be successful and as a result they are not always happy or healthy.

sponsive to the needs of others, good at problem solving, and unlikely to give up on themselves or others. They are *not* necessarily intellectually superior. In fact, research shows that IQ, as measured by standard intelligence tests, is not highly correlated with productivity (Gilmore, 1974).

Success can be defined in terms of productivity. One person may be successful as a teacher, another as a homemaker. Accomplishments may be large (such as a major discovery) or small (like an A on a high school math test). A series of small accomplishments can result in a much larger one; for example, a series of good grades in high school may result in an academic scholarship or admittance to the college of your choice. To be successful you do not have to be brilliant or exceptionally talented. In general, each one of us has the potential to be productive in some way. What facilitates productivity is a positive sense of self-esteem and the ability to deal effectively with change and adversity.

Self-Esteem Defined

Self-esteem is your attitude about yourself. It is your estimate of how capable, worthwhile, and successful you are. Self-esteem is distinctly different from conceit. A conceited person has an insecure and unrealistic estimation of self and in order to maintain this inflated sense of worth needs to see others as less capable and expert. Conceit is generally a sign of poor self-esteem. In direct contrast, persons with positive self-esteem perceive themselves realistically. They own up to their strengths and weaknesses and are not driven to compare themselves to others or devalue the success of those around them.

How do you know if someone has positive self-esteem? Usually you can tell by how people carry themselves and behave. People from Western cultures who have high self-esteem stand straight, have no problem looking another in the eye when speaking, and generally have a smile on their face. They are not afraid to speak their opinion in a polite and appropriate fashion, and they are likely to seek out opportunities for self-development. They are not threatened by others' successes and express a number of appropriately positive self-statements. The impression you get of people who have positive self-esteem is that they are self-assured—without being overconfident. Here are two typical profiles of children, one with negative self-esteem, the other with positive self-esteem:

Sarah, age ten, is a physically attractive child. An A student, she is also a proficient dancer and an excellent actress. She seems to command the short-term admiration of her peers. Closer investigation of Sarah's peer relationships, however, indicates that they are not as positive as they seem at first glance. Sarah is envious of anyone whom she perceives as better than she is. She seizes every opportunity to denigrate accomplishments of the peers she finds threatening. She is also very exclusive about her friendships, choosing to associate only with the more popular members of the group. She has a need to be the center of attention, which serves to alienate her from her friends over time. Sarah steals the show in a number of direct and indirect ways. She will, for example, monopolize conversations, manipulate others to get her way, and refuse to participate in activities or discuss topics she has no interest in or knowledge of. Adults find Sarah demanding and insecure. She constantly seeks their approval; when she does not receive it, she pouts or cries. She rarely smiles and hardly ever extends herself to anyone unless she perceives it to be self-advantageous.

Sarah is a good example of a child with poor self-esteem. On the face of it, this seems surprising, for Sarah has the basic ingredients for success. She is attractive, bright, and talented. Yet she exemplifies the characteristics of insecurity: she is jealous of other children's achievements, is too dependent on adult approval, and is overly self-centered and rigid in her social interactions. Should Sarah continue this course of development, she may not reach her full potential. She may actually become an unhappy and unhealthy adult.

Jessica, unlike Sarah, is an example of a child who is well adjusted and secure. Jessie is also ten years old. She is an average student with average to above average potential in extracurricular activities. Jessie's teacher refers to her as a "delight." She is accepted by most of her peers, hardworking in school, and not at all discomforted by the success of others. In fact, Jessie often praises her peers for their accomplishments. She will verbalize her own desire to be as good as others whom she perceives as outstanding but is not jealous or demoralized when she does not reach their levels of achievement. Jessie rarely gives up in the face of disappointment. Her parents and teachers perceive her as being persistent and not easily frustrated. "I do the best I can," says Jessie, "and I just try to do better each time."

Jessie is inclusive about her friendships and always ready to help. She does have her favorite friends, but her criteria for accepting a peer as a friend include shared interests, values, or proximity—not who is popular this week. Jessie does not require the constant approval of adults. Sure, she needs periodic feedback from adults—all children do. But she is also capable of monitoring herself in between those feedback lapses and is not immobilized or given to poor performance when feedback is not forthcoming.

Jessie's behavior pattern indicates that she has positive self-esteem. Her chances for a successful career as an adult are excellent. Why? you ask. She does not have the natural talents of Sarah. True, but what Jessie does have is what researchers refer to as a productive personality. She is self-motivated, self-assured, persistent, and responsible. Sarah is not, and that's what makes the difference. Because Jessie has these traits, she is able to expend all of her energy on goals and self-development. She is not bogged down with worries about how she compares to others or how much praise she is going to receive from adults. She is generally liked by others and therefore receives positive feedback, which serves to further enhance her self-esteem. Her persistence and her positive attitude about mistakes help her stick with goals until she reaches them. Because school success does not come naturally to Jessie, she has developed excellent study and work skills that will remain with her all of her life.

Is there hope for Sarah? Yes, definitely. To understand how Sarah's self-esteem can change and how Jessie's has developed, we need to consider how self-esteem is formed and nurtured.

The Development of Self-Esteem

The psychologists William James and C. H. Cooley explained the development of self-esteem in two very different ways. James believed that self-esteem is the result of the difference between what I want to be and what I think I am or could be. If what I ideally want to be is close to what I am or think I can be, then I like myself. If my view of myself is not what I would like it to be and if I think I can never reach my ideal, then I devalue myself and have poor self-esteem. Cooley, on the other hand, felt that a person's self-esteem comes from feedback, real or imagined, received from others. In other words, Cooley felt that we tend to value ourselves in the same way that we believe other people value us. He referred to this as the "looking glass self."

How much value can be placed on the theories that these two men proposed about self-esteem? Maryanne Harter (1983) has recently examined the formation and development of self-esteem in children. She found that children have a relatively well defined sense of self-esteem by the time they reach the age of eight. They tend to make estimates of their own self-worth in five important areas: physical appearance, social acceptance, scholastic competence, athletic and artistic skills, and behavioral conduct. These judgments of self-worth are made on the basis of expectations, as William James suggested, and on the basis of our beliefs of how others value us, as Cooley proposed. Let's say you are academically successful but possess little athletic talent. You may generally like yourself if you and those important to you value academic excellence over athletic prowess and if you feel that your performance is up to your own expectations. On the other hand, you may have a very poor view of yourself if you and the significant persons in your life value athletics over academics and if you feel that your performance does not measure up to your own expectations.

Applying these findings to Sarah and Jessie, we find that there are a number of reasons for the difference in self-esteem between the two girls. Sarah may have unrealistic expectations for herself whereas Jessie's expectations may be realistic. Another explanation for the difference in self-esteem has to do with the reactions the girls receive from the adults in their lives whom they value. Parents, teachers, coaches, and peers communicate powerful expectations and evaluations that influence the development of self-esteem. To better understand what influences the development of self-esteem, let's briefly review what experts have determined about the formation of self-esteem.

The psychologist Abraham Maslow believed that healthy self-esteem is necessary for a person to be truly productive and successful. He argued that self-esteem comes from two basic sources: the love, respect, and acceptance we get from significant others and our own sense of competence and achievement. Psychologists Carl Rogers and Albert Bandura have addressed each of these basic sources of self-esteem. Their ideas are useful to discuss.

Rogers emphasized the role played by unconditional love and acceptance in the formation of positive self-esteem. He used the term "unconditional positive regard" to refer to the no-strings-attached love that one person has for another. This unconditional positive regard communicates that the person is valued just for existing. "I love you because you are you" is the message that this kind of acceptance communicates.

To provide this kind of love, parents don't have to approve of everything their child does. On the contrary, parents and teachers need to give children accurate and direct feedback about their shortcomings as well as their strengths. In the case of unconditional positive regard, there is a clear distinction between the feedback that is given for behavior and performance and the general love and acceptance that one person has for another; parents and teachers may need to deal with a child's behavior, but their love and caring for that child is always there. In the case of conditional positive regard, there is a contingency placed on approval: acceptance of the child is dependent on the child's behavior and performance. The child is approved of only when measuring up to others' expectations.

Unconditional positive regard is a self-esteem enhancer for several reasons. First, positive regard provides a person with a sense of being loved and valued, one of the conditions that Maslow felt was necessary for self-esteem. Unconditional positive regard makes this source of self-esteem a certainty. Second, if I believe that I am loved no matter what I am or accomplish, then I will have less reason to fear negative evaluations or mistakes and will therefore be more likely to take advantage of new opportunities for self-development. Because I don't have to worry about losing the security of the basic love and acceptance from the significant people in my life, I have more energy and time to spend pursuing goals and self-development. Finally, having someone value me just for being me always leaves me with something to fall back on when I receive negative feedback. It is like having unlimited bank credit to draw upon in times of need.

As might be expected, conditional positive regard does not have the same effect. Because it is conditional, the individual cannot *rely on* this kind of acceptance and therefore might hesitate to risk failure in a new venture. Moreover, because acceptance is contingent on meeting a standard, the child feels worthwhile only as long as the standard is met. If for some reason the child does not measure up, then that basic level of support is withdrawn. If there is nothing else to replace it, the child becomes stuck and unable to proceed toward self-development.

Do we need unconditional positive regard from everyone in our lives in order to maintain positive self-esteem? No. Evidence indicates that we need this level of acceptance from at least one person in our life at any one point in time. It is particularly critical during the early childhood years because this is when the basic notions of self-esteem are forming. Most of the acceptance we receive from others (peers, employers) is conditional. This is all right so long as there is one source of unconditional positive regard to rely on.

Aside from the need to belong and to be loved, an individual's self-esteem is also dependent upon feeling basically competent. Albert Bandura (1977) refers to this sense of competency as "self-efficacy," which is our evaluation of our own ability to handle life situations, our judgment about how well we are able to perform particular tasks or activities. For example, we have expectations about our ability to parent, work at our job, and engage in other activities, like sports or dancing. Naturally, we tend to avoid activities that we feel are beyond our ability level and to gravitate toward those activities in which we expect to do well. If children believe they are good readers, they will look for opportunities to read and will persist if they run into obstacles. But if they believe they are poor readers, they will avoid reading and will likely give up in the face of any reading difficulty.

Self-efficacy expectations, then, influence our choice of activities. They also influence how hard we try and what we do when we meet obstacles. What determines our self-efficacy judgment? Bandura believes that our competency judgments about ourselves are based on four sources of information: the successes and failures we have had in a particular situation, the successes and failures of others in that situation, the feedback we get from others about how successful we will be, and our own internal physical state (tense, tired, anxious, etc.). A child begins to form ideas about competency based on these pieces of information.

To illustrate how the various sources of information determine competency judgment, let's take the example of a child facing a reading exercise. To have a sense of self-efficacy about reading, the child needs to have met with previous success at reading. It would also be helpful for the child to have seen other people reading successfully, to have received assurance from others, and to feel alert and well rested, in order to concentrate.

The power behind these self-efficacy judgments can be seen both in the research and in clinical examples. Bandura and his associates have shown that you can change a person's judgment about competence and thereby improve performance. In one study (Weinberg, Gould, & Jackson, 1979) women were led to believe that they were strong and physically competent whereas men in the same study were led to believe they were weak and less competent; the typical sex differences that we see in physical tasks disappeared on a subsequent test of physical strength. In another study Schunk (1984) took a group of children who were failing math and changed their expectations of success and failure; the children became more competent at mathematical tasks.

Following this line of research, I have had similar success changing the performance of children who had been experiencing academic difficulties. Susie, a fourth grader, has dyslexia, a rather significant learning disability in reading. She would make all kinds of excuses to avoid reading. She would, for example, get a headache and have to go to the nurse's office during reading time. She even got to the point where she would claim that reading gave her a headache. Susie had a low estimate of her own self-efficacy and therefore engaged in avoidant behavior. This in turn led to a vicious cycle of self-defeating thoughts and behaviors: the more Susie avoided reading, the stronger she felt about not being able to read and then the poorer she did on reading tasks. While she had a genuine reason for her difficulties with reading, her own self-defeating thoughts about her competence as a reader just made her reading disability worse. To help remedy the situation her teacher, her parents, and I designed a plan to change Susie's self-efficacy expectations:

1. We provided Susie with reading material on a level that was slightly below what we knew she could handle. This was done to reestablish a success record for her. In most cases expectations can be set a bit higher than the expected level of achievement, but in the case of the low achiever it is sometimes important to establish a record of success first.

2. We paired Susie with another child who was also having difficulty reading but who had persisted on the reading tasks and was making progress.

3. Susie received positive feedback from both her teacher and her parents for sticking with the task. The teacher also had a

classroom-wide recognition program for good effort and trying to do one's best on difficult tasks. The end result was that the whole class became a support to Susie.

4. We instructed Susie on how to deal with her headaches (by rubbing her temples or putting her head down on the table). We also educated her as to why she was getting the headaches; we explained that the headaches were her body's way of saying that she was thinking about reading as impossible and awful. We asked her to think a little differently about the reading and suggested that she think of it as being hard but as something important that she could do. (We used some guided imagery exercises to help Susie with this.)

The plan for Susie changed all four major pieces of information she used to judge her competence for a task. Within six weeks Susie was no longer having headaches at reading time and was no longer avoiding reading. In fact, she volunteered to read to the class! Susie's proficiency in reading improved as well. While she still was not up to grade level, she was making progress. Most significantly, Susie believed that she could read. Who could ask for anything more?

To summarize, we know that self-esteem is dependent upon the feedback that we receive from others and upon the evaluations that we make of our own accomplishments. The unconditional acceptance that we receive from other persons contributes significantly to the security of feeling valued. Our self-efficacy judgments influence our expectations and the goals we set for ourselves and are therefore the basis for our ideas of what we can ideally be. These expectations are the other ingredient for self-esteem development.

Self-Esteem Enhancers

How can a parent or teacher optimize a child's self-esteem? On the basis of available information about self-esteem, there are several practical suggestions that can be made.

Value Your Child Unconditionally

Unconditional positive acceptance is a self-esteem enhancer. But how is it communicated to the child? One way unconditional acceptance is expressed is by the quality (as opposed to the quantity) of time spent with the child. Quality time is time marked by focused attention. This means that the adult concentrates on the child instead of doing other things or becoming preoccupied while the child is attempting to communicate.

Adults cannot give children undivided attention all of the time. Clearly, this is impossible and unnecessary. But it is necessary to give a child at least 20 minutes of quality attention three to four times a week. All of us will occasionally ask a child a question and allow ourselves to become preoccupied and not really listen when the child responds. We may respond to the child with a standard "uh-huh," but we are not really paying attention or showing genuine interest in the conversation. The child then feels ignored. (Indeed, an adult would feel quite the same way.) If this happens frequently, the child begins to feel unimportant and devalued by that adult. If there is never anyone willing to provide quality attention, the message communicated to that child is "You are not an important person." Showering children with material things does not communicate the idea that they are valued. Quality attention does, however, because it requires you to give something of yourself—your time and your attention. And that is far more difficult to do.

Quality attention, then, is characterized by focused and active listening. The listener shows undivided attention by looking directly at the child, putting aside any distracting activity or object, and asking questions that reveal an interest in what the child is saying. (Details of how to structure communication to the child so that it reflects this quality attention are further discussed in Chapter 4.)

Another way that quality time is expressed is by the effort we make to show that we value the child. This occurs when we actively show interest in the activities and projects that are important to the child. For example, helping with homework, listening to ideas, going to games or recitals, or just playing with the child indicates that the child is important to us. This is a powerful affirmation of the child's self-worth.

As with quality attention, there are guidelines for how to spend quality time with a child. The kind of feedback we give the child while we are so engaged conveys very definite ideas about what we think of the child. I will be discussing this point in more detail shortly and in other chapters of this book.

In addition to time spent with the child, there are other, more subtle, cues that communicate to the child that she or he is valued. It is easy to go along with activities that you personally enjoy or that do not compete with your other priorities; it is much more difficult to be inconvenienced or to have to choose among priorities. When we make the child the priority, we are making that child feel important. This point was reinforced for me in a conversation I had recently with my ten-year-old daughter, Katie. She had a talent show at school during school hours and wanted her father and me to attend. Both of us have busy schedules. It was impossible for my husband to get away from his job on that particular day. My schedule was packed, but with a great deal of effort I was able to rearrange my activities in order to attend the show. My husband explained to Katie that he really wanted to go but could not do so this time. That night at the dinner table Katie turned to me and her father and said, "Mom, thanks for coming today. I know that you went out of your way so that you could be there; that meant a lot to me. And Dad, I know you would have been there if you could." Katie is a verbal child, but what she expressed is what most children feel when the important adults in their lives do go out of their way to be present at the events that are important to them. If you think about it, most adults feel the same way. When you as an adult want other adults to know that you care about them, don't you go out of your way for them? When you perceive that others are in fact going out of their way for you, you infer that they genuinely love you. Children make the same inferences about our behavior toward them. When we extend effort on their behalf, they also infer that we love and value them.

Clearly, we cannot always drop what we are doing and make the child the priority. Children do need to learn that sometimes other people's needs have to come first. Secure children accept this. However, if the child is never the priority for an adult, the message that is received is that he or she is not as important as everything else—is second-rate at best! Remember also that priority is expressed by quality attention and by the willingness to become personally involved with the child. Using material substitutes, that is, buying the child gifts, does not communicate this sense of value.

Another issue that often comes up when expressing unconditional acceptance is the question of selective attention. Consider this example: Mom is a softball fan whereas little Jenny, who is not interested in softball, really loves ballet. Mom tells Jenny that she has to play softball if she wants to take ballet lessons, so Jenny does both activities. Mom shows up for every softball game and practice but rarely makes the effort to go to Jenny's ballet practices or recitals. When Jenny practices ballet at home, Mom shows no interest. If Jenny wants her mother's attention, she has to talk only about the activities her mother is interested in.

While it is natural for us to have our own particular interests, to blatantly ignore our child when she or he expresses interests that are different from our own is to give that child conditional acceptance only. Essentially, what we communicate to that child is that her or his preference has no value. It is a way of invalidating that child. Parents and teachers need to support children when they are engaged in productive and appropriate activities. So, for example, while Jenny's mom may have a strong interest in softball, she needs to accept and value her daughter's interest in ballet. Here's another example: A mother I know has a son who is highly involved in hockey. This particular mother hates hockey but makes it her business to attend the hockey games and some of the practices. She does so with an honest but positive attitude. She does not play martyr, giving her son the idea that she goes because she has to. He is aware that hockey is not her favorite sport and that she comes to the games only because it is important to him.

This kind of behavior communicates unconditional love loud and clear.

There are literally thousands of ways that we communicate our love and acceptance to our children. Making their special meals, laughing at their silly jokes, reading them their favorite stories, and genuinely enjoying their company are inexpensive but nonetheless potent activities that support the message "I love you because you are you."

Set Your Child Up to Succeed

Parents and teachers can guide children under their care to succeed. But in order for children to succeed they must first become aware of and accept their own strengths and weaknesses. Children come to accept themselves by knowing that their major caregivers understand and accept them as individuals. This requires being able to assess the academic, athletic, artistic, technical, and manual aptitudes that each individual child possesses. It also requires an understanding and acceptance of the child's unique temperamental profile. Chapter 3 discusses in detail how one goes about assessing the particular attributes of a child. Chapter 3 also discusses how much of a child's aptitude and temperament can be changed by the environment and how much is genetically predetermined. This information is vital for establishing realistic goals and expectations. It is also useful in fitting the environment to the individual.

Individuals well suited to their general environment are much more likely to succeed. This is because they are able to use the environment as a resource. A simple example will illustrate the point. Consider the case of a child who is athletically inclined but not musically endowed. That child is much more likely to succeed if he or she is provided an opportunity to compete in athletics. If the child is placed in an environment where evaluation is primarily on the basis of musicality, however, success is far less likely. The consequence of not accepting or knowing our own natural abilities and temperaments is that we then set inappropriate expectations.

In essence, we set ourselves up to fail. This is the case since goals and expectations are the core of our ideal self-image.

A similar example can be made for temperament. If my child is bothered by noise, forcing her to work or play in a noisy environment for an extended period of time is setting her up to fail. She will not be able to concentrate. She may even be more irritable and difficult to manage. The end result is that she receives negative feedback about herself from others and from her own poor performance. But knowing her temperament and working with it will optimize the probability of her success.

There are other factors that also set the stage for success. Knowing how to set goals, establishing a good plan to reach those goals, and managing disappointments constructively are important lifelong tools for the building and maintaining of positive self-esteem. (These skills are covered in various chapters of this book.) When we establish reasonable goals and develop good problem-solving skills, we increase our own self-efficacy ratings. Likewise, maintaining a positive attitude in the face of failure allows a person to grow from mistakes, which then promotes positive self-esteem.

Parents can also help their children succeed by providing productive feedback. This is an evaluation we make of another person's performance and behavior that is direct, specific, objective, and accurate. It is not value-laden or derogatory in nature, and it is provided for positive as well as for negative behavior. Here is an example of what might be called productive feedback: "Mary, I like the way you handled the disappointment of not being able to go to the movies. I know that you were a little upset. You handled your feelings well. You told me you were mad, and then you went into the other room and found a craft project to do." Notice that the message is very specific and objective. The parent here pointed out to the child exactly what she did that was productive. This kind of feedback is instructive to the child; it reinforces good problem-solving skills and good communication skills.

Let's now consider another example of productive feedback, this time directed toward negative behavior: "Mary, I do not like the way you handled not being able to go to the movies. I know that you were disappointed. I would be, too. But when you are disappointed or upset, you cannot kick the door or damage your things. You need to handle your upset feelings differently. What do you think you can do instead to get your angry feelings out?" Notice again that the feedback is direct and to the point. While the parent gives the child the message that her behavior is unacceptable, the child herself is not derogated. It is the old saying "I love you but not your behavior." This kind of feedback is not offensive in nature and therefore does not usually provoke a defensive response. Of course, there are those who take offense with any criticism, even constructive criticism. But, in general, productive feedback is more likely to be accepted and acted on.

Productive feedback is also accurate. The parent provides the child with honest information about the behavior, performance, or situation. When parents or teachers give children inaccurate feedback, the children are unable to trust or benefit from it. Telling a child that he or she is the best reader in the class when this is clearly not the case is an example of inaccurate information. Even though a parent's motivation for providing this inaccurate information is admirable, in the long run it does more harm than good.

Productive feedback enhances a child's self-esteem. It provides the child with information about how best to manage self and environment. With this information the child can then modify behaviors and expectations to increase the likelihood of having successful relationships and achieving goals. Successful relationships and successful performance promote our own estimates of self-efficacy and contribute to the positive image we present to others and the positive feedback that we receive in return. Positive feedback from others and high self-efficacy ratings are the basic ingredients for positive self-esteem. (Chapter 4 provides a framework for how to give productive feedback.)

Empower Your Child

An empowered child is one who believes that his or her destiny is under control, who feels confident that the world can be managed and that goals can be achieved. When individuals feel a sense of personal competency, they are empowered. To use Bandura's term, the person has self-efficacy. Parents and teachers can promote this sense of empowerment in children in several ways. A number of chapters in this book elaborate on how parents and teachers can empower children; what I would like to do here is simply outline what some of these ways are.

Making the child take responsibility for feelings and actions is the first step toward empowerment. Responsible individuals do not wait for someone else to do their work or meet their needs. They take the initiative themselves and as a result meet with success more often than not. Responsible individuals acquire the skills and resources to manage the tasks of everyday life. They are self-disciplined and generally self-controlled. They have a take-charge attitude and an assertive manner. Such children sometimes misdirect their need for control and engage in behavior that is perceived as obstinate and stubborn. They give their caregivers a run for their money. I am fond of a story involving our second child, Jessica, that illustrates perfectly her take-charge attitude, which was evident early in her life. Jessie was three years old when she wanted candy for breakfast. When we said no, she disappeared for about two minutes. When she returned, she announced that I was not in charge. When I asked her who was in charge, she responded that God was in charge and that she had just talked to God and He had put her in charge. Let me tell you, Jessie is a headstrong child, but when this attitude is appropriately channeled, it leads to an adult who is a real go-getter and leader.

How do we make a child a responsible little person? There are several ways. First of all, we have to allow children to own their own feelings. We cannot protect them from all negative experiences or emotions. This does not mean that we deliberately frustrate the child. Nor does it mean that we should put children in situations where they are likely to be traumatized. What it does mean is that we take advantage of naturally occurring situations that may lead to disappointment and refrain from always trying to eliminate that disappointment for them. For example, if a child is involved in a spat with another child and no one is being physically hurt, it may be better to let the child own the hurt and resolve the conflict independently. Too often, parents are only too ready to intervene and solve the problem for the child. What children conclude from this kind of intervention over the long run is that they cannot handle things themselves. This kind of parental pampering serves to undermine a child's sense of self-efficacy.

In a similar vein, parents sometimes disempower their children by making excuses for them and protecting them from the natural or logical consequences of their own actions. When this happens repeatedly, children never have to take responsibility for themselves. Consequently, they fail to develop self-control and self-initiative; they also come to expect others to manage their problems for them and therefore never develop good coping skills. A good example of the overprotective parent is one who genuinely feels that his or her child can do no wrong and that when the child does get into trouble, it is someone else's fault. Another example of an overprotective parent is one who has to make sure that everything goes right for the child. They contrive situations so that the child benefits without having to put forth any effort; consequently, that child becomes an adult without developing the work skills or self-discipline necessary to deal with the adult world. These contrivances serve to weaken the child's sense of self-efficacy.

Giving children responsibilities around the house and reinforcing responsible behavior are other ways to empower them. Home is a great classroom for the real world. If the home environment does not provide the child with the opportunity to learn responsibility, it will probably not develop. The irresponsible adult is evaluated negatively by others and often fails as well. This of course impacts negatively on self-esteem.

Parental discipline style has been definitely shown to influence feelings of empowerment in children. Discipline styles influence self-esteem because they influence the development of the child's behaviors and attitudes. Children who engage in productive behaviors and have positive attitudes receive positive feedback from others. They also succeed more often. Diane Baumrind (1977, 1983) has done a great deal of research on the discipline styles of parents with productive and nonproductive children. She has found that parents who use a democratic discipline style produce children who are self-directed, self-controlled and socially adept—all traits of the successful adult. A permissive or an overly authoritarian parent typically produces a child who is not self-directed or self-controlled and has a poor or marginal interpersonal style for interacting with adults or peers. (The characteristics and techniques of a democratic discipline style are detailed in Chapter 4.)

I would like to make one last point before proceeding with the next suggestion. Language (that is, how we verbally express ourselves) greatly influences how we think and how we act. We believe what we say to ourselves, and we use a form of internal language to monitor and control behavior. Using the language of responsibility helps the child internalize a productive attitude. So when parents use words and phrases like "take charge" or "in control" or "responsible," they are programming their child to be responsible.

Help Your Child Develop Good Social Skills

The ability to get along with others is one of the best predictors of adult productivity and health. Social skillfulness is the ability to function with others at work, home, school, and play. The socially skillful child is not necessarily the most popular or the one with the most friends but, rather, the child who is able to initiate and maintain friendships, use social resources as supports, and obtain a sense of satisfaction from those relationships.

To be socially skillful the child needs to know how to take the perspective of another, communicate effectively and productively, show empathy, negotiate, and problem-solve in an objective and assertive way. (These skill areas are discussed in the chapters that follow.) There are natural differences among people in their level of social sensitivity and awareness. Some children are naturals, others clearly are not. Let me offer an example: Terry is an eight-year-old child whom most adults and peers rate as socially very adept. What does Terry do to give other people this impression? She smiles, is generally pleasant, and seems to know just what to say and do in most situations. She expresses interest in what they are doing and can compromise when there is a conflict of interest. She is considerate and polite and is always willing to lend a helping hand when there appears to be a need for one . And because Terry also has a wonderful sense of humor, she is enjoyable to be around.

If we analyze what Terry is doing in order to be perceived as socially adept, what we find is that she is pleasant and positive. Most of us prefer the company of people who are generally positive. Depressed, morose attitudes are very wearing on companions, even those who have a high degree of tolerance for this kind of behavior. We also find that Terry is able to "read others" very well; that is, she is able to decode the various verbal and nonverbal behaviors of others. She is not self-centered, so she can show interest in others. People like to be around those who are oriented toward others. Terry is able to compromise. This means that she is willing to meet the other person halfway. She does not need to have her way all the time, but she is not a doormat, always giving in to what others want. Finally, she is helpful, courteous, and kind. These are traits that endear a person to others.

Help Your Child Become a Self-Reinforcer

To maintain a sense of positive self-esteem a child needs to be able to make accurate, positive self-statements, keep a healthy and productive perspective, and forgo immediate gratification in favor of long-term goals.

To encourage children to make appropriate self-statements, a parent or teacher can reinforce accurate self-evaluations. Let's consider a typical scenario: Jessie comes home with her report card. She has obtained a B average, a very good grade for Jessie. Her father asks her how she thinks she has done. Jessie responds positively, and her father then reinforces her for feeling good about her B average. The dialogue might go something like this:

FATHER: I'm proud of your report card, Jessie. I know you did your very best, and that's what counts. How do you feel about your report card?
JESSIE: I feel good. I did try to do my best. Maybe the next time I can do even better.
FATHER: I'm pleased. You can be proud of yourself. I'm sure that you will do this well or even better the next time. We're here to help in any way we can. We're proud of two things, Jessie: we're pleased you put forth your best effort, and we're proud of you because you're proud of yourself for doing your best.

The parent in this scenario made a number of statements that reinforce accurate self-evaluations and positive self-esteem. He praised good effort. He also validated for the child a realistic performance expectation. By praising Jessie for her B average when B is her true potential, the message to the child is that a B is perfectly acceptable. Now, if Jessie were really capable of A's and was achieving only B's without expending any effort, the father's response to Jessie should be quite different. This is where knowing and accepting your child's potential is so important.

The parent in this scenario also clearly and objectively praised Jessie for being a self-reinforcer (". . . we're proud of you because you're proud of yourself"). These types of parental behaviors go a long way toward socializing accurate self-evaluations, which in turn promote the development of self-control and self-direction.

Encourage Your Child to Be a Positive Thinker

Maintaining a positive perspective is essential both for self-esteem and for coping skills. A positive perspective is the ability to minimize the negatives in a bad situation and maximize the positives in every situation. It's appreciating what you have now and not lamenting what you don't have or what someone else has that you want. (Chapter 7 describes in detail how parents and teachers can teach this kind of positive perspective taking.)

Teach Your Child to Delay Gratification

A child who is willing to give up an immediate reward in order to reach a goal is a child who is more likely to gain self-esteem in the long run. This is because children who can delay gratification are better problem solvers and therefore get better results. Let me illustrate the point with an example: If Tony wants an A on his oral report, he has to work hard and practice giving the report. To do this he may need to give up some of his playtime. The payoff is that he does better on his oral report. Getting a better grade on his report increases Tony's feeling of self-efficacy. Also, he is more likely to get positive feedback from others, which also increases his self-esteem.

Parents and teachers can promote this kind of behavior in children by rewarding them when they choose to forgo immediate rewards in favor of long-term goals and by instructing them on the merits of such behavior. So, for example, I might point out to Susie the benefits of giving up ten minutes of playtime to review her spelling words and raise her spelling grade. I would then reward Susie for putting the playtime aside and for the improved spelling grade. This helps Susie understand the merits of delaying immediate gratification. (Chapter 8 elaborates on the techniques of teaching children how and when to balance the need for immediate rewards with long-term gains.)

Be a Positive Model Yourself

Children imitate what they see. Therefore, as parents and teachers we need to be good role models ourselves. This means that we need to accept ourselves. We need to take responsibility for our actions and show by explicit example how to productively manage disappointments and mistakes. We need to be good communicators who are sensitive to other people; at the same time, we need to recognize and take care of our own needs as well. We need to be able to set realistic goals and expectations for ourselves. This means understanding and accepting our own strengths and weaknesses. Finally, we need to be good problem solvers and effectively balance the needs and rewards of today with the needs and rewards of tomorrow.

This is a lot to ask of anyone. But raising children is the most important challenge there is! The world's future productivity and security depends on how well we do as parents and teachers. Hopefully, we can learn from each other and support each other in our role as the socializers of tomorrow's adults. The chapters that follow are designed to provide support and direction. The material presented comes from both experts and the many parents and children whom I have had the good fortune of sharing experiences with over the years.

Chapter 2

Resilience

Is self-esteem the only factor responsible for the development of a productive and healthy personality? Clearly not. Self-esteem is certainly important, but it is not in itself always sufficient to ensure the development or maintenance of a productive and healthy personality. An individual also needs resilience, the glue that keeps us functioning when we are confronted with life's misfortunes or challenges. It is the attitudes, coping behaviors, and personal strength that you see in people who manage adversity and adjust well to the changes demanded of them by their life circumstances. Resilience is the ability to bounce back from a bad or difficult situation.

Consider Eleanor Roosevelt, for example. Despite the fact that she was born to a wealthy, aristocratic family, her childhood was far from happy. Her mother was cold and rejecting. Her father was an alcoholic (on more than one occasion in her early childhood he left her deserted outside a pub while he drank himself into a stupor). Both her parents died before she was ten years old, and she was raised by her maternal grandmother, who was aloof and emotionally distant like her mother. Nor was Eleanor's adult life stress-free: she had to endure an overbearing mother-in-law, almost continuous rejection from her husband, and the death of an infant son. But instead of wallowing in the misery of these hardships, Eleanor directed her energies toward community and world peace. She became one of the most influential women in American politics, earning from President Truman the title "First Lady of the World" (Cook, 1992).

Then there is the case of Terry Fox, an ordinary college student distinguished by his sense of challenge and commitment. Early in his high school career, Terry faced disappointment with a sense of determination characteristic of a resilient personality. When the coach told him that he was too short to play basketball, Terry worked harder on his skill and agility to compensate for his size and earned a prominent place on the team. This sense of determination and this ability to see hardship as a challenge was again elegantly demonstrated during his fight against cancer. In March of 1977, when Terry was a freshman at Simon Fraser University, he was diagnosed with osteosarcoma, a relatively rare form of bone cancer. The disease necessitated the amputation of his right leg. At first Terry was devastated by his fear of the cancer and the loss of his leg, but the despair was short-lived. To the amazement of friends, family, and the basketball coach, Terry adopted the cancer as his challenge. He decided to run five thousand miles across Canada to raise money for cancer research. Running with an artificial leg, he managed to personally raise $2 million and prompted other celebrities and citizens to raise an additional $25 million. Terry died on June 28, 1981. He had fought hard and long, but, more importantly, he had proven that personal misfortune can become an opportunity to grow and contribute in a big way to oneself and to society. Terry lost his own personal battle against cancer, but he gained a lasting place in Canadian history as a national symbol of courage, hope, and determination.

There are plenty of other examples of resilient individuals. I can cite numerous stories from my own clinical practice as a psychologist. John, for example, was hit by a car during his sophomore year of high school and suffered a number of life-threatening injuries along with a serious head injury. The doctors offered little hope to John's family for his survival, much less for any substantial recovery from the head injury. John, however, with the aid and support of his family, made a remarkable come-back. He refused to be intimidated by the poor prognosis and, like

Terry Fox, accepted his medical hardship as a challenge. Today John is once again an A student in honor classes. He has resumed his position on the football team and continues to be involved in a number of community projects. One year after the accident, one year after being told he would never fully recover physically or mentally, John ran in a marathon to raise money for multiple sclerosis.

Then there is Mary. She was born prematurely and experienced a number of medical crises during her first year of life. Her mother was hospitalized for depression four times before Mary's 12th birthday. Her father was an alcoholic who would frequently drink away his paycheck. As a result, the family did not always have money even for basic necessities. Mary, who was the eldest of the four children in this dysfunctional family, assumed the role of parent for her younger siblings, one of whom was afflicted with cerebral palsy and mental retardation. It would have been easy for Mary to allow her life situation to discourage her from personal growth and development. But this did not happen. With the aid of sympathetic and dedicated teachers, Mary was able to achieve personal goals and provide her family with support. Today she is in her second year of medical school. She is still a major support to her family and expects to work with VISTA (Volunteers in Service to America) for two years after she completes her medical education.

What made Eleanor Roosevelt and Terry Fox resilient? What is behind the continued resilience of John and Mary? Recently, researchers have begun to understand why some people bear up well and sometimes even thrive under stress. This research provides some important guides for parents and teachers to promote resilience in children and maintain it for themselves. Let me briefly review what the experts have discovered about resilience as a trait in children and adults.

Traits of the Resilient Personality

The research on resilient children comes from a number of sources. Some of the major findings are from studies that followed the same children from infancy through adolescence (Block, 1981; Block & Block, 1980; Murphy & Moriarty, 1976; Werner & Smith, 1982). Clark (1983) and Garmezy (1983) studied the lives of minority children who had succeeded in school. Others, such as Anthony (1974), looked at the traits and factors surrounding resilient children from highly dysfunctional families, and still others examined the resilient survivors of wars and concentration camps (Moskovitz, 1983). Emmy E. Werner (1984) summarized all of these studies to find that resilient children share four central characteristics.

Resilient children take a proactive rather than a reactive or passive approach to problem solving. This means that they tend to take charge of their life situation. This is in contrast to children who wait for others to do things for them or react negatively to situations that they can't control. This proactive approach to problem solving requires children to be self-reliant and independent while at the same time socially adept enough to get appropriate help from adults and peers. Eleanor Roosevelt learned early in life to be independent. She dealt with the emotional rejection of her mother and husband by getting involved with projects and community activities and by finding alternative sources of unconditional love (her father in early life and her teachers during childhood and adolescence). In so doing, she was able to find a refuge from the social rejection of her mother and grandmother and alternative sources of positive feedback to fuel her own sense of self-esteem and self-efficacy.

Resilient children are also able to construe their experiences in positive and constructive ways. This is true even when those experiences are painful or negative. Terry Fox's run for cancer research is a good example of this characteristic in action. Terry Fox took what was a threat and made it his personal challenge. By making the cancer research his goal, Terry gave a positive meaning to his condition and was therefore able to grow and deal effectively with it. He was not permanently discouraged from developing his physical prowess. After losing his leg and undergoing chemotherapy, he trained for one year and ran across Canada with an artificial leg. And why? To raise money for cancer research. The cancer became the impetus for this admirable goal and drive.

Resilient children are good-natured and easy to deal with. As a result, they gain other people's positive attention. These children usually establish a close bond with a least one caregiver during infancy and early childhood. This caregiver is not always the child's parent. It can be another relative or a neighbor, friend, coach, or teacher. Mary's case is particularly good example. During infancy she was nurtured by her grandmother, and during her elementary and high school years she had a few dedicated teachers who befriended and guided her. Mary managed to get the nurturing that she needed from caregivers outside her immediate family because her good-natured and affectionate disposition made her highly attractive to the adults in her life.

Of course, a good-natured disposition is to some extent innate. This does not mean, however, that a child not so blessed is doomed to failure. It simply means that such a child is at risk, especially in homes that are fraught with problems or otherwise less than ideal. (I will be discussing temperament in Chapter 3 and will provide suggestions about how to manage and nurture the more difficult child.)

Finally, resilient children develop early in life a sense of what Antonovsky (1979) calls "coherence," defined as a basic belief that life makes sense and that one has some control over what happens. This sense of coherence keeps resilient children strong through the more difficult times. According to the research done by Moskovitz (1983), children subjected to the trauma of war and concentration camps were able to love and behave compassionately toward others despite the horror that surrounded them. They were able to do this because they saw and construed a higher purpose for their lives. Similarly, for Eleanor Roosevelt that sense of coherence translated into a mission for community and world well-being. For Terry Fox, the sense of coherence was evident in his goal to raise a million dollars for cancer research. For John, it was the belief in his own ability to heal and recover. And for Mary, it is a personal mission to make the world just a little better. All of these individuals placed a sense of meaning on their suffering, which in turn contributed to their ability to persevere and function against all odds.

The research on stress-resistant adults has turned up some of the same characteristics of resilience. Suzanne Kobasa and her colleagues have studied those individuals who perform well physically and mentally under stress. Her original research was done in the late seventies on high-powered business executives who refused to buckle under pressure (Kobasa, Maddi, & Courington, 1981). Since that time researchers have noted similar findings among other populations, including lawyers (Kobasa, 1982), teachers (Holt, Fine, & Tollefson, 1987), and nurses (McCranie, Lambert, & Lambert, 1987), as well as among people who suffer from chronic illnesses like rheumatoid arthritis (Okun, Zautra, & Robinson, 1988). The characteristics that seem to underlie the resilient individual are a sense of control, challenge, and commitment. These three characteristics have been collectively defined as "the hardy personality."

Admittedly, not all researchers have been supportive of the hardy personality concept. Some (Funk & Houston, 1987; Hull, Van Treuven, & Virnelli, 1987) have argued that the three characteristics are not independent of each other. They have also questioned the measurement of hardiness and its exact causal connection to stress resistance. Despite these objections, however, the research clearly indicates that the characteristics included in the hardy personality do at different times distinguish resilient from nonresilient individuals. It is also true that the hardy attitudes identified by Kobasa in adults are similar and even equivalent to those found in the studies of resilient children. Let me then discuss in more detail the three component traits behind the hardy personality. Hopefully, this discussion will provide a basis for what we, as the caregivers of children, can do to develop the "mental muscle" that children require to be resilient.

The first of the components, a sense of control, refers to the basic belief that I as an individual can influence what happens to me. This does not mean that I can always control the situations or people around me. Rather, it means that I can control *myself* and accept responsibility for my own decisions and their consequences. Psychologists refer to this belief as an "internal locus of control" (Rotter, 1966). Persons who have an internal locus of control take responsibility for themselves. They believe that taking charge of the situation will result in management of the stressor. Internal-locus-of-control people do not expect others to do for them what they can do for themselves. They are active, independent people who live by the motto "God helps those who help themselves." This internal locus of control is what Werner (1984) talked about when she described the proactive approach to problem solving of resilient children.

An internal locus of control is certainly evident in all of the examples I cited earlier. Eleanor Roosevelt assumed responsibility for her own happiness by finding other sources of acceptance and areas where she could contribute and be successful. Terry Fox took charge of his medical situation when he decided to use it to benefit others, and John demonstrated this sense of control when he decided to take the necessary steps to push himself toward recovery. Mary managed her poor home environment by finding a refuge—school and her grandmother.

The sense of challenge, the second of the characteristics of hardiness, is the ability to see the positive aspects of change and to minimize or get beyond the negative aspects of a situation. A person who sees life as a challenge is not only positive about life in general but also able to defuse the threat behind misfortune and extract opportunity from the change. Terry Fox's run for cancer is an example of this challenge orientation. He mitigated the threat of the cancer by making it his challenge. To have this kind of positive perspective, a person must be able to think flexibly. This means that one has to be able to see a situation from different perspectives and generate different solutions for problems. In Terry's case, he construed the loss of his leg and the end of his basketball career as an opportunity to start a new venture as a runner, albeit one with an artificial leg. The threat of cancer and the loss of his leg did not immobilize him. They became the reason for and the drive behind a bigger and better goal.

This challenge orientation can be seen in the positive attitude that resilient children maintain when confronted with problems. For example, John's remarkable recovery resulted from his ability to see his prognosis as a challenge and not a threat. Interestingly, the professionals involved with John felt that his optimism was due to denial of his real condition. But John was realistic. He set little goals for himself and made alternative plans in case he did not recover completely. He was in many ways more flexible about his condition than the professionals and was able to remain positive in spite of their negativity.

The third characteristic of the hardy personality is a sense of commitment, that is, the ability to find meaning and value in what one is doing. It is the ability to see a reason or purpose behind one's existence. Commitments are the goals we set and the effort we put forth to reach them. Commitments are stress inoculators and achievement motivators because they focus human energy toward goals. In times of adversity or task difficulty a goal-oriented perspective motivates the person to persevere. Individuals who lack commitment are alienated from self and others, and in stressful times they, lacking reasons for continuing, are likely to give up. Commitment is what Werner talked about as the fourth characteristic of the resilient child. A child who is able to see a meaning behind suffering is a child with a sense of commitment. The resilient children in Werner's studies often found this sense of purpose by assuming the role of caregiver to others in their negative situation or by choosing alternative life paths as adults. Mary is a good example of a resilient child who saw a purpose in her negative situation. She was the caregiver to her siblings and to her parents. Even as a small child Mary realized the need she met for these individuals. As an adolescent she decided on a life course different from that of her family, while at the same time remaining supportive of them. What is more, Mary is still able to see a purpose for those early experiences. She claims that her family situation motivated her to go to medical school and to eventually work on research related to alcoholism and depression.

A resilient individual is a person who is responsible, positive, self-reliant, committed, and socially skillful. All of these traits can be socialized and reinforced. In the next section of this chapter some of the skills and conditions that promote resiliency in children and adults are discussed. The recommendations offered come from research (Kimchi & Schaffner, 1991) and from my own experiences as a clinician and parent.

Resiliency Enhancers

Research on resilient children and adults (Kimchi & Schaffner, 1991) offers implications for the socialization and development of the resilient personality. These implications involve skills and attitudes as well as what the research refers to as protective conditions. In the following pages I present ways to foster the skills and attitudes characteristic of children with resilient personalities.

Help Your Child Develop Skills

All resilient children do well in at least one activity. They are often good students and excel in some activity, like sports, art, or music, that brings them praise. They are not necessarily outstanding in any of these areas, but they are recognized because of their efforts and the outcomes they produce. Skills are resilience enhancers because they are resources we can use to deal with stress. They also gain us the respect of others because they produce tangible evidence of what we can contribute. Skills and talents aid in the establishment and pursuit of goals, and goals give people reasons for persevering. Mary's academic skill is a perfect example. Her interests in biology and her aptitude for the subject gained her the support and respect of a number of individuals outside her family. Her academic interests were also influential in the design of her career goals and gave her the focus she needed to get beyond the negativity of her immediate situation.

In order to develop their own unique aptitudes children must first feel that those skills and interests are of some value. Especially early in life, adults provide children with feedback about the worth of their skills. Children also need the support and encouragement of adults to develop their *natural* aptitudes and interests. I emphasize natural aptitudes because it is important to value what the child has and not what you as the parent or teacher would like the child to have. So if Jimmy has an aptitude for dance but not for sports, then dance is what needs to be encouraged and valued. One of the major threats to the development of a child's resiliency and self-esteem exists when caregivers deny or minimize the child's natural talents and attempt to impose their own preferences instead.

Help Your Child Develop Other Interests and Hobbies

Resilient children's hobbies and interests—music, art, watching football games, fishing, and so on—are consistent sources of satisfaction and enjoyment for them. Katie, our eldest child, loves to read, dance, play the piano, and get involved in drama. When she has had a particularly stressful day at school or at home, she will play the piano, choreograph a piece of music, or read as a way to "de-stress." For many adults, watching a football or basketball game provides the same kind of relief. The point is that hobbies and interests are stress buffers. They allow us to take a time-out from the stressful situation. Because we tend to find them satisfying, they also help us to rejuvenate and feel good again.

As parents and teachers, we need to encourage our children to develop healthy hobbies and interests. This means reinforcing them for occupying themselves with worthwhile activities. By praising Katie for using her hobbies to de-stress, we help her see that hobbies are useful as stress relievers. And I can't tell you the number of unique gadgets we have on display and the experiments we have observed and tested as a result of our second daughter's interest in science. Simply paying attention to her inventions and encouraging her to get involved in one of her projects when she is "stressed out" reinforces a positive use of hobbies. At the same time, of course, we have to teach our children how to balance these other interests with job and school responsibilities. It's sometimes very easy to allow hobbies or interests to interfere with our responsibilities or keep us from dealing with the stressor in a timely fashion. This is inappropriate and a potential source of distress.

Help Your Child Develop Social Skills and an "Other-Orientation"

Resilient individuals tend to be socially skillful. They are typically well liked and therefore able to solicit support and help from others when needed. The research on resilient children supports the importance of a positive disposition and a smooth style of social interaction. The research on stress resistance in adults draws a similar conclusion: social support is a stress neutralizer and socially skilled individuals are typically more socially connected.

Resilient individuals are also "other-oriented." Werner (1984) refers to "required helpfulness" on the part of resilient individuals as one of the experiences that contribute to their strong character. This "other-orientation" gives these children a purpose and a focus that allow them to transcend their immediate negative conditions. Mary did not feel powerless in her situation because she had a job to do: she had to care for her siblings. Because she assumed that role, she did not concentrate on her own misery, and she found that she was an effective caregiver, a discovery that served to boost her own sense of self-worth.

Help Your Child Become Responsible

Resilient children are responsible individuals. They initiate ideas and do their share when working in groups. They take charge of themselves and actively seek out solutions to problems. This take-charge attitude is an asset in good and bad times. In good times, responsible individuals take advantage of the opportunity open to them and in times of trouble they take the necessary steps to manage the problem. A child or adult who has not developed this sense of responsibility depends on others or on fate. The outcomes under these circumstances are generally negative. Eleanor Roosevelt, Terry Fox, John, and Mary are examples of individuals who assumed responsibility for themselves (and sometimes for others). Eleanor assumed responsibility for her own identity and happiness when she developed an interest in world peace. John accepted the responsibility for his own recovery, and Terry took charge of his negative prognosis and made it count for something. Mary never excused herself from responsibility for her own success—even though she had good reason to.

According to the research done by Rutter (1979), Clark (1983), and Garmezy (1983), household rules and chores promote a sense of responsibility in children by providing them with an opportunity to be accountable. They communicate to children the adult's expectation that they be responsible. (Chapter 4 deals extensively with how parents can create this sense of responsibility in their children.)

Help Your Child Develop Coping Skills

Coping skills are essential for a person to be psychologically resilient. Good coping skills are defined as the effective management of stressors. "Effective" means dealing with a stressor in a way that minimizes its negative impact and maximizes its positive impact on the individual or group. Terry Fox dealt with his stressor—cancer and the loss of his leg—by making cancer research his goal and by figuring out other ways to compensate for the amputated leg. As a result, he could manage the cancer and function without the lost leg.

More specifically, coping is the mental effort and physical actions applied to managing those events, people, and situations that we perceive as negative or potentially negative. There are two kinds of coping: emotion-focused and problem-focused (Lazarus & Folkman, 1984). Emotion-focused coping has to do with managing the feelings that arise in response to a problem and is especially important in situations where the outcomes are not controllable. There are any number of emotion-focused forms of coping: wresting the good out of a bad situation (e.g., recognizing that losing your job frees you to do something you like better); finding a diversion (e.g., going to a movie as a break from a stressful task); reappraising the negative situation so that it does not appear as bad ("I decided it was not as bad as I thought" or "I know I can handle this"); making positive comparisons to another situation ("It could have been worse"); and selectively attending to one part of the problem and putting the rest of the problem on hold. These strategies can be helpful to the individual when they are applied appropriately to a situation. In the chapters that follow I will be discussing these coping strategies in more detail with some ideas about the parameters of their usefulness.

Problem-focused coping attacks the problem directly. Such a strategy might involve decisions that directly affect the outcome (e.g., getting the chemotherapy to deal with the cancer). It may mean that we bring together the appropriate resources to solve the problem, or it may involve changing aspects of ourselves (getting new skills) to deal with the stressor. The point here is that a coping skill is any of an array of different strategies that can be used to control the course and outcome of a problem situation.

How effective our coping skills are will depend on the magnitude of the problem and our own ability to think flexibly. Psychologists refer to the ability to see a situation from many different perspectives as "cognitive flexibility." It is also the ability to be a creative problem solver. Cognitive flexibility strengthens our ability to maintain resilience because it allows for the consideration of a number of different alternatives, one of which might solve the problem. The issue of cognitive flexibility will be addressed in several of the chapters that follow. It is perhaps the single most important defense we have against stress. A number of stress researchers (Antonovsky, 1979; Kobasa, 1979; Lazarus & Folkman, 1984) have emphasized the importance of flexible thinking as a stress inoculator.

Successful coping is enhanced when physical health is optimized. Relaxation skills, good nutrition, and exercise contribute in a positive way to physical health and effective coping. Relaxation skills, for example, assist in physically managing the side effects of stress. (Chapter 6 provides an overview of the more popular relaxation strategies.) Good nutrition and regular physical exercise are prerequisites for both emotion-focused and problem-focused coping. Eating a well-balanced diet and getting enough exercise reduces stress. Additionally, good nutrition enhances problem solving because good nutrition allows us to think and feel optimally. Poor nutrition can contribute to negative moods and irrational thought patterns. Exercise is a form of physical relaxation as well as an adjunct to good nutrition. (Chapter 6 discusses in more detail the basics behind good nutrition and exercise and how they add to our overall resilience and self-esteem.)

In summary, coping skills are important for building and maintaining resilience. Sometimes, however, stressors are so overwhelming that even the most resilient individual has difficulty coping and requires a break or assistance. Such behavior is not an indication of weakness or poor coping. Knowing when you need help is itself a good coping skill.

Teach Your Child How to Set and Stick with Goals

Goals and commitments are important for productivity and resilience. Goals serve as motivators of human action. However, overcommitment to one goal (putting all your eggs in one basket) can represent a problem for resilience, since failure to attain the goal is stressful. So while we need to teach children to have goals, there are guidelines for how to teach them to set goals.

First of all, there should be more than one goal and the goals need to be realistic. A child who sets his sights on being a pro football star but has no athletic ability is setting himself up for failure. This is especially true if he has no other goals to pursue.

But even if the child is gifted athletically, having more than one goal decreases the threat to resilience because there are other realistic goals to rely on as motivators if one of the goals is thwarted. Eleanor Roosevelt pursued several different goals at one time, and Mary always has three goals (she refers to them as "projects") that she dedicates herself to.

The second general rule is to help the child think about different ways to attain the goal in question. By helping children brainstorm different means to ends we are essentially increasing their ability to think flexibly about attaining goals. Along these lines, it is important to help children understand that they may have to start at the bottom in order to get to the top. Success sometimes comes very slowly and in ways we least expect. Mary worked as a lab technician for three years before she was able to go to medical school. She also was resourceful in the way she found funding for medical school. She learned early in life to think flexibly and to not be discouraged by having to work her way up.

Persistence is the third key to successfully reaching a goal. Children need to tolerate a certain degree of frustration in the process of pursuing goals. They also need to learn when to give up on one goal and pursue another. Giving up simply because things are difficult or not going your way has negative implications for two reasons: you never succeed and you never develop the stamina to "tough it out" during difficult times. On the other hand, holding on to an unattainable goal or one that taxes your resources beyond reasonable limits is equally damaging. Consider this example: Suppose I set a goal for myself of finishing college in three years instead of four. Then I find that I'm having trouble keeping up with the extra course load even though I'm working very hard. I also find that I'm getting C's instead of my customary A's. If I analyze the situation, what I find is that my goal of completing the degree in three years is not compatible with my goal of doing the best I can and keeping up a good grade point average. I might at this time reconsider my original goal and adopt the alternative one of completing my education in four years instead of three. There's a fine line between giving up too soon and "beating a dead horse." The general rule of thumb is first to give it your all. If the resources are not available or if the goal is causing too much stress, then you may need to reconsider the goal. This is a time when good decision-making skills are helpful. Young children do not have the ability to do this kind of decision making. They require adult guidance. However, as the child matures and has instruction in goal setting, this kind of goal-setting sophistication can be developed.

Give Your Child a Meaningful Philosophy to Live By

In addition to goals, we need to have a philosophy of life that gives what we do some focus and meaning. For some people religion fills this need well. Commitment to family, community, and nation are examples of principles resilient people use to persevere. During the course of his recovery John was fond of saying that no one in his family was a quitter. Family pride gave John a focus when he needed it most, and his religious beliefs also provided him with a sense of hope and meaning. Another example of how commitment to a group motivates perseverance includes the athlete who pushes just a little harder for the sake of the team or the school. Indeed, national pride partly fuels the drive behind those who compete in the Olympics.

To develop these higher-order values, parents and teachers would do well to promote community spirit. The greatest threat to the acceptance of such values is an overemphasis on self and the "me only" attitudes that we sometimes see in our society. Totally self-centered people have nothing to look to when they are personally stressed and in a muddle. A higher-order philosophy expands a person, providing reasons and goals that help the individual transcend the immediate situation. Stories are good sources of inspiration and information about higher-order values. (Chapter 5 discusses how parents can use stories to instill these values as well as the attitudes and beliefs that are important for resilience.)

Help Your Child Develop an Attitude of Excellence

The attitude "I will do my best" is useful for the development of resilience because it helps the child develop "mental muscle." To do one's best one has to push beyond what's expected in order to get into the habit of working hard and sticking with the task. This same kind of stamina is what is needed to be resilient in the face of a stressor. John was used to working hard because his family instilled in him this sense of excellence and need to excel. When he was confronted with his own medical crisis, he was able to respond with vigor because he was used to pushing himself. Because he had already developed the habit of working hard, he had the proper attitude and skills to do so when he pushed himself to recovery.

Help Your Child Become "Change Skilled"

Change is a permanent fixture of existence and for some people a chronic source of distress. While the ease with which we deal with change is partially determined by our temperament, how we perceive and manage it also influences how stressful change will be. Chapter 7 provides some tips for how to teach children to deal effectively with change. In addition to the suggestion provided in that chapter, it is also helpful to give your child and yourself opportunities to get used to change. To do this, you may want to occasionally introduce innocuous changes, for example, in the seating arrangement at the dinner table or in the arrangement of furniture in a bedroom. These changes should be done only during relatively calm times and should always be prefaced by an explanation. For example: "We are going to switch seats at the dinner table this week [or month] so that we can get used to making changes when we are at school and when you are older." Getting used to small, insignificant changes helps us prepare for more substantial changes later on. People who are "change skilled" are better able to deal with stress and are therefore more likely to be psychologically resilient.

Provide Your Child with Nurturance, Structure, and Good Role Models

Nurturance, structure, and good role models promote resilience in children. In Chapter 1, I discussed the importance of nurturance and structure for the development of self-esteem. The same points apply here. Werner (1984) found that stress-resistant children had at least one nurturing adult during their early childhood years; sometimes this special person for the child was someone other than the child's natural parent. The early unconditional love of a nurturing adult, who becomes an important role model for the child, helps the child develop a basic sense of trust. Her maternal grandmother was an important source of nurturance during Mary's preschool years. To this very day Mary strives to be like her grandmother; she takes pride in her ability to take care of others and to manage "no matter what," just as her grandmother did.

Structure, rules, and chores promote resilience. Why? you ask. External structure promotes internal structure. This means that a child learns self-control from the clear expectations, rules, and reinforcements in the environment. A child who has no structure to model has more difficulty developing self-control and a sense of responsibility; both are essential for the development of one of the characteristics of a hardy or resilient personality: the sense of control. Resilient children subjected to discrimination, trauma, or poverty all seem to have this kind of structure in their background (Clark, 1983; Garmezy, 1983; Rutter, 1979).

Finally, the research of Rutter and his colleagues indicates that a good school environment mitigates the ill effects of other stressors. In other words, the teacher and the school can make a difference. Qualities identified for the more successful schools are the following: the use of positive incentives and praise, clearly specified rules and structure, an emphasis on making the student a responsible individual, good role models, appropriately high standards, and consistent feedback from the teacher. These characteristics make sense because they promote a sense of control and challenge in the child. Reinforcing responsible behavior and setting reasonably high standards for the child help develop that "mental muscle" referred to earlier. The structure, positive role models, and praise aid in the development of self-control. The case studies of Eleanor Roosevelt and Mary speak to the importance of a good school environment. Eleanor Roosevelt felt that her boarding school experience was challenging and that it provided her with a strong sense of responsibility and self-pride. And Mary, too, found a source of personal support and reinforcement for her academic interests in school.

In conclusion, resilience is the ability to manage change and adversity. The research on resilient children and stress-resistant adults has provided us with an understanding of the ingredients of a resilient personality as well as of some of the factors responsible for its development and sustenance. The challenge for those of us responsible for the development of tomorrow's adults is to promote these characteristics in the children under our charge. The chapters that follow provide guidance and suggestions based on both research and my own experience gathered over the years. I hope they prove useful.

Chapter 3

Sizing Up Your Child

Is a person destined from birth to be successful and resilient? The answer to this question is not simple or straightforward. Behavioral geneticists are now suggesting that our genes determine the range of traits we might exhibit and the capabilities we might possess (Hoffman, 1991; Kagan & Snidman, 1991; Plomin, 1989). In other words, our genetic makeup sets the outer limits of what we are and can be physically, mentally, and perhaps emotionally. The environment, that is, the experiences we have as members of a family and a community, has a lot to do with how those traits and abilities are expressed. For example, I may be short, artistic, and emotional. Whether I allow my shortness to aid or impede me or whether I am able to develop my artistic abilities and use my emotionality constructively is influenced by my experiences with the world, by the models in my environment, and by the reinforcements I receive from the significant persons in my life. If there is a good fit between me and my environment, the probability of my becoming successful and resilient is increased. If there is a poor fit, I will have more difficulty being productive and resilient. In order for there to be a good fit, I need to have an understanding of my general temperamental characteristics, as well as my capabilities and limitations. This chapter discusses the individual differences that exist in temperament, learning styles, stress tolerance, and aptitudes. Hopefully, the information will provide a better understanding of the genetic parameters that influence an individual's behavior, interests, and goals.

Temperament

Temperament is our general predisposition to behave or respond in a given way to the people, places, and events around us. Temperament is what people refer to when they describe the differences between two children from the same family. Experts who have studied temperament have identified several different temperamental categories and some general features of temperament that are useful for helping us understand our child—and even ourselves.

Hans Eysenck (1982) was one of the first psychologists to popularize the notion that certain aspects of our personality are biologically based and determined. Eysenck identified two global traits, extroversion and neuroticism, which seem to encompass a number of different temperaments. Extroverts are highly social individuals who thrive on activity and stimulation. By contrast, introverts (the opposite of extroverts) prefer quiet, calm environments; they tend to think things through and prefer small, rather than large, social gatherings. Neuroticism refers to the degree of emotionality experienced by an individual. A person high on the neuroticism scale tends to be emotionally very unsteady. A person low on the scale is more even-tempered. Alexander Thomas and Stella Chess are psychiatrists who have studied temperament profiles and changes over the life span. They have identified the following nine temperament characteristics, which are useful in helping parents better understand themselves and their children.

Activity Level

How physically active do you need to be? Activity level refers to a person's preference, and perhaps need, for physical movement. Children and adults who have a high activity level are always on the go and require opportunities to move around. They have a difficult time sitting still and prefer activities that are physically active in nature. If these individuals have sedentary jobs, they require periodic physical activity. For example, the business executive who is high on this temperament trait may need to use the lunch hour engaged in some form of physical activity (e.g., taking a walk, playing tennis). A highly active child may need an opportunity to move around frequently during the school day. Persons who are low on this trait are quite the opposite: they prefer sedentary activities and are quite content to stay in one place for long periods of time; they won't drive you nuts on long car trips!

Rhythmicity

Rhythmicity is defined as the temporal consistency characterizing our bodily functions like sleep, hunger, and elimination of bodily wastes. Persons who are highly regular tend to eat, sleep, and eliminate about the same time each day. You can set your watch by them! Individuals who are irregular have inconsistent patterns; they don't get tired or hungry or eliminate at the same time each day.

Approach/Withdrawal

This temperament category refers to the positive or negative response a person has initially to a new situation. The infant or toddler who shows little hesitation trying new foods or playing with new toys has an approach disposition. A withdrawal tendency is exhibited by the infant who immediately spits out any new food or who generally prefers the old thing over the new. A child with a withdrawal disposition is uneasy in new situations and will often cry and cling to the familiar adult. Adults who have an approach temperament will often seek out new situations; they chance a new restaurant and new foods. Those who are disposed toward the withdrawal side of the scale would just as soon stick with what they know they like; they are far more hesitant and therefore more cautious about trying anything new.

Kagan and his associates (1985) have identified a similar temperament pattern. They call it the Inhibited–Uninhibited approach to novel stimuli. Children who are inhibited approach new situations in a cautious, controlled, and reserved fashion. They are slow to explore new things. In contrast, uninhibited children are spontaneous and eagerly approach novel events. Interestingly enough, Kagan and Snidman (1991) have found some preliminary evidence to suggest that the brain chemistry of inhibited children is distinctly different from that of their uninhibited counterparts. There actually may be a physical reason why people differ in their orientation to novel situations and things.

Adaptability

Where approach/withdrawal refers to the nature of a person's initial response, adaptability refers to how long it takes the person to get used to something new. The infant who three months later is still fussing over a change in schedule is temperamentally slow to adapt. The child who initially rejects a new toy but then in a day or two accepts it with no trouble is adaptable. The child who is initially uncomfortable about a new class in September but fits right in after a few weeks is adaptable; the child who is still having difficulties three months later is slow to adapt. Similarly, adults who are uncomfortable with changes in routine or with major changes in the work or home situation are slow to adapt. Those who seem to go with the flow are adaptable. These individuals experience little discomfort and adjust to new situations very readily. Highly adaptable individuals can go from a work or school schedule to a vacation schedule with little difficulty. Those who are slow to adapt take a while adjusting to the change and would, for example, have more trouble unwinding on vacation.

Threshold of Responsiveness

Threshold of responsiveness refers to the smallest amount of change a person needs before he or she knows that there is a difference in the environment. Some people know when there has been a two-degree change in the weather. Others simply don't register the change until the temperature has risen or fallen five or eight degrees. Some people are sensitive to noise, hearing the slightest change in noise levels, whereas others are quite tolerant of noisy environments. Some people have a low sensory threshold for vision: they will take note of the little changes that occur in their physical world. Others, by contrast, are quite oblivious to those changes. Threshold of responsiveness applies to the senses; vision, taste, smell, audition, and touch. It also includes the perception of pain. Some of us have low sensory thresholds for all our senses. This means that we will respond to very slight changes in our environment. Other people have high thresholds for some of the senses but low thresholds for others. For example, a given person might have a low threshold for pain but a high threshold for everything else.

Intensity of Reaction

Once a person has recorded a change in the environment, there is a response to that change. Intensity of reaction is the strength with which a person responds to the people, things, and events in the environment. Some personality researchers (Plomin, 1989) refer to this trait as emotionality. Some people respond with a lot of gusto, others are far more reserved. The child who cries hard usually also laughs hard. The mild-mannered child generally has a softer response to the world.

Quality of Mood

Believe it or not, mood (or shall I say, the manifestation of mood) is temperamentally based. Quality of mood refers to the degree of friendliness and cooperativeness typical of a particular person across a number of different situations and over the course of time. It is the natural tendency to see the cup as half full instead of half empty. A positive quality of mood exemplifies itself in infancy with the baby who is usually smiling and cooing. During childhood and even into adulthood, it is demonstrated by the child or adult who is generally cooperative and upbeat. A negative quality is characterized by a person who is frequently pessimistic and ornery. Statements like "There is no pleasing him" are indicative of this negative quality of mood. Statements like "She is a joy to have around" or "He cooperates and pitches right in whenever asked to" are characteristic of the positive side of this temperamental trait.

Distractibility

Distractibility refers to how easily a person's attention can be diverted from one thing to another. A person who is highly distractible will be interrupted by the slightest distraction. Individuals who are not distractible are captured by what they're involved in and therefore are not easily distracted. Statements that are indicative of high distractibility include "He goes and starts one thing, sees another and then goes to it." In contrast, persons who are low on distractibility will become so engrossed in an activity that they become totally oblivious to what is going on around them.

Attention Span and Persistence

Thomas and Chess feel that attention span and persistence are usually related. Attention span refers to how long a person can sustain attention on a task, and persistence refers to the stick-to-itiveness that a person generally exhibits for a task. Attention span, of course, depends on age. For an infant, a long attention span is a half hour and a short one is a minute or two. Children and adults who have a long attention span can stay with a task for hours. A highly persistent individual will pursue a task until it's finished. "She kept trying and trying until she got it right" is a statement describing a persistent individual whereas the following statement is characteristic of a person with low persistence:

"He gives up as soon as he has any difficulties with it." Thomas and Chess claim that sometimes a person can have a high attention span but low persistence or a short attention span and high persistence. They can be equally low or high on each trait as well. The point is that attention span and persistence, like other temperaments, are individual differences that exist for each one of us.

Temperamental Differences between Children

The combination of some of these traits makes some children more difficult to deal with than others. Thomas and Chess have identified the difficult child as one who is irregular, has negative withdrawal responses to new stimuli, is slow to adapt, and has intense reactions that are typically negative in nature. The easy child is on the opposite end of the temperamental spectrum. Such a child is typically regular, has a positive approach to new stimuli, adapts well and positively to change, and responds in a mild to moderate way to events in the environment—in short, an "absolute delight." The "slow to warm up" child is in between the difficult and the easy child: she or he is by nature slow to adapt to change but less intense and less negative than the difficult child. To get an idea of your child's temperamental profile, answer and score the questions that appear in the Temperament Assessment on page 81.

When rated, the nine temperament characteristics give us an idea of the temperamental makeup of the child. Accepting the child's basic temperament traits and working with those basic dispositions instead of against them does two things: it reduces the stress on the child, and it reduces the stress on the parent. Some children are naturally more difficult than others. These basic dispositions are not anyone's fault. They are the raw material we have to work with. Sometimes the children who are the most difficult to handle become strong leaders as adults. A child who is persistent may develop a strong character and persevere when others are likely to give up. The same traits that predispose children to be highly sensitive and to react strongly to the things and people in their environment also provide the energy and life behind the great works of art, music, and drama. One has only to peruse the life histories of the great musicians and artists to see that many of them were intense and sensitive people. Learning about what we are temperamentally and then adapting our environment to best fit those characteristics allows us a better opportunity to use our own natural resources to be productive and cope with the stresses in life. Accepting the temperamental characteristics of our children and fashioning a "good fit" with their environment enhances their productivity and coping effectiveness. To illustrate my point, let me give you an example of two children with two very different profiles.

George is a strong-willed youngster. He has difficulty adapting to change and reacts intensely to both positive and negative events in his environment. George is also very sensitive to changes in his physical environment: he has a low threshold for noise, odors, touch, and pain. When you show George a picture, he is able to see the detail in the picture, and his own drawings are very detailed. He tends to worry a lot, and his natural propensity is to view the glass as half empty rather than half full. George is, in a word, difficult. When his parents first sought professional assistance, they blamed themselves for their child's behavior. Most parents do. But George was set up temperamentally to be difficult. This does not mean that George is doomed to be nonproductive and unhappy.

The good news about George is that today he functions quite well as a young adult. He is an A student in college and gets along well with his professors and peers. He has a few close friendships, including a serious relationship with a girlfriend. He still needs a few hours to himself each day and he is still intense, but he worries less than he did and he makes a conscious effort to look for what is right in a situation. George looks and acts happy and now admits to feeling "pretty good" most of the time.

But raising George was a real challenge. George's parents had to stop blaming themselves for George's basic temperament and accept and love him for what he was. To do that they first had to see the positives behind his individual temperament traits.

George's sense of persistence allows him to stick with tasks he is personally committed to. He has a strong need to be in control and is not easily influenced by the crowd; as a result, George had no desire to party or do drugs, like some of the other kids in his high school. George stands up for what he believes—even if what he believes is not popular with the rest of the folks. George learned to direct his worry toward productive planning, and for the most part he is able to laugh at his own negative propensities. At the same time, his tendency to worry helps him plan ahead for problems that might occur. In other words, the temperamental traits that George exhibits are good *and* bad, not good *or* bad.

George's parents understood and appreciated him for what he was. They also had to help him understand his own temperament, and they taught him how to adjust the environment, when possible, to suit himself. For example, George has learned to take change slowly. If he goes on vacation, he takes at least two weeks off from his schedule because he takes longer to adapt to the new routine. By taking at least two weeks off George benefits from the vacation; shorter vacations are simply more stressful for him because he is expending a lot of energy simply adjusting to the change in routine.

George's parents had to work with him on perspective taking, a skill that keeps counterproductive worry and negativity under control. (Chapter 8 addresses this skill.) As a result of being taught how to think more positively, George gets the best mileage out of his negativity. That is, he still thinks about what might go wrong, but now he is able to look at what he is thinking, reject needless concerns, and plan only for the problems that might feasibly occur. George's parents also had to teach him how to identify the early signs of arousal and how to channel his intensity appropriately. They also had to learn to give him space and time to defuse when angry. Trying to discipline and deal with George when he was highly aroused resulted in a further deterioration of the situation; waiting until tempers cooled worked much better. George now assumes that responsibility for himself. He asks for and takes the time and space he needs when he feels himself losing control.

George's parents had to use parenting strategies and communication techniques with him that were different from those they used with their other children (those strategies are highlighted in Chapter 4). Because George is slow to adapt, his parents had to prepare him for routine changes. Now George prepares himself. If he is going to take a new summer job, he finds out everything he can about the particulars before he actually starts the job. This helps him get used to the new situation faster and significantly reduces the distress. And, finally, George, with the guidance of his parents and counselors, chose a course of study in school that best fits him and that will allow him a career that suits his temperament. He is an accounting major, a choice that suits his aptitude in math and his ability to deal with details.

Alexander is temperamentally very different from his brother George. Alex is friendly, easygoing, moderately intense, and sensitive to things in his environment. He likes change and can adapt to a new situation easily. Because change is not a problem for him, it is not difficult for Alex to be spontaneous, to do something out of the ordinary on the spur of the moment. He was an easy child to raise and nurture—far easier than George. In contrast to his brother, Alex is far less likely to think a situation out fully; sometimes he makes mistakes because of this. Everyone likes Alex; his open and friendly nature makes him a natural "people person." Because he was more social in nature than George, Alex experienced more difficulty with peer pressure during high school. He made the right decisions, but the kind of guidance his parents had to give him was quite different from the guidance given to George. Alex's choice of career is consistent with his temperament: he intends to pursue a career in politics.

Fitting the Environment to Temperament

What these examples show is how different two children from the same family can be and how flexible parents need to be because of those differences. To give you some idea about how to fit the environment to temperament, I have briefly outlined what each temperamental extreme would optimally require from the environment.

Activity Level

A child who is highly active requires frequent physical outlets. By contrast, a child who is by nature on the inactive side may be stressed by days that are highly physical, and a child who is moderately active will do well with a mix of physical and sedentary activities. Sports and physically active recesses are "good fits" for physically active children. Likewise, frequent stops on long trips and opportunities to walk around during the schoolday are examples of ways parents and teachers can arrange the environment to fit the active child. Inactive children, on the other hand, need time for quiet activities. They need to be encouraged to engage in enough physical activity to remain healthy, but they need the time and the opportunity for nonphysical activities. These children have no trouble with the physical pace of the typical schoolday because the sedentary nature of traditional academic tasks fits their temperament. Schedules that require a continuous physical pace (e.g., summer sports camp), by contrast, may be uncomfortable for the inactive child because they do not "fit" the child's natural temperamental tendencies.

Rhythmicity

Children who are highly regular are likely to feel better with regular eating, sleeping, and elimination cycles. When these cycles are disrupted, they may feel distressed until a new regular pattern is established. A highly regular child may become very distressed by a schedule that is constantly shifting. So, parents of highly regular children need to establish regular meal and bed times, as a way of providing a "good fit" with the environment.

Approach/Withdrawal

The person who is disposed toward the approach dimension of this temperament continuum will prefer new things and will most likely seek out new experiences. A person who is inclined to withdraw from new situations will require time to adjust and will actually need to pace the number of new things experienced. Children who tend to withdraw from novel situations are sometimes helped by a "gradual transitioning" to the new situation. This can be accomplished in a number of different ways. Let's take the first day of school as an example. Children who basically withdraw from new situations will find the first day of school more stressful than other children will. Helping such children prepare by familiarizing them with the new situation in advance of the first day of school is what I mean by gradual transitioning. Having children begin a school schedule for awakening and retiring at night the week before school starts is a way of transitioning. Allowing them to bring something familiar to school is another way of helping them make the transition. And allowing these children an opportunity to meet their teacher and see the classroom prior to the opening of school is yet another way of helping them make the transition.

Adaptability

People who are slow to adapt require more time than highly adaptable individuals and need to prepare for those changes that they can predict. Parents who have children who are slow to adapt have to be particularly careful not to overwhelm them with too many changes at one time and have to teach them how to pace themselves. One of my favorite examples of this principle involves one of my all-time favorite persons—Jacob. Jacob was seven years old when I first met him. Like George, he has difficulty adapting to change. Jacob's family moved from the city to the suburbs when he was 12. This involved a change of school district as well as the change of residence and neighborhood. Jacob was, as you might expect, apprehensive about the move and the new school. When I discussed the situation with him, he—not his parents or I—had the following analysis and solution: Jacob knew that he didn't like change and that this move represented a major change. He also knew that he would eventually get used to the new house, neighborhood, and school but that it was best for him to take all of this very slowly. So he decided that moving in June would give him the whole summer to get adjusted to the new house and neighborhood. He would need the first semester to adapt to the new school and classmates, and then, he figured, he could handle the bus. So he asked me and his parents if we could arrange to take him to school in the morning. He also reasoned that the car trip with me could serve as a session and save me time! I was so impressed with his forethought that I did arrange my schedule to take him to school once a week. Luckily, his parents were also able to implement his plan. While it is not always possible to arrange rides to school in the morning, this particular example shows the importance of accepting one's own temperament and planning around it. Expecting everyone to adapt equally easily to change is an error. There are natural differences; it makes sense to work with them.

Threshold of Responsiveness

Children with low sensory thresholds are more sensitive and are likely to respond readily to slight changes in their physical world. They may require environments that restrict the level of a particular stimulus. For example, a child who has a low sensory threshold for noise will do better in a quiet environment. Those who have a high threshold for noise are not bothered as much by loud noises and will fare better than the low-threshold child in a noisy environment (although noisy environments do eventually take a toll on everyone). The point is that persons with low sensory thresholds are aroused more easily and therefore may not tolerate a particular situation as well as their high-threshold counterparts. The implication of all this is that some children are more likely than others to become overaroused by the typical kinds of situations all children encounter, for example, playgrounds, school cafeterias, noisy bus rides to school, and birthday parties. A parent needs to determine if noise is bothersome to the child, and if so, whenever possible, to arrange a quieter environment. A child who has a low threshold for touch may be bothered by frequent hugs or tight-fitting clothes. Providing loose-fitting clothes and respecting the child's tactile sensitivity are examples of "fitting" the environment to the child.

Intensity of Reaction

Parents of high- or low-intensity-reacting children could provide a "good fit" for these children by respecting their natural reactivity tendencies. A high-intensity child needs to know how to vent his or her feelings appropriately. Forcing them to stifle their expression of emotion actually goes against their natural grain and is itself stressful. So, parent and child might negotiate on what is and is not appropriate "venting." Hitting another person or shouting obscenities is not an acceptable outlet for their intensities. But, discussing the issue in a very animated way with you may be most appropriate. The same consideration needs to be given to high-intensity children for positive situations. They require a socially appropriate outlet for their emotional expressions.

At the other end of the continuum are low-intensity reactors. Low-intensity reactors find it distressing when they are forced to be highly emotional and demonstrative with their feelings. Respecting their "reserved" response to a situation as a genuine expression of feelings allows for a comfortable fit between them and their environment. On a day-to-day level, this means accepting the fact that they are less likely to laugh or cry hard. They may even be more hesitant to offer public displays of affection (e.g., hugs and kisses).

Quality of Mood

It's easy for some people to look at a situation and see the opportunity and goodness in it. It is far more difficult for others to do the same, but this does not mean it's impossible for people to learn to think more positively even though their natural tendency is to think negatively. The implication of this temperament characteristic for parenting is this: Children who are negative or who are worriers need to be taught how to manage their thoughts so that this temperamental characteristic works for, instead of against, them. In the example cited earlier, George was taught how to channel his negative mood disposition toward a productive expression. (Chapter 8 covers techniques parents can use to teach their children these perspective-taking strategies.)

Distractibility, Persistence, and Attention Span

Children with short attention spans need work and concentration schedules that allow them to take short breaks. Breaking up their homework assignments, for example, so that such children can do different parts at different times may be the key to making homework less onerous for them.

Persons differ in their ability to persist. Some individuals are stressed by jobs that require them to move from one project to another before completing the first. Others have a hard time sticking to a project that is long and involved. In the latter case, breaking the project up so that is has separate components is sometimes helpful for ensuring that the project is completed.

Learning Style Differences between Children

Temperament is just one of the many factors that one has to consider in sizing the child up. Learning styles and learning modalities are equally important since a great deal of the child's time is spent learning. Educators Rita Dunn and Kenneth Dunn (1977) as well as Bernice McCarthy (1987) have studied the different learning styles and modalities that people use to learn. The Dunns have identified four major factors that affect how children learn:

1. The child's immediate environment, specifically, its design and the degree of sound, light, and heat
2. The child's own emotional status, specifically, how the child is motivated (by self, teacher, adult), how responsible and persistent he or she is, and how much structure in the environment he or she requires to be a successful learner
3. The child's sociological needs, specifically, whether she or he prefers to study alone, in pairs, or with an adult or to alternate between these possibilities
4. The child's physical needs, specifically, whether he or she is auditory, kinesthetic, or a combination modality learner, and whether he or she learns better at a certain time of day, requires movement, and does better if he or she eats small snacks while studying

Bernice McCarthy discusses four different learning styles, which address the unique ways people generally think and learn and are similar to the formulations offered by other researchers and theorists who have studied differences in thinking styles. Type I learners learn better when the material presented has personal relevance. They need, in other words, to know why the material is important to them. They like to deal with concrete concepts and to problem-solve by looking at different alternatives. They are sensitive to feelings, they like subjects dealing with people, and they do best under cooperative learning conditions. Type I learners do better when they have an opportunity to directly experience what they are learning. Thus, field trips and roleplay activities suit this learning style. Additionally, encouraging Type I learners to integrate subjective experiences and helping them relate new material to things already known maximizes their learning potential. For example, a parent or teacher might suggest role playing to teach children about the American Revolution. Playing the role of, say, George Washington helps children learn relevant facts and issues and encourages them to feel personally involved in the decisions he made. Reading assignments that hold no personal interest and research projects that are abstract are the kinds of assignments Type I learners have the most difficulty with.

Type II learners require a different learning setting. They are analytical, have a fascination for ideas, and like details and abstractions. They are logical, industrious, and thorough. Type II learners like learning environments where they have the opportunity to explore a given subject in detail. They like assignments that require them to draw conclusions, analyze content, and compare and contrast. To learn about the American Revolution, for example, a Type II learner might prefer to analyze the strategies used by the colonists and contrast them with the British strategies. The younger Type II learner might learn the concept of measurement by measuring different things (e.g., liquids, solids, shoe sizes, height) and then analyzing how such measurements are similar or different. Type II learners find role plays and creative assignments the most difficult.

Type III learners like to take abstract information and apply it to practical problems. They are pragmatists who enjoy finding answers to questions and problems themselves. They tinker and experiment with things until they get them to work. They are intolerant of fuzzy ideas but value strategic thinking and skills-oriented instruction. The Type III learner would approach a history lesson about George Washington from the point of view of the strategies he had to use in order to win the war against the British. A Type III learner also does well with math concepts that are tied to practical problems. For example, the older Type III student might learn the principles of calculus or geometry in the context of flying a plane from New York to Los Angeles. Younger Type III learners also do well with problems that simulate real-world tasks; for example: "You have $50. Go to the grocery store and purchase what you would need to eat for a week. The groceries have to be nutritious, and your meals have to be well balanced." Such a project requires the integration of information about health and about food prices and also calls upon addition and subtraction skills. Type III learners have the most difficulty with assignments that require them to do busywork and with reading assignments that are not connected to some project.

Type IV learners are "what if?" thinkers. They like to integrate what is being learned with experience. They learn through trial and error and tend to be independent and self-reliant. They like change and will sometimes jump from one project to another before they finish the task at hand because they are so excited by novelty. They like open-ended problem-solving situations. They love to learn through self-discovery and excel by adding to or improving on what already is. They like variety in instructional method. Using the George Washington example, a Type IV learner might learn about the American Revolution by writing a role-play skit; to enhance understanding, a number of "what if?" statements based on the facts could be generated as the impetus for the role plays. Type IV learners have the most difficulty with tasks that require a lot of detail and assignments that require specified steps. This is the case because Type IV learners are creative and need the opportunity to find the answers for themselves.

To get a general idea of your child's learning style and the modalities that your child favors, answer the question in the Learning Style Questionnaire on page 91. Examining the responses that you have given for your child will provide some insight about what conditions are most conducive for your child's learning. While it's not possible to always set up the optimal learning conditions for a child, working with learning styles can lead to a better fit between child and environment. Homework time, reading time, and the general academic environment are enhanced when we work with the child's natural learning style. This point was certainly reinforced for us with our second child, Jessica. She requires short study times with activity and is primarily a Type III learner. She is a problem solver and has a tremendous amount of common sense. To encourage Jessie to read, we focused on her natural interest in science and math and found science experiments and kits that required her to read and experiment at the same time. This particular strategy worked like a charm. Her reading and language arts skills improved tremendously. Fortunately, her second-grade teacher was attuned to the different learning styles of children. She created a teaching approach entitled "Workshop," which involved a set of activities designed to convey various academic concepts. The children were required to complete certain exercises but could choose others. The activities were varied and were designed to accommodate the various learning styles. Jessie was so motivated to complete the exercises that she would often finish them before the deadline. She loves school and she loves learning. Working with her natural tendencies instead of against them certainly was crucial to the development of this healthy learning attitude. Table 3.1 summarizes the four different types of learning styles and the kinds of learning environments that are best suited to them.

Stress Tolerance Levels and Triggers

Each and every one of us needs a certain amount of stress (discussed in Chapter 6) to be productive and successful. Too much or too little stress threatens our productivity and well-being. Stress researchers have discovered that we all have different stress tolerance levels. This level varies from time to time and is set off by various triggers. It has been useful to me both personally and professionally to communicate ideas about stress by using the analogy of a water barrel. When the water barrel is empty, there is room for more water. When the water barrel is full, adding more water to it simply causes a spillover; the barrel needs to be drained before you can possibly add any more water to it. The water barrel represents our everyday experiences and demands. The water level in the barrel is our tolerance level; it tells us how much more we can tolerate before we experience the spillover effects, which are experienced as distress symptoms (see Table 6.1). Some of us have barrels that are naturally half full to begin with. Some of us have a propensity to fill those barrels faster than others. What fills my barrel can be different from what fills yours. The kinds of things that fill our barrels are what stress researchers call stress triggers. Knowing what those are and managing them appropriately helps us keep a sense of personal control. Helping our children understand their own stress triggers and tolerance levels

TABLE 3.1.   Learning Styles

Type	Basic characteristics of child	Needs
I	People and feeling oriented Needs to know the reason for learning Relates experience to different perspectives Likes to get involved in the material Imaginative Perceives information concretely and then thinks about it	Opportunities to listen and share ideas Self-involving activities Discussions
II	Abstract thinker Likes theory and facts Likes logic Likes lectures Detail oriented Processes information abstractly and then thinks about it	Traditional classrooms Activities that involve comparisons, synthesis, and analysis Lectures
III	Pragmatic Values strategic thinking Skill oriented Likes to experiment Processes information abstractly and then acts on it	Opportunities for hands-on activities Opportunity to test theories Projects that allow for experimentation
IV	Enthusiastic Intuitive Learns by trial and error Likes change Takes risks Perceives information concretely and acts on it "What if?" thinker	Variety in activities Some freedom of choice in how to learn Open-ended assignments

contributes to the resources the child needs to be successful and resilient.

The question is, How do you know what your stress tolerance level and stress triggers are? A stress diary is sometimes a useful tool for discovering them. It helps us identify our symptoms of stress and the kinds of things that set us off. A model for constructing the stress diary is provided on page 90. (It is designed for both parents and children; parents can complete one for themselves and one for their children.) The diary is set up to look at the child's behavior at three different times of the day.

Common Stress Triggers

Too Much or Too Little Sleep. One of the more common stress triggers or "barrel fillers" is sleep deprivation. People vary in the amount of sleep they require to stay healthy and well rested. Some people require only four to six hours, others eight hours, and still others ten hours. Most children require at least eight hours of sleep—and when they don't get it, you know it. Sleep allows the body to repair itself and refuel. Sleep deprivation prohibits this, leaving us less able to deal effectively with everyday stressors. Sleep deprivation fills that barrel a lot! Likewise, too much sleep can leave the person groggy and sluggish. The effects on our barrel of too much or too little sleep are the same: we are in a compromised position to deal with everyday stressors and concerns.

Diet. Proper nutrition is of paramount importance for optimal mental and physical functioning. Poor nutrition, on the other hand, is a major barrel filler. Poor nutrition upsets our body chemistry to some degree. For some people—adults as well as children—poor nutrition is a major stress trigger. This is certainly the case for our second child, Jessie. When Jessie's blood sugar levels are low, she becomes irritable and oppositional. She does best when she eats often and eats the right carbohydrate–protein combinations. Parents interested in how diet affects behavior in children would do well to read Dr. Lendon Smith's (1976) book on this subject, *Improving Your Child's Behavior Chemistry*. Dr. Smith argues that individuals differ in enzyme and endocrine activity, in blood and body fluids, and in the way they react to drugs, chemicals, and disease. The delicate balance of hormones, blood sugars, and other biochemicals affects our functioning. Because nutrition affects this balance, it is worthwhile for parents to become aware of what their children eat and what effects their diet has on them.

Allergies. Dr. Smith, as well as Dr. Rapp, argues that children don't act well because they don't feel well. While there is certainly controversy about this issue, allergies can and do affect our stress tolerance levels. For some children, allergies may contribute in a significant way to how fast and how much the level in their stress barrel rises. I have recently been made more aware of the role allergies play in the behavior of children: I have two boys in my practice whose major depressive symptoms were significantly relieved by eliminating milk from their diet and molds from their environment. Another child had such severe symptoms that she required psychiatric hospitalization; she is currently being treated for severe allergies, and her behavior and general functioning have certainly improved.

Do allergies explain all stress reactions? For some children and some adults, allergies are a major stress trigger; for others they are not. You don't know until you start to observe and keep track of the particular triggers and the child's reaction to them. We are all unique and therefore respond differently to different things, allergens included. For those of you interested in learning more about allergies and the effects they have on children, I suggest you read Dr. Doris Rapp's (1991) *Is This Your Child?*

Seasonal Effects. Recently, psychiatrists and other researchers have discovered that a few people (mostly women, ages 21 to 40, although men and children can be similarly affected) suffer from what is now referred to as seasonal affective disorder

(SAD). This disorder is marked by a depressive syndrome that generally strikes during late autumn, peaks in winter (usually February), begins to improve in March, and is typically gone by spring. Some people experience a reverse seasonal effect; that is, they experience the depressive symptomatology during the summer months. The incidence of SAD is greater at higher latitudes: persons living in the northern states are more likely to experience the disorder than those living in the southern region of our country (Wurtman & Wurtman, 1989). The symptoms of Winter SAD include fatigue, a marked tendency to oversleep, and depressed mood, as well as extreme irritability at times, difficulty concentrating, and carbohydrate cravings in the late afternoon and evening. Summer SAD peaks in July and August and includes agitation, insomnia, and appetite loss. The disorder is caused by a disturbance in our brain chemistry, specifically, in the levels of the hormone melatonin, which affects mood and subjective energy levels, and the neurotransmitter serotonin, which controls a number of functions, including mood, concentration, appetite for carbohydrate-rich foods, and, possibly, the immune system (Wurtman & Wurtman, 1989). Both the hormone melatonin and the neurotransmitter serotonin are influenced by photoperiodism, the earth's daylight cycle; levels of these chemicals in our brain vary, depending on the time of year and, therefore, the length of day and night. While the number of people who have to be clinically treated for SAD is relatively low, the change in seasons may affect all of us to some degree. Most people refer to their negative feelings as the "winter blues." Taking note of these seasonal changes in ourselves and our children gives us a little more information about what factors operate as stress triggers.

Medical or Other Existing Conditions. Our physical status contributes to how full our barrel is because physical ailments tax the body's natural resources and at the same time present conditions that require attention. Ailments can influence what alternatives we have to choose from and how much energy we have. If I have the flu or a cold, my ability to handle the kinds of stress I normally manage is compromised. I might not be quite as able to effectively write or read or manage a problem. I might need to curtail some of my activities and rest more. It's not unusual to observe more irritability in a child who is getting sick. Illness is a stress trigger that can fill a child's barrel (and our own barrel as well).

Likewise, existing chronic conditions like diabetes, learning disabilities, depression, or hyperactivity (also called attention deficit hyperactivity disorder, or ADHD) can become stress triggers. This is especially the case when the person's chronic condition fits poorly with environmental demands. For example, hyperactive children who eat lunch in a noisy cafeteria and then play outside in an unstructured setting are much more likely to misbehave because their barrel, which fills faster than that of other children in unstructured and noisy environments, is spilling over. Similarly, diabetics who do not have the opportunity to eat when and what they should are more likely to have difficulty because their bodies and barrel levels are naturally sensitive to diet. Learning disabled children who have to compete in a learning environment that is not suited to their disability are likely to experience stress, thus raising their barrel level and further impeding their progress. Tables 3.2 and 3.3 provide the common characteristics of learning disabilities and attention deficit hyperactivity disorder. For those readers interested in finding out more about these two conditions, a bibliography is provided in Appendix 1 of this book.

Poor Fit between Person and the Environment. We have already seen how a good fit between person and environment increases the probability of success and productivity. Mismatches between temperament and environment or between ability level and expectations are sources of distress. Persons who are reserved and inclined to prefer quiet environments will be taxed in situations that require them to be outgoing or in environments that are chaotic and noisy. Children who attempt to meet the unrealistic expectations of their parents (or who set unrealistic goals for

TABLE 3.2. Characteristics of Learning Disabilities

Academic achievement that is significantly below the child's academic potential

Poor motor coordination (i.e., unable to throw ball, color, or do other age-appropriate gross- or fine-motor activities)

Difficulty understanding age-appropriate material

Confuses left and right

Poor handwriting

Transposes information from book, board, or mind to paper incorrectly

Has trouble with spelling, even after much attention and practice

Has trouble following directions

Has trouble scanning written material and as a result loses place when reading

Has reading comprehension difficulties

Mixes up the order of words in a sentence

Mixes up the order of letters in a word

Reverses letters or numbers

Has trouble expressing self

Has trouble with math

Has trouble remembering what he or she has learned; requires repetition

Reads very slowly

Has inconsistent performance pattern: sometimes does very well, sometimes not

---

Note: A given child will not typically exhibit all of these characteristics. If your child shows a number of them, consult your child's teacher or school psychologist.
Source: S. M. Miller, The School Book (New York: St. Martin's Press, 1991).

themselves) operate under chronic pressure, which in turn serves to lower their stress tolerance level. For example, if John expends a great deal of emotional and physical energy perfecting his soccer skills, he has less energy available for other pursuits. If he succeeds and meets his expectations, the positive feelings he experiences serve to lower the stress level in his barrel. But if he desires to be a soccer star and has absolutely no aptitude for the sport, the energy and frustration he experiences will simply serve to fill his barrel. There is a distinction to be made between working hard in

TABLE 3.3. Characteristics of Child
with Attention Deficit Hyperactivity Disorder (ADHD)

Has difficulty sitting still
Is almost continuously fidgeting
Is impatient (i.e., has difficulty taking turns or awaiting a turn)
Is very easily distracted
Has trouble completing tasks
Is disorganized for age (i.e., is always losing things)
Has trouble paying attention for age-appropriate time span
Talks excessively
Is impulsive (i.e., engages in dangerous acts without thinking, blurts out
   answers, interrupts others without thinking)
Does not learn from mistakes
Has trouble following directions
Does not seem to listen

Note: The ADHD child may not exhibit all of these characteristics. The American Psychiatric Association's *Diagnostic and Statistical Manual of Mental Disorders*, 3d ed., revised (1987; DSM-III-R) states that the child must exhibit at least eight of the characteristics for six months or more and the symptoms have to be apparent before the age of seven.

order to achieve a realistic goal and working hard and not reaching an impossible goal. Sometimes knowing the distinction between the two kinds of goals is difficult. A realistic assessment of our strengths and weaknesses is, of course, a prerequisite for setting realistic goals.

Erroneous Assumptions and Self-Defeating Attitudes. The assumptions we make about situations and the attitudes we hold about ourselves and others are sometimes sources of distress. (Chapter 8 addresses erroneous assumptions and self-defeating attitudes and offers suggestions on how to alter them.) Attitudes and assumptions are the filters we use to evaluate ourselves, others, and situations. If they are self-defeating or inaccurate, they will lead to erroneous perceptions. Perceptions in turn influence how we feel and react in a situation. For example, if Susie believes that her parents should give her everything she wants, she will most likely feel very angry and act out in some way when they don't, or can't, comply. Her negative emotions, along with her negative actions, serve to fill her barrel. Additionally, the attitude that her parents should give her whatever she wants sets up unrealistic expectations in Susie that are themselves stress triggers when they are not met. How do you know what assumptions the child is making or what that child's attitude is? Often we can tell from behavior. For example, when Susie has a temper tantrum after not getting her own way, we can be reasonably sure that she believes she should have her way. Asking children what they think about a situation is of course a direct way of assessing their attitudes and assumptions. The point is, becoming aware of how you or your child views a situation enables you to identify and modify the sources of much distress.

Everyday versus Major Stressors

Everyday Stressors. Table 3.4 provides a brief overview of the normal developmental stressors that occur for children at various ages. They represent the typical kinds of issues that children face as they proceed through the developmental stages. For example, children ages one to four experience separation anxiety; how much and to what degree it fills a particular child's barrel depends on the child and the environment. Other normal stressors include changes in routine, social disappointments, having too much or too little to do, and changes required when advancing from one grade to another in school. As with developmental changes, whether or not these normal events are stressful for the child depends on the child and on the environment. Routine changes are likely to be more stressful for children who are temperamentally slow to adapt than for highly adaptable children.

Major Stressors. Divorce, family trauma, relocation, and the like are major stressors for children and adults. Sometimes

TABLE 3.4. Normal Childhood and Adolescent Stressors

Developmental stage	Normal stressor
Preschool (1–4 years)	Not having control over immediate environment Birth of sibling Transition to nursery school Separation from attachment figures Adjustment to child care
School age (5–12 years)	Transition to school Homework Competition with peers Peer relationship changes Grades in school Disappointments connected to sports or other extracurricular activities Peer teasing Pressure to go with the fad Sibling reputation pressures Conflict with teacher Child–parent conflicts Special recognition for outstanding performance Oral reports Worry about tests Time pressures (i.e., balancing extracurricular activities and schoolwork demands)
Adolescence (13–19)	Hormonal changes Growth changes Peer pressure Heightened sexuality Dependence–independence issues Relationship issues Increased responsibility for self in school Social responsibility Career and college choices

(continued)

TABLE 3.4. (*Continued*)

Developmental stage	Normal stressor
Adolescence (13–19) (*continued*)	Transition to work
	Part-time jobs
	Gender role issues
	Dating issues
	Self-evaluations and acceptance of strengths and weaknesses

Source: L. Arnold, *Childhood Stress* (New York: Wiley, 1991).

these traumatic situations give the individual the opportunity to develop resilient attitudes and skills. At the same time, such stressors drain the person emotionally and physically. At these points in our life, we typically experience decrements in performance and have less tolerance for everyday irritants. This is because stressors such as these fill our barrels very quickly and fully. As a result, we have to allow ourselves the time and space to "de-stress," or, to continue the analogy, drain the barrel. We can accomplish this by simply staying with a familiar routine, refraining as much as possible from making major decisions, and engaging in enjoyable hobbies and activities. (Table 3.5 lists the major life event changes that studies have found to be stressful for children and adolescents.)

The foregoing discussion covered the typical kinds of stress triggers that might operate for you and your child. There are, of course, others. Sometimes particular situations, people, or events trigger a child. By keeping a stress diary, you and your child will become more aware of what those idiosyncratic triggers are. Awareness is the first step toward control.

Stress Assessment

To introduce the idea of stress and the stress diary to your child, you might try the following procedure:

TABLE 3.5.   Major Childhood Stressors

Death
parent
sibling
close relative
close friend
favorite pet

Serious illness
self
parent
sibling
close relative
close friend

Other extraordinary trauma
(e.g., war, fire, legal problems, sexual abuse)

Parental
divorce
remarriage
job loss
job start
abuse
alcohol abuse
incarceration

Change in
standard of living
school district
residence
number of people living in home
parental contact

Source: L. Arnold, *Childhood Stress* (New York: Wiley, 1991).

Step 1: Sit down with your child at a time that is convenient and free from other distractions and commitments.

Step 2: Explain to the child what you mean by stress. I find the analogy of the barrel very helpful, but there are other, equally good, strategies for getting the concepts across.

Step 3: Describe the stress diary.

Step 4: Discuss what you mean by stress symptoms. You can use Table 6.1 in Chapter 6 for guidelines.

Step 5: Complete the diary for two or three weeks. That is usually a sufficient amount of time to recognize the pattern of everyday stressors and their effects.

Step 6: Review the diary with your child.

Step 7: Periodically review a day with your child, using the format of the stress diary. This helps the child develop the habit of analyzing his or her own stress triggers and patterns.

The following example of how a discussion might go with a young child is from a conversation I had with a six-year-old boy:

Alex, I would like to talk to you about something very important. I would like to talk to you about what makes us feel good and what makes us feel bad. Look at this picture. What is it? Yes, it's a barrel. I want you to pretend the barrel holds all the things that you have to do and all the things that you are thinking about. The barrel even holds all the things you eat. So when you wake up in the morning and you have to fix your bed, imagine that your barrel fills up just a little. If you have a fight with your sister, then your barrel fills up a whole lot more. If your barrel fills all the way up and you get very tired, guess what happens? That's right—the barrel spills over and you feel very bad. How do you know that you are feeling bad? Do you smile when you feel bad? Do you cry? Do you get a headache? I know when my barrel is spilling over because I get grouchy and sometimes I even get a stomachache or a headache. We are going to play a little detective game. I am going to ask you how you are feeling, and we are going to try to figure out what your body and brain feel like. We are also going to try to figure out what is filling up your barrel.

With an older child, of course, you can be much more direct and to the point. The trick is getting your child to cooperate with you. Providing incentives and doing it yourself sometimes legitimizes the task and elicits more compliance from the child. It is also possible to gather the information by just observing your child and keeping track of the diary yourself. For very young children this is, of course, the most reasonable strategy.

Finally, it is necessary to recognize that individual differences exist for various aptitudes. I have already mentioned that it's important for parents, teachers, and child to establish expectations based on the child's natural abilities. It is also important to help children develop interests in activities and hobbies that enhance their natural potential. In order to establish reasonable expectations for performance, it is helpful to first discuss what the experts know about the various forms of intelligence.

Aptitude Assessment

Most experts now agree that intelligence is multidimensional and difficult to measure objectively through standardized tests. Theorists have offered different ideas about the several components of intelligence. H. Gardner (1983) suggests that there are six major kinds of intelligence: musical, linguistic (verbal), logico-mathematical, spatial (an aptitude that an artist or architect might need), bodily kinesthetic (aptitude for dance, sports, etc.), and personal (self-knowledge and interpersonal skills). R. B. Catell (1971) classifies intelligence as either fluid or crystallized. Fluid intelligence, which refers to those abilities that are relatively independent of the person's culture or environment, are innate and include the ability to solve abstract problems, general reasoning abilities, memory, and analytical abilities, whereas crystallized abilities are greatly influenced by educational background and include vocabulary, general information, and arithmetic skills. R. J. Sternberg (1985) argues that there are adaptive and contextual qualities of intelligence. For Sternberg, intelligence is the ability to adapt to a situation. It includes the knowledge of how to organize the environment in order to learn (called metacognition) and a performance component, which involves the ability to do what has to be done, and a knowledge-acquisition component, which is what is actually learned and used through the process of learning. What are the implications of all these ideas for the development of self-esteem and resilience?

Well, just as it's important to accept and work with your child's temperament, learning styles, and stress factors, it's equally important to accept and develop the abilities the child comes to this world with. Experts have identified several different kinds of aptitudes that go into a person's intelligence. A given individual may be high, low, or average on one or all of these aptitudes. For example, a child might have great musical and verbal abilities, average people skills, and no athletic aptitude. It is essential to find out what your child's profile is so that you can work with it. The problem for parents and teachers alike is that we sometimes misjudge a child's potential. This is the case because we do not always have objective ways to assess it and also because our own expectations and aspirations for our children influence our perceptions of them. Measured IQ (i.e., intelligence as measured by standardized IQ tests) is not an absolute index of native intelligence or future success. The best that we can say about measured IQ is that it predicts school performance reasonably well for most, but not all, children.

We all have hopes and dreams for our children. We must be careful not to impose those expectations on the child if he or she is not capable of achieving them. So what do we do to find out what the aptitude profile of our child is? Perhaps the following guidelines will prove helpful:

1. Expose your child to different activities. Observe how the child does. If the child appears to be putting forth a reasonable amount of effort, accept the performance as an indicator of his or her level of competence.

2. In academic areas, talk to your child's teacher. A good

teacher is a reliable source of information about your child's academic potential. Grades in school are the teacher's view of your child's achievement relative to her or his potential. There are also standardized achievement tests. These tests suffer from a number of shortcomings, but if they are consistent with the child's grades and with the teacher's and your perceptions, then they are probably indicative of your child's achievement and potential relative to other children of the same age and grade. If the grades and standardized test scores are inconsistent, you may need another measure of what the child's academic potential is. If you are uncertain, you may want to elicit the aid of the teacher or the school psychologist.

3. Set the child up to succeed. Cater as much as you can to your child's learning style and natural aptitudes. Whenever possible, make use of the child's individual learning style and natural intelligence to master competencies in school or at home. Providing an optimum learning environment will give your child the opportunity to best realize his or her potential.

Adam, age six, had difficulties mastering his list of spelling words. His mother would use the rote kind of drill that many of us have tried with our children. This strategy simply did not work for Adam because he was not a traditional kind of learner and not at all interested in lists of spelling words. Adam was a Type I and Type III learner. He was also a child with very strong spatial, kinesthetic, and musical abilities. When Adam's mother put his spelling words to music, he mastered the list in record time. Essentially, what she did was to use Adam's natural musical intelligence to master the spelling task. This strategy personalized the learning experience for Adam, and as a result he succeeded in learning the spelling words. Similarly, Jessie's dad used Jessie's natural spatial and kinesthetic aptitudes to improve her reading comprehension. By encouraging Jessie to visually diagram the plot and characters in the story, he helped her improve her comprehension. Her willingness to read also increased. Sometimes her dad would ask her to give a book report using dance and music; on those occasions Jessie would put together a collage of classical music pieces to illustrate the themes in the book. These are examples of how parents can make use of their child's natural abilities to master a task.

4. Encourage your child to always do his or her best. Pay attention to what the child says and how the child acts when engaged in activity that requires an aptitude. Children who show signs of distress may be mismatched for their potential, and a child who is seemingly breezing through may require more of a challenge and higher expectations.

5. If the child shows a strong interest in an activity, encourage it even if the child does not excel in it. Remember that interests and hobbies are great stress relievers. You don't have to be a Mozart to get something out of music.

6. Ask your child how he or she feels about the task. Often the child has a good handle on how much to expect. If you or a knowledgeable adult feel that your child is ready for a challenge and the child expresses concern, ask the child to give it a try. Explain that it's reasonable to give a short trial period for something new and difficult. Then respect the child's evaluation of the situation. An example will help to clarify the point: Jane was a gifted child. It was suggested that she be given an opportunity to try an accelerated math program. At first Jane was hesitant to do so. Her parents and teachers asked her to give it a try for three weeks, promising that she would be allowed to switch back to her former program if she felt the program was too intense for her. After two days Jane loved it. When she discussed her experience with her parents, they were able to help her see that allowing herself the opportunity to try out something difficult resulted in a positive outcome for her.

7. If your child appears gifted in some area (see Table 3.6 for criteria), be careful not to overburden him or her. Often a child is gifted in one area but not in another. For example, a child may be gifted artistically but not academically. Or a child may have superior academic skills but be somewhat immature. There is a

TABLE 3.6.   Characteristics of a Gifted Child

Has excellent memory
Learns new concepts and skills easily
Is very self-sufficient for age
Has a special talent in an area like art, music, dance, athletics, or language
Excels academically
Has excellent reasoning abilities
Has a long attention span
Has a love for learning and seeks out new information
Reads on a level considerably above grade level
Has an excellent vocabulary
Has scored over 125 on a test of intelligence

Note: These are general guidelines. School districts and experts differ on the criteria used to identify gifted children.
Source: S. M. Miller, *The School Book* (New York: St. Martin's Press, 1991).

tendency for parents and teachers to expect gifted children to be uniformly superior. They may not be. Be careful to assess the component aptitudes of your child—for the child's sake and your own.

8. Finally, remember that children mature over the whole course of childhood. Sometimes they do not initially demonstrate their full potential. Research has shown that academic aptitude can fluctuate greatly during the early childhood years. Therefore, we need to keep an open mind about the child's interests and abilities.

In summary, this chapter examined the basis for individual differences. When we accept ourselves for what we basically are, we are then in a better position to fashion our environment to fit our unique personal characteristics. Individuals who experience a good fit with their environment cope better with the stresses and strains of everyday life and are more likely to succeed. The combination of self-acceptance and good environmental fit sets the foundation for self-esteem and resilience.

Temperament Assessment

Scoring Directions: Add up the scores for each of the temperaments and plot them on the scale below. Compute the score by adding up the numbers you circle. For example, if you circled a 1 for each of the items under activity level, the total score would be 5. Plot the sum on the scale appearing below the questions.

Directions: Circle the number of the statement that best describes your child.

Activity Level

A.0 My child usually sits quietly when engrossed in an activity.

1 My child sometimes sits quietly when engrossed in an activity.

2 My child has difficulty sitting quietly even when engrossed in an activity.

B.0 My child can usually sit through a meal without causing a commotion.

1 My child sometimes has difficulty sitting through a meal and sometimes causes a commotion.

2 My child has difficulty sitting through a meal and frequently causes a commotion.

C.0 My child can usually tolerate a long car trip.

1 My child sometimes tolerates long car trips.

2 My child is restless on long car trips.

D.0 My child usually prefers quiet play activities.

1 My child sometimes prefers quiet play activities and at other times prefers physical play.

2 My child always prefers physical play.

E.0 My child stays in one spot at night while sleeping.

1 My child sometimes stays in one spot while sleeping and sometimes does not.

2   My child is all over the place when sleeping at night.

0	5	10
low activity	moderate activity	high activity

Intensity of Reaction

A.0   My child is not very expressive emotionally; my child does not typically show emotions with facial expressions, body language, or verbal intonations.

1   My child is somewhat expressive emotionally.

2   My child is very expressive emotionally.

B.0   My child has a mild reaction to stressful events and disappointments.

1   My child has a moderate reaction to stressful events and disappointments.

2   My child has a strong reaction to stressful events and disappointments.

C.0   My child approaches special events with a laid-back kind of attitude.

1   My child approaches special events with a moderate degree of enthusiasm.

2   My child shows a great deal of enthusiasm for special events.

D.0   My child reacts in a calm manner when his or her rights have been violated.

1   My child shows a moderate degree of anger when his or her rights have been violated.

2   My child reacts strongly when his or her rights have been violated.

E.0   My child relates stories and events in a calm, matter-of-fact manner.

1   My child expresses some enthusiasm when relating a story or event.

2   My child expresses a great deal of enthusiasm when relating a story or event.

0	5	10
low reactor	moderate reactor	high reactor

Quality of Mood

A.0   My child is rarely in a good mood.

1   My child is sometimes in a good mood and sometimes in a bad mood.

2   My child is generally in a good mood.

B.0   My child is difficult to console or comfort; when my child is upset, it takes a long time for him or her to snap out of the negative mood.

1   It's sometimes difficult to console or comfort my child; when he or she is upset, it takes a little while for him or her to snap out of the negative mood.

2   My child is easy to console; when he or she is upset, it takes very little time for him or her to snap out of the negative mood.

C.0   My child is noncooperative when asked to do things around the house.

1   My child is sometimes cooperative when asked to do things around the house.

2   My child is usually cooperative when asked to do things around the house.

D.0   My child will report the bad things that happen before any of the good things.

1   My child reports an equal number of good and bad things that happen.

2   My child reports the good things that happen before any of the bad things.

E.0   My child will argue and complain for a long time about things that don't go his or her way.

1   My child will argue and complain for a little while about things that don't go his or her way.

2   My child argues just a little about things that don't go his or her way.

0	5	10
negative mood	moderate mood	positive mood

Distractibility

A.0   My child's concentration is not easily broken by noise.

1   My child's concentration is sometimes easily broken by noise.

2   My child's concentration is easily broken by noise.

B.0   My child's concentration is not easily broken by other activities going on at the same time.

1   My child's concentration is sometimes easily broken by other activities going on at the same time.

2   My child has a hard time concentrating when there is something else going on.

C.0   My child's concentration is not disturbed by the presence of other people.

1   Sometimes my child's concentration is disturbed by the presence of other people.

2   My child's concentration is almost always disturbed by the presence of other people.

D.0   My child will come back to an activity after being called away from it.

1   My child will sometimes come back to an activity after being called away from it.

2   My child will seldom return to an activity after being called away from it.

E.0   If my child is involved with a toy or activity, it's not easy for me to substitute another toy or activity; my child wants to return to the original toy or activity.

1   If my child is involved with a toy or activity, it's sometimes easy for me to substitute another toy or activity.

2   If my child is involved with a toy or activity, it's easy for me to substitute another toy or activity.

0	5	10
low distractibility	moderate distractibility	high distractibility

Sensory Threshold

A.0   My child notices details in pictures, slight changes in a room, and little things that are out of place.

1   My child is moderately observant; he or she notices some details in pictures and things that are obviously out of place.

2   My child is oblivious to the physical world; he or she does not notice details in pictures and hardly ever notices when changes have been made to a room.

B.0   My child is sensitive to noise; he or she complains when there is even a little noise.

1   My child is moderately sensitive to noise; he or she complains only if there is a lot of noise.

2   My child seems to have a high tolerance for noise; he or she rarely complains about loud noise.

C.0   My child is very sensitive to odors.

1   My child is moderately sensitive to odors.

2   My child is not very sensitive to odors.

D.0   My child has a low tolerance for pain; he or she cries or complains about the slightest injury or discomfort.

1   My child has a moderate tolerance for pain; he or she will cry or complain about injuries or discomforts that are substantial.

2   My child has a high tolerance for pain; he or she rarely cries or complains about injuries or discomforts.

E.0   My child is sensitive to touch; he or she often complains when clothes are tight-fitting; he or she does not like to be cuddled or held.

1   My child is moderately sensitive to touch; he or she complains only if clothes are very tight; he or she likes to be held and cuddled some of the time.

2   My child has a high tolerance for touch; he or she rarely complains about tight-fitting clothes; he or she likes to be cuddled and hugged.

0	5	10
low threshold	moderate threshold	high threshold

Rhythmicity

A.0   My child does not have a predictable time when he or she gets tired.

1   My child sometimes has periods when he or she gets tired at about the same time each day.

2   My child generally gets tired at about the same time each day.

B.0   My child does not have a predictable time when he or she gets hungry.

1   My child sometimes has periods when he or she gets hungry at about the same time each day.

2   My child gets hungry at about the same time each day.

C.0   My child does not have regular bowel movements.

1   My child sometimes has periods when he or she has regular bowel movements.

2   My child has regular bowel movements.

D.0   My child sometimes eats a lot and then other times eats a little.

1   My child sometimes has periods when he or she eats about the same amount each day.

2   My child generally eats about the same amount each day.

E.0   My child sometimes sleeps a lot and then on other days sleeps very little.

1   My child has periods when he or she sleeps about the same amount of time each day.

2   My child generally requires about the same amount of sleep each day.

0	5	10
low rhythmicity	moderate rhythmicity	high rhythmicity

Approach/Withdrawal

A.0   My child prefers old clothes and toys to new ones.

1   Sometimes my child prefers old clothes or toys to new ones.

2   My child prefers new clothes and toys to old ones.

B.0   My child is very reluctant to try new foods.

1   Sometimes my child will try new foods.

2   My child will willingly try new foods.

C.0   My child does not like going to new places.

1   My child sometimes likes going to new places.

2   My child often likes going to new places.

D.0   My child does not like to meet new people.

1   Sometimes my child likes to meet new people.

2   My child generally likes to meet new people.

E.0   My child is reluctant to get involved with new situations (e.g., new school year).

1   Sometimes my child is eager to get involved with new situations.

2   My child is eager to get involved with new situations.

0	5	10
withdrawal	moderate	approach

Adaptability

A.0 It takes my child a long time to adjust to a new situation.

1 It takes my child a little time to adjust to a new situation.

2 It takes my child very little time to adjust to a new situation.

B.0 My child has difficulty accepting the rules of a new situation.

1 My child sometimes has difficulty accepting the rules of a new situation.

2 My child readily accepts the rules of a new situation.

C.0 It takes my child a long time to get used to new foods and places.

1 Sometimes it takes my child a long time to get used to new foods and places.

2 My child learns to like new foods and places quite quickly.

D.0 It takes my child a long time to adjust to new routines.

1 It takes my child a little time to adjust to a new routine.

2 It takes my child very little time to adjust to a new routine.

E.0 It takes my child a long time to warm up to new people.

1 Sometimes it takes my child a long time to warm up to new people.

2 My child warms up to new people quickly.

0	5	10
slow to adapt	moderate	quick to adapt

Persistence and Attention Span

A.0 My child has a tendency to give up and look for assistance when tasks are difficult to master.

1 My child will sometimes give up on a task and look for assistance; it depends on the task and the circumstances.

2 My child seldom gives up on a task even though the task is difficult to master; he or she generally tries to figure things out without assistance.

B.0   My child accepts "no" from me as an answer and will go on to some other activity.

1   My child sometimes accepts "no" for an answer and will go on to some other activity.

2   My child rarely accepts "no" for an answer and will continue to ask permission for a long time.

C.0   My child rarely finishes an activity that he or she starts.

1   My child will finish some activities and not others.

2   My child usually finishes an activity that he or she starts.

D.0   My child does not like doing any one activity for a long period of time.

1   Sometimes my child will want to do the same activity for a long period of time.

2   My child generally gets engrossed in an activity and will spend long periods of time on it.

E.0   My child loses interest easily when I am telling a story or when he or she is watching a program or a movie.

1   Sometimes my child loses interest when I am telling a story or when he or she is watching a program or a movie.

2   My child rarely loses interest when I am telling a story or when he or she is watching a program or a movie.

0	5	10
low persistence/ attention span	moderate persistence/ attention span	high persistence/ attention span

---

A similar assessment scale appears in B. Kuczen, *Childhood Stress* (New York: Delta Books, 1987).

Stress Diary

Time of day	Distress symptom (See Table 6.1.)	Stress trigger (See Chapter 3 for common stress triggers.)
Early morning		
Midmorning		
Noon		
Midafternoon		
Early evening		
Late evening		

Learning Style Questionnaire

Directions: Check as many as apply.

1. My child studies best when:
   _____ the lights are bright
   _____ the lights are dim
   _____ does not matter

2. My child seems to study best when:
   _____ the room is slightly warm
   _____ the room is slightly cool
   _____ does not matter

3. My child does better if she or he:
   _____ studies alone
   _____ studies with me
   _____ studies with friends
   _____ studies with another adult
   _____ does not matter

4. My child studies best while sitting on:
   _____ something soft, like an upholstered chair or a couch
   _____ something hard, like a straight chair
   _____ does not matter

5. My child learns best when:
   _____ told exactly what to do
   _____ allowed to determine how to structure his or her study time or
   project
   _____ given some guidelines and some freedom to choose
   _____ does not matter

6. My child learns best by:
   _____ hearing and discussing the material
   _____ seeing and reading about the material

_____ experimenting with the material

_____ does not matter

7. My child needs to:

_____ move about periodically when studying

_____ sit still while studying

_____ does not matter

8. My child's motivation for learning is affected by:

_____ positive feedback from the teacher

_____ negative feedback from the teacher

_____ positive feedback from me

_____ negative feedback from me

_____ positive feedback from another significant adult

_____ negative feedback from another significant adult

_____ feedback from peers

_____ his or her own performance

_____ nothing seems to motivate my child to learn

9. My child seems to study best when:

_____ allowed to eat a snack while studying

_____ not allowed to eat a snack while studying

_____ does not matter

10. My child seems to study best:

_____ with background music

_____ when it's completely quiet

_____ does not matter

11. My child concentrates better in the:

_____ morning

_____ afternoon

_____ evening

_____ does not matter

12. My child is:

_____ very organized and hardly ever loses things

_____ somewhat organized, sometimes loses things

_____ hardly ever organized, always loses things

13. My child likes to:

_____ read about new things

_____ listen to discussions about new things

_____ do projects to learn about new things

_____ none of the above

14. My child learns best when:

_____ he or she can learn and apply (Type III)

_____ he or she can express an opinion (Type I)

_____ he or she has time to think about the new material (Type II)

_____ he or she becomes actively involved while learning the new material (Type IV)

15. When my child is learning:

_____ he or she likes to determine how to learn (Type IV)

_____ he or she tends to observe (Type I)

_____ he or she tends to think and ask a lot of questions (Type II)

_____ he or she tends to think about how the material can be used (Type III)

16. My child:

_____ gets excited about learning new things (Type IV)

_____ has to analyze everything and understand every detail of a subject (Type II)

_____ likes to try new things out to see if she or he can use them (Type III)

_____ likes to know how other people feel about the subject (Type I)

17. My child likes:

_____ subjects and assignments that deal with feelings (Type I)

_____ subjects and assignments that are logical and methodical (Type II)

_____ subjects and assignments that are practical (Type III)

_____ subjects and assignments where he or she can see results and learn independently (Type IV)

18. I would say my child likes instruction that incorporates:

_____ personal relationships (Type I)

_____ observation and experimentation (Type III)

_____ rational explanations (Type II)

_____ opportunities to practice and then try again (Type IV)

19. My child:

_____ is intuitive (Type IV)

_____ is a thinker (Type II)

_____ has a lot of common sense (Type III)

_____ is very sensitive to feelings (Type I)

20. My child learns through:

_____ the discussion method (Type I)

_____ the lecture/information method (Type II)

_____ the coaching/facilitator method (Type III)

_____ the self-discovery method (Type IV)

Chapter 4

Promoting Self-Esteem and Resilience
The Role of Parenting

Of all the professions, parenting is the single most important and, at the same time, the most difficult. Socializers of children (parents, teachers, grandparents, and other significant adults) contribute in a significant way to children's self-esteem and resilience. There are no formal training requirements, no professional unions, and very few established support systems for parents. Nevertheless, there are good parents and good children. In this chapter, I will explore the components of good parenting and the connection it has to the development of self-esteem and resilience.

Components of Good Parenting: Parental Discipline Styles

What exactly have the experts learned about good parenting, and how does good parenting promote success and resilience? Diana Baumrind (1970) has identified five different parental styles and their effects on the development of what she calls the "competent child." The five styles include the authoritarian, the permissive, the rejecting-neglectful, the traditional, and the democratic-authoritative. Baumrind characterizes competent children as those who function well with peers and adults, have a strong sense of personal identity, and are confident about their skills and aptitudes. Competent children are responsible and independent, other-oriented, trustworthy, positive, assertive, persistent, self-motivated, and good at problem solving. They are respectful of authority figures but able to question adult directives when necessary. Sounds familiar? As you can see, many of these characteristics are typical of resilient children and adults. Is there a connection between parenting style and the development of competent children? Yes. The relationship is not perfect, but evidence from Baumrind's studies, as well as the studies of others, indicates that parenting has a strong effect on the emotional, social, and intellectual development of a child.

Authoritarian parents are strict and autocratic. They establish rules independent of any input from the child. The rules in an authoritarian home are generally overly restrictive, and punishment is severe and harsh. The principal means of control used by authoritarian parents are coercion and intimidation. Authoritarian parents believe that children owe them obedience and respect. Disobedience is interpreted as an assault on the parent's power base. As a result, such parents react to the child's noncompliance with anger and reinforce the power differential between the child and themselves by becoming even more dogmatic and punitive. There is absolutely no attempt to see things from the child's point of view or involve the child in decision making of any kind. The child is dictated to and is expected to obey without question, in the same way a good subject responds to an autocratic dictator.

If there is a parental style diametrically opposed to the authoritarian parent, it is permissiveness. Permissive parents believe in the natural goodness of children. Children have no limits or demands imposed on them by the parents, and there is no consistent set of rules. Permissive parents are overly responsive to the needs of their children. They allow their own schedule and needs to be determined by the child's every request and demand. They expect nothing from the child, and when they do attempt to discipline they are weak and inconsistent. In short, permissive parents expect that children will raise themselves. When there's a problem with the child, the permissive parent is often overwhelmed and incapable of dealing with the situation. In *Summerhill: A Radical Approach to Child Rearing*, A. S. Neill (1977) argues for a more permissive parental style.

Rejecting-neglectful parents are uninvolved and detached. These parents are disengaged from their children and "motivated to do whatever is necessary to minimize the costs in time and effort of interaction with the child" (Maccoby & Martin, 1983). They keep their children at a distance, showing little interest in their activities, accomplishments, and behavior. With older children, such parents have no awareness or interest in the child's whereabouts, friends, school performance, or health. When they are forced to interact with the child or deal with the child's behavior, they are typically hostile and rejecting. With younger children, this parenting behavior is characterized by a disruption in the parent–child bond. These parents are sometimes neglectful of the child's basic needs and almost completely unresponsive to the child's emotional and intellectual needs. The message the child gets from rejecting-neglectful parents is "Leave me alone, I can't be bothered."

In the traditional parenting style one parent (usually the father) operates in an authoritarian style while the other (usually the mother) is nurturing and permissive. The authoritarian parent sets strict rules and limits and is the disciplinarian. The permissive parent sets few limits and is very responsive to the child. To use Glenn Austin's (1988) description, the traditional parenting style is characterized by "father knows best" and "mother loves more."

The final parental style is the democratic pattern (called the "authoritative parental type" in Baumrind's study). The democratic parent commands respect from the child and establishes rules that are consistently enforced. However, the democratic parent, unlike the authoritarian one, considers the child's wishes and solicits the child's opinion when appropriate. The democratic parent gives feedback to children about their behavior, correcting negative behavior and reinforcing positive behavior. Responsive, warm, and firm, parents of this sort encourage excellence and provide educational and culturally enriching experiences for their children. Discipline in a democratic setting is proportionate to the transgression and involves the use of reason, concern, and positive guidance. Democratic parents are respectful of their child. This respect is reflected in the way the parents communicate and relate to the child. Although there are times when children and parents are less than thrilled with each other, it is generally true that children from democratic homes enjoy their parents and their parents enjoy them! Rudolf Dreikurs (1964) promotes a democratic parental style in his book *Children: The Challenge*.

To better understand the differences among parenting styles, consider the following scenarios, each illustrating the way a parent with an authoritarian, permissive, democratic, or rejecting-neglectful style would respond.

Susie, age nine, has been invited to a skating party after school. The party is scheduled for the same time as her piano lesson. The authoritarian parent might respond like this: "How could you even ask to go? You know you have a piano lesson, and a lesson is more important than a party." And when Susie attempts to plead her case (if she does), the response from the parent might be, "Don't you dare argue with me. I said no, and no is no. Now go to your room, young lady." The permissive parent's response might be, "If you want to go, sure, go ahead. I will cancel your piano lesson." The democratic parent's response would be: "Well, Susie, you do have a piano lesson, and it is important to keep the appointment with your teacher. I know you want to go to the party. Let's think about how we can solve this problem together." The rejecting-neglectful parent either fails to give the child an answer or gives a response that would result in the course of least resistance for the parent.

Now consider a scenario where discipline is needed. Susie is told that she can play outside after dinner for one hour. She loses track of the time and comes in after two hours, one hour past her curfew. The authoritarian parent would react with, "Susie, you're late and because you're late, you're grounded for the rest of the summer. From now [early July] until school starts, you're to go to you room after supper. There will be no TV and no company. Do you understand? That will teach you to disobey me!" The permissive parent might comment on the child's being late and might even complain to the child but would fail to do anything definitive about it. The democratic parent's response to the situation might go something like this: "Susie, I asked you to come in at seven o'clock. It's now eight o'clock. What happened?" Susie might then explain that she did not realize the time and the parent would respond with, "Tomorrow you will need to come in an hour earlier. Maybe you can think about how you can keep better track of the time. I would be glad to help if you would like some help thinking about it." Rejecting-neglectful parents would probably not notice or care if the child is late so long as it does not interfere with them or their routines.

From these examples you can see that the democratic parent's style encourages children to assume responsibility for themselves. The style seems to combine and balance the best features of the authoritarian and permissive households. It promotes problem solving and it also models good interpersonal skills. The permissive home offers no guidelines for the child. The fact that Susie is excused from the piano lesson and suffers no consequences for being late teaches her nothing about making commitments and sticking to them. Nor does it model how the real world reacts when a norm or expectation has been violated. In short, children from permissive homes do not learn how to organize or control themselves because a framework of rules and commitments is simply nonexistent. The opposite extreme is apparent in the authoritarian household. Because the parents are so controlling, the child either comes to rely on them for self-control and decision making or rebels in either an overtly aggressive or passive manner. Moreover, the authoritarian parent is a poor example of how to interact with others. Finally, the rejecting-neglectful style is the most destructive of them all. The message the child gets from such a home is "Do what you want but don't bother me."

According to research conducted by Baumrind (1977, 1983) over a 30-year period, there were more competent children from the democratic homes studied than from any other home environment. In Baumrind's sample of children, 85% of those raised by democratic parents were judged competent and 15% were considered partially competent. This is in direct contrast to the children coming from rejecting-neglectful homes: none of these children was judged fully competent, although half were found to be partially competent. The outcome statistics for the permissive and authoritarian households are equally interesting. None of the girls coming from authoritarian homes was judged to be incompetent, although more than half were evaluated as only partially competent. Boys from these households had more of a problem: approximately a quarter were considered totally incompetent while half were evaluated as partially competent and only 18% were seen as fully competent. Girls seem to have problems in homes that are permissive. None of the girls from the permissive homes was fully competent; 70% were judged partially competent while the remaining 30% were evaluated as completely incompetent. Sixty percent of the boys from permissive homes were partially competent, 20% were fully competent, and the other 20% were considered to be totally incompetent. Finally, the data from traditional homes are certainly more encouraging than those from permissive, authoritarian, or rejecting-neglectful homes, but they still do not equal the outcome seen from the democratic parenting style. Half of the girls coming from traditional homes were perceived as fully competent, 33% were partially competent, and 17% were completely incompetent. None of the boys coming from traditional homes was judged completely incompetent. Most (57%) were partially competent, while the remainder were considered competent.

While it's true that you can't always generalize the results of one study to the rest of the population, other researchers and clinicians have come to similar conclusions about parental styles. Stanley Coopersmith (1967) found that children whose parents use a democratic parenting style have higher self-esteem, and

Glenn Austin (1988) argues a similar point on the basis of his work as a pediatrician. The democratic parental style appears to be superior to all others. But is parental style the only factor responsible for the development of competent children? No. Parenting is a complex issue and involves several interacting variables. One such variable is the interpersonal warmth that the parent exhibits toward the child. Maccoby (1980) defines a warm, nurturing parent as one who is "(1) deeply committed to the child's welfare, (2) responsive to the child's needs, (3) willing to spend time (within limits) in joint enterprises of the child's choosing, (4) ready to show enthusiasm over the child's accomplishments and acts of altruism, and (5) sensitive to the child's emotional states" (p. 392). Hostile parents are not committed to their children and are quite open and vocal about their negative feelings toward them. Maccoby found that children whose parents were warm and nurturing tended to be more considerate of other children, to have higher self-esteem, and to do better in school. W. C. Becker (1964) found that the interpersonal warmth of the parent influenced the development of competence in children; this finding may explain why there was a scattering of competent and incompetent children across parental discipline styles in the Baumrind study. Becker found that restrictive parents who are warm and loving are likely to have children who are obedient, polite, and nonaggressive. Children of permissive, warm parents are socially outgoing, independent, active, and somewhat domineering. In addition, warm parents produce children who are likely to be socially competent with peers and open to adult guidance and direction.

Taken together, these results suggest that a warm democratic home produces the best overall results for most children. The question is, What does an adult need to do in order to be a warm and democratic parent? Baumrind (1970) claims that parents need to (1) be good models themselves of socially appropriate behavior, (2) adopt firm standards of behavior and enforce these standards with rewards and punishments, (3) be committed to their child, (4) have high but reasonable expectations for achievement, and (5) provide their child with a challenging and stimulating environment. Specifically, democratic parenting involves a set of guidance techniques collectively referred to as "positive discipline." Democratic parenting also makes use of constructive communication skills. Let's look at each of these components in more detail.

Components of Good Parenting: Positive Discipline

The major elements of positive discipline are (1) attending to and reinforcing appropriate behavior, (2) setting realistic rules and expectations, and (3) enforcing those rules and expectations.

Pay Attention and Reinforce Good Behavior

Parental attention is a powerful reinforcer. Children prefer negative attention over no attention at all. Parental attention helps children focus on their behavior and understand the connection between behavior and consequences. It provides children with direct feedback about the efficacy of their actions and attitudes. The problem for most people is that they tend to pay attention only to negative behavior. Social psychologists refer to this tendency as a "negativity bias." When parents pay attention only to their child's negative behavior, they inadvertently reinforce that behavior.

Democratic parents pay attention to their child's good and bad behavior and know how to reinforce appropriate behavior. Their children know that appropriate behavior is noticed and occasionally rewarded. Commenting positively every so often when children do what they are supposed to increases the probability that they will continue to execute their responsibilities. This does not mean that you need to praise children every time they do what is expected; this is unrealistic and indeed not very good for the child. Nor is it good to pay attention only to your child's negative behavior. Authoritarian parents and rejecting-neglectful parents tend to punish negative behavior and essentially ignore appropriate behavior. When such an attitude is prevalent and when parents attend to children only when they are misbehaving, children will misbehave when they want and need the attention. Or they'll develop unrealistic and unhealthy attitudes about being perfect in order to avoid a parent's wrath or disappointment. We all need to know that we are important and valued by those whom we judge to be important and significant. Parents, teachers, and other significant adults fit this role for children. Attending to the positive traits and behaviors of another is one way of communicating that person's value and worth.

There are a number of methods one can use to reinforce behavior, the more popular techniques being reward, praise, and encouragement. Each of these practices has advantages and disadvantages as well as uses and misuses.

Rewards. Rewards are tangible objects or gestures children receive when they behave in a way that is consistent with the expectations of the person who has the power to reward. Rewards can be material objects like allowances, toys, and food; they can also be hugs, kisses, pats on the back, trips to the playground or movies, and privileges. Finally, a reward might be inclusion into a friendship or small group. For example, the reward for good grades in junior high or high school is election to the honor society. Or a reward for appropriate behavior on a shopping trip with Mom or Dad might be an invitation for another such trip.

Rewards can be useful incentives, but their effectiveness in promoting resilience and self-esteem is dependent on their proper use. Rewards that are outrageously disproportional to the deed undermine the value of the deed. That is, parents or other adults who overreward or underreward children give them a wrong message or leave them feeling controlled or resentful. Consider this example: Tommy, age ten, is given $25 for taking out the garbage each week. Tommy, of course, has everything he could possibly want; the $25 means very little to him. So Tommy sometimes takes the garbage out and sometimes doesn't. His parents are having difficulty finding rewards that mean anything to him. This pattern of overreward is typical of how Tommy's parents treat him in general. Tommy now expects other people to treat and reward him in the same fashion. Unfortunately, his home situation does not mirror reality, and Tommy has difficulty motivating himself to do what he is supposed to do in school and elsewhere. He has developed the attitude that the world owes him, and he has become increasingly resentful of the responsibilities that teachers and others expect him to assume. Moreover, because Tommy has never had to work very hard for any of his material possessions, he has not learned to value hard work. Overrewarding focuses his attention on the reward and not on the task. Some psychologists claim that it actually destroys the person's interest in the job. According to these psychologists, people who are overrewarded believe that they do their job only because of the reward and not because they like the job. In other words, the reward controls their interest and motivation for the job. The external reward, and not their own internal interest, is what keeps them working. When this happens to children, they come to rely on external rewards as motivators. This is a problem when a child is in a difficult or stressful situation where there are few external rewards. If children have not learned to call upon their own internal interests and motivations, they will not have the necessary drive to get through the difficult task or situation. In short, overrewarding represents a threat to a person's internal sense of control because it makes the person dependent on other people and situations. Internal control is one of the necessary ingredients for resilience. Therefore, overrewarding detracts from a person's sense of resilience.

Underrewarding has the same effect on resilience, but for different reasons. When people receive too little for their efforts, they infer that their efforts and work have little value. This can lead to feelings of resentment and hopelessness. As a result, a person may simply give up. A child who works hard to get a B in math and is rewarded with a neutral response like "Oh, that's nice" is left feeling "Why bother?" Think about yourself. Adults who receive small bonuses for major accomplishments at work often become resentful of their jobs and, unless there is good reason not to, will eventually put less and less effort into their work. Underrewarding, like overrewarding, undermines a person's internal motivation and sense of control.

Obviously, a reward needs to be the right kind and the right amount to have beneficial effects. But how do you know what the best kind and right amount are? There are no definitive answers. But here are some general guidelines:

Rewards need to be relevant and desired by the child; in other words, they should be age-appropriate. A good idea is to allow the child to choose from a range of rewards. When you involve children this way, the reward means more to them. Think about the magnitude of the reward. Ask the question "Is this reward reasonable, given my child's age and the situation?" If the child seems to be demanding bigger and more frequent rewards, it may be necessary to use other incentives. The magnitude of the reward should vary according to the difficulty and length of the task and the age of the child. For example, it would not be unreasonable for a child to earn half the cost of a new bike for reaching some major goal when that goal meant working hard and consistently for a long period of time (e.g., four to eight weeks). Older children have a need for larger rewards that they earn over longer periods of time; younger children need smaller but more frequent rewards.

There are definitely individual differences among children with respect to the efficacy of rewards; you need to gauge the effect of this method of reinforcement on your child. Use physical rewards sparingly. Don't get the child into the habit of expecting a physical reward each and every time he or she does what's expected. The real world does not operate this way, and teaching the child to expect something that the real world does not offer is to set that child up for disappointment and frustration as an adult. Also, too-frequent rewarding detracts from the power and novelty of rewards.

Praise and Encouragement. Besides physical rewards, parents can also use praise and encouragement to reinforce desired behavior. Praise is a positive statement that one person makes to another. When we praise others we provide them with our judgment about how well they did. For example, the statement "You're such a good piano player" is a praise statement; "I like the way you're behaving" is another example of praise. Encouragement, on the other hand, promotes self-evaluation and focuses on the actions of the doer. "Thank you for picking up" is an example of encouragement. A statement that directs the child to his or her own evaluation of behavior, like "Tell me how you managed to keep such good control," is another example of how a parent provides encouragement for the child's positive behavior. Jane Nelsen (1987) does a very good job of describing the difference between praise and encouragement in her book *Positive Discipline*. She offers the following guidelines for determining whether a statement is praise or encouragement: Statements that promote self-evaluations and empathy for the child's point of view ("I can see that you enjoyed that"), address the deed, involve self-disclosing messages ("I really appreciate your sense of humor"), or ask questions to cue appropriate behavior ("What do you need to do to avoid trouble in the future?") all meet the criteria for encouragement.

The appropriate use of praise encourages resilience and self-esteem because it provides children with feedback about the usefulness of their behaviors and attitudes. Praise is one piece of information children can use to determine which behaviors and attitudes to keep and which to discard. Nelsen argues that the overuse of praise may encourage children to become "approval junkies," a trait that may persist into adulthood. These children are overly dependent on the positive evaluations of others and require frequent approval and support. If they don't get it, their self-esteem suffers. Clearly, then, praise needs to be balanced and combined with encouragement. Also, children have to learn to become accurate self-evaluators and reinforcers.

Encouragement is a powerful socializing tool for resilience and self-esteem. It teaches children how to evaluate and monitor their own behavior. Good self-evaluations increase a person's internal sense of control. Self-evaluations followed by self-reinforcement and self-correction reduce reliance on other persons and on external controls. Children who learn to monitor themselves develop self-control and are better able to carry on in stressful times because they have the internal and personal resources to do so.

To use praise effectively, the adult must be careful not to overdo it. As with physical rewards, too much praise minimizes the impact of praise and can result in a person becoming overly dependent on the evaluations of others. Similarly, praise needs to be meaningful, specific, and sincere. Praising a child with a sarcastic tone or for trivial kinds of achievements serves to devalue the worth of your praise. Encouragement, on the other hand, can be used more frequently, although again it is unrealistic to think that a parent needs to comment continually on everything the child does. The example that follows will illustrate how positive discipline techniques can be used to reinforce responsible, take-charge behavior.

Darren's parents noticed that he would go to his room every night after supper and do his homework. They rarely had to speak to him about assuming this responsibility and decided that they needed to reinforce this appropriate behavior. So one night during dinner Darren's father said, "Darren, Mom and I noticed that you've been taking responsibility for your homework. We want you to know that we appreciate your decision to assume this responsibility [encouragement]. What made you decide to do your homework without being told [encouragement]?" The following week Darren had an invitation to go to the movies with some friends. Mom used this opportunity to reinforce Darren's responsible attitude and behavior toward homework: "Sure you can go. You've earned the privilege. Doing your homework with no prodding from us proves to me that you're a responsible person [praise], and because of your responsible behavior you can take this opportunity to go to the movies [reward]." Darren's parents took note of his responsible behavior, encouraged him to continue, and then used the movie as a reward. Darren learned several points from these interactions. First, he learned that responsible behavior is noticed and that it pays off at least some of the time. These are exactly the kinds of messages that children need to hear if they are to develop the internal controls they need for self-esteem and resilience.

Rewards, Praise, and Encouragement Applied to Resilient Behaviors. Rewards, praise, and encouragement can be used to instill the kinds of resilient behaviors and attitudes discussed in Chapter 2. To illustrate, allow me to discuss examples of the kinds of behaviors parents need to notice and reinforce.

Responsible and Self-Reliant Behavior. Examples of responsible behavior include doing homework, handing in assignments, doing chores, keeping curfews, owning up to mistakes, and accepting credit for success when appropriate. These behaviors increase a person's general feelings of self-efficacy and internal control. Being responsible and independent helps establish the right mental set for taking charge in difficult times and for pursuing and sticking with goals in order to be successful.

Behavior That Shows Initiative. Examples of this kind of behavior include showing interest in a topic area without undue prodding and taking responsibility, when appropriate, instead of expecting or relying on a parent or other adult. An example involving our second child, Jessica, illustrates this point very nicely: Jessica, then a second grader, wanted to go ice-skating after school. She took the initiative of finding out all the necessary information. She asked her older sister to help her look up the telephone number of the skating rink. She phoned the rink, asked all of the appropriate questions, and even recorded the number for me in case I felt the need to check on the information. She was going with a friend who had been skating all year, so she arranged to have the friend's mother phone me in case I had any questions! This is a good example of proactive problem solving. This kind of behavior certainly builds on the child's sense of internal control. It also develops the problem-solving skills that help the child see adversity and change as manageable. Parents must look for this kind of behavior and reinforce it. There are numerous examples of how children show initiative. When toddlers attempt to dress themselves and when children successfully occupy themselves, they present opportunities to parents to attend to and support their initiative.

One of the major threats to the development of initiative are parents who do too much for their children. The psychologist Alfred Adler claimed that parental pampering inhibited children from reaching their full potential. Parents who feel they are responsible for their children's entertainment all of the time are *pampering their children*. Parents who feel the need to fight all of their children's battles are *pampering their children*. Parents who do for their children when their children could easily do for themselves are *pampering their children*. Parents who overindulge their children are *pampering their children*, and parents who expect little and are overly protective and controlling are *pampering their children*. Pampering inhibits the development of both self-esteem and resilience, because it gives children the message "You cannot do it yourself and the world owes you." Both of these attitudes interfere with the child's sense of internal control.

Self-Control and Self-Discipline. When children refrain from getting into trouble or resist an impulse to do something that could result in trouble, they are exhibiting self-control behavior. Similarly, the child who refrains from acting out when upset or the child who goes to practices or studies for the long-term goal instead of giving in to the gratification of the immediate situation is demonstrating self-control and self-discipline. Self-control is a prerequisite for a number of the traits needed for resilience. Indeed, it's the basic foundation for our feelings of internal control. Self-control and self-discipline are necessary during times of stress and adversity. Self-control provides people with confidence that they have what it takes to face a challenge, hence promoting a challenge perspective. Self-control and self-discipline are necessary if a child is to reach high academic or career goals.

Other-Oriented Behavior. Children need to think of more than themselves. In Chapters 1 and 2 I discussed why thinking about others and social skills in general are so important for resilience and self-esteem. Examples of the kinds of socially skillful behaviors that children need to develop and parents need to reinforce are discussed in detail in Chapter 10.

Persistent Behavior. Examples of persistent behavior include finishing a task, sticking with something difficult until it is mastered, and some forms of what would be considered stubborn behavior. There are, as mentioned in Chapter 3, natural differences among individuals in terms of frustration tolerance and persistence. This means that being persistent is more difficult for some children and requires creative thinking in order to make it happen. For example, it may be necessary for a child low on the persistence scale to work for a short while on a task and then do something else before completing the task. Children who have naturally low persistence may require more encouragement from parents and teachers.

It's also the case that children (and adults, for that matter) are sometimes steadfast in their positions on certain issues. For example, a small child may want the candy that is in the cupboard. While the child's persistence may be a problem for the parent, the fact that the child persists in the attempt to secure his or her own way is an example of persistence, a trait that, when directed appropriately, will serve the child well. So a parent might want to show the child that the kind of stick-to-itiveness that was demonstrated to get the candy from the cupboard can be used to get other tasks done. For example, suppose that Jane doesn't think she can put the puzzle together. Jane's parents can help her persist with the puzzle by directing her natural persistence appropriately. The direction might go something like this: "Jane, you think you'll never get that puzzle together. But I think you can because you know how to try hard and not give up. Remember how hard you tried and how you just wouldn't give up trying to get the candy from the cupboard the other day? Well, if you think about the puzzle the same way, I know you'll solve it." Now Jane might argue that putting the puzzle together is harder than getting the candy. Her parents' response in this case would be to first express an understanding that it may be harder for her to persist with the puzzle and then to convey their confidence that she has what it takes to stick with it. The fact that the child has the persistence to seek something desired means that it can be directed toward the mastering of challenges. In any case, persistence is important for resilience and self-esteem because difficult tasks and accomplishments require a person to persevere.

Personal Drive for Excellence. Parents need to reinforce their children's achievements. And, more importantly, they need to recognize and then support their children's efforts at perfecting whatever skills they have. There are two components for excellence: the raw talent and the effort one expends in perfecting that talent. Talent alone does not ensure success or resilience. The willingness to work hard and perfect one's skills is crucial for success and contributes to the kind of persistence needed to be resilient. Behaviors that are indicative of a drive for excellence are the willingness to work and the setting of realistic high goals. Suppose a child comes home and says, "I'm going to get an A on the spelling test," then proceeds to study very hard but secures a grade of B+. In this case the parent needs to praise and encourage the effort and, if the child's potential is a B+, help the child accept that level of performance. The fact that the child desires to excel is healthy. The desire, of course, needs to be balanced with the potential. What's important is that parents expect and support the attitudes and behaviors that lead to achievement by their children.

Good Decision Making. Examples of good decision making in children include choosing to keep rules, choosing the right foods, and choosing productive activities. Good decision making is at the core of good problem-solving skills, and problem solving is critical to good coping. Coping enhances self-esteem and resiliency. (Decision-making skills are discussed in detail in Chapter 8.)

Perspective-Taking Skills. Examples of perspective-taking skills include balancing the positive with the negative, accepting disappointments with grace, being a good sport, putting distance between yourself and an adverse event, and seeing the negative as time limited. I had a terminally ill child in my practice whose ability to put things in perspective was beyond belief. Jane told her mother that she knew there was no cure for her cancer but that she was going to fight until the time that they did have a cure. When the cancer advanced to the point where it was clear that she was not going to survive, her message to me and her parents was that she was looking forward to heaven. Jane concluded, "God must want me pretty bad to be calling me so soon." Jane's sense of humor and perspective were remarkable and inspirational (Jane is one of the reasons why this book is being written). She was resilient—right to the end of her 13 years! Her ability to put her disease in perspective helped her adopt a challenge orientation toward the fight with cancer and, finally, accept death. (Details on perspective-taking skills are provided in Chapter 7.)

Establish Realistic Rules and Expectations

The second component of positive discipline is to establish realistic rules and expectations. Democratic parents have rules and provide structure. The rules in a democratic home are clear, simple, and reasonable. The parents involve their children in rule setting and listen to what their children have to say. The parents ultimately establish the rules, but they explain the reasons behind them and change them in appropriate circumstances. When it's possible to give children choices, democratic parents do. For example, Mr. and Mrs. Jones had a discussion with their three children (ages 10, 12, and 14) about cleaning their rooms. They felt it was time the children were given the responsibility for keeping their rooms clean and tidy. The parents explained their criteria for a clean and tidy room and then gave the children the choice of how they were going to meet those criteria. Once the children decided on who was going to what, Mr. and Mrs. Jones reviewed their plan to be sure that it was doable. They adopted the plan and held the children accountable for their respective jobs.

By giving children the opportunity to become involved in rule setting, parents not only optimize the probability of compliance but also give children an opportunity to learn decision-making skills. To ensure that rules are not forgotten or misconstrued, it's sometimes helpful to use contracts for older children and provide cues and signals for younger ones. (An example of a contract is provided in Appendix 2.) For younger children, parents might use a picture of a toothbrush to remind children to brush their teeth or they may have a designated signal that indicates a certain behavior needs to take place. In one family I know, the mother uses the phrase "code red" to indicate that the noise level is too high and needs to be lowered.

When a child has difficulty keeping or remembering rules, it may be necessary to review and practice. Parents should avail themselves of opportunities to share the model with the child. For example, Lisa, a hyperactive child, has trouble in restaurants and stores where there's a lot of social stimulation. Before going to the grocery store, Lisa's mother explained to her exactly what she expected of her in the store: "Lisa, you will need to stay with me in the grocery store. You can hang on to the shopping cart. I will ask you if you want something, but you're not to ask me." Her mother then asked her to repeat the instructions and briefly set up a role-play situation at home for Lisa to practice the rules. The two went on a brief shopping trip, and because Lisa was self-controlled, her mother praised her and allowed her to pick out a treat from the store. You should know that Lisa's mother doesn't always use physical rewards, but in this case she thought it wise to. Lisa has an especially hard time in the grocery store. Her natural inclination is to run all over the store and ask her mother for everything in sight. Because her mother knew that taking her to the store would be taxing for both of them, she set Lisa up to succeed by reviewing the rules very carefully and keeping the shopping trip short. Rewarding Lisa for rule keeping in the case was appropriate; this time Lisa was successful, and that needed to be noticed. The next time out, her mother may use only praise or encouragement. She might also lengthen the time span for the shopping trip.

To summarize, rules are important because they give children the structure they need to develop self-control and self-discipline.

The research cited earlier certainly supports appropriate rule setting. On the other hand, arbitrary rules and rules that are overly restrictive are destructive to the development of self-control and are likely to invite rebellion or unhealthy passivity. Appropriate rules are rules that are reasonable, necessary for the child's safety or the smooth functioning of the family, and clear and well understood by the child and that, when possible, involve the child's input and choices.

Enforce the Rules

Democratic parents are generally consistent and enforce the rules they put in place. To enforce the rules, parents of this persuasion use natural and logical consequences and positive reinforcement. A natural consequence is one that happens without adult intervention. An example of a natural consequence might be a situation where a child leaves a bike out in the front yard instead of putting it away. As a result, the bike is ruined or stolen. In this case the parent did not intervene, and the consequence occurred very naturally. Once a natural consequence has taken place, a parent need not moralize about it. Preaching to the child at this point serves only to detract from the power of the natural consequence. In fact, at this point parents might use some active listening and encouragement to help the child learn from the mistake. Consider this example: Alex leaves his bike in the driveway. Dad pulls out of the driveway and runs over it. Alex is devastated by the loss of the bike and comes and cries to his parents. His parents empathize with Alex's loss and ask if he might be able to think of a way to remember to put his bike away when he gets a replacement next year. The dialogue might go something like this: "I'm sorry your bike got ruined. I imagine you feel pretty bad about losing it. Maybe you can think of a good way to remember to put the bike away when you get your new bike next year." If the child gets upset because you won't fix the problem, the best you can do is remain emotionally calm, express your feelings and your understanding of the situation to the child, and remain firm in your position. Sometimes parents have to remove themselves from their children temporarily in order to maintain composure and control. For example, Alex might want his parents to fix his broken bike. He might even try to get them to believe that the broken bike was their fault. Or he might attempt to pull on the heartstrings of his kind and empathetic parents so that they then take responsibility for his problem. If this happens, Alex has not experienced the natural consequence of his behavior. Moreover, by rescuing Alex, his parents may inadvertently communicate the expectation that others will fix the problem he creates for himself. This is not a resilient expectation or message.

Natural consequences can be a powerful discipline technique when parents can allow them to happen, since children learn the direct connection between their actions (or lack thereof) and the effects their actions have in the real world. This kind of feedback helps children learn to moderate their behaviors so that they can effect the best results. When children learn to control their behavior in this way, they increase their own feelings of self-control.

Natural consequences have limitations as well: they cannot be used when they involve harm to the child or someone else or are ineffective in cases where the child is not bothered by the consequences. In these cases a parent can apply logical consequences. (A word of caution about both natural and logical consequences: the child, especially the difficult child, may initially escalate the behavior as a way of testing the system. Be patient and firm. Eventually, these virtues pay off, as the child realizes you're not going to back off from the consequences.) Logical consequences, which require the intervention of an adult, involve the application of a consequence following a transgression or an act of noncompliance. For a consequence to be logical it must be related in some way to the offense, it must be reasonable, and it must be administered in a respectful (as opposed to a hostile) manner. Jane Nelsen (1987) does an excellent job explaining logical consequences in her book *Positive Discipline*. Using the work of Adler and Dreikurs as a foundation, Nelsen argues that the purpose behind the parents' use of logical consequences is instruction, not punishment. Thus, if a consequence is applied to a child's misbehavior in a demeaning way or if the consequence far exceeds the crime, the consequence is not a logical one. It becomes a punishment and has few long-range benefits.

To ensure that the consequence is logical, a parent would be wise to ask the following questions:

1. Does the consequence last for a long time?
2. Is the consequence highly punishing for the child?
3. Is the consequence likely to engender a high degree of anger in the child?
4. How would you feel if you were the child? Would you feel overpunished?

If the answers of any of these questions are yes, then the consequence is probably unreasonable and needs to be rethought. Remember that the major point of a logical consequence is to instruct. When consequences are severe, they lose their directive quality and become justification for a child's self-pity and feelings of victimization. Again, think about those times when you felt that the consequences for yourself or someone else were a little too severe. What is remembered in such cases is the unfairness of the punishment, not the poor decision making that caused the behavior being punished. Sure, a child might not repeat the behavior in the presence of the punishing agent when the consequences are severe. Punishment surely does inhibit negative behavior—at least for a while—but it does little else and can create a number of negative side effects.

Let's talk about ways parents can maximize the instructional effectiveness behind logical consequences. Consequences that are of short duration and proportional to the offense and that have either a relational quality or a negotiated connection to behavior work the best. So, for example, requiring a child who violates a curfew by an hour to come in one hour before the regular curfew the next time meets all the criteria of a logical consequence. It is of short duration, it is directly proportional, and it is highly related to the misconduct being addressed. Sometimes it's impossible to find a consequence that's exactly like the misbehavior or noncompliance. In these situations, parents have to select a consequence. For example, if Susie fails to do her chores, a logical consequence might be a deduction in her allowance for the week. Such a consequence might be negotiated with Susie at the time the chore list is drawn up. The actual amount of the deduction would be proportional to the number of times Susie failed to do her job that week.

In addition to the use of natural and logical consequences, rule enforcement requires that parents have a dialogue with their children concerning the rules and rule violations. Some clinicians suggest a "gripe session" for this purpose. During a gripe session children have the opportunity to discuss their feelings about the rules and parents have an opportunity to listen. This is a forum where parents may choose to amend the rules or the consequences. Or they may choose to keep the rules and to help the child problem-solve. Family meetings are a more formal way of accomplishing the same thing. (Appendix 1 contains lists of resources that address the benefits and mechanics of family meetings.)

Rule enforcement is enhanced when natural and logical consequences are occasionally paired with rewards, praise, or encouragement. Rules are viewed more favorably when associated with these positive reinforcements. Doing homework has more appeal if every so often the child gets a pat on the back from Dad or Mom or a "Good job" from the teacher. Indeed, adults like to hear words of appreciation from employers even though they know that failure to do a good job might also result in the loss of that job. The association of positives with the natural and logical consequences makes the rule or job less onerous.

Components of Good Parenting:
Constructive Communication

"Every time you talk to a child you are adding another brick to define the relationship that is being built between the two of you.

And each message says something to the child about what you think of him. Talk can be constructive to the child and to the relationship, or it can be destructive" (Gordon, 1975, p. 46).

In addition to using positive discipline, democratic parents communicate constructively with their children. Constructive communication promotes self-esteem and enhances social skills. It also encourages an open (as opposed to a closed and defensive) line of communication. Communication is the transfer of information between two or more people. It involves words and actions—what we say and write to each other, the "looks" we give, the faces we make, the tone of voice we use when addressing another person, the actions we perform or fail to perform. All these forms of communication put together build relationships and lead children (and adults) to make judgments about what another person thinks of them. In fact, Virginia Satir (1972) claims that communication is the most important influence on the relationships people have with each other.

The hallmarks of effective, constructive communication are its congruence and its open, supportive and instructive nature. Communication is congruent when there's a consistency between what people say, how they say it, and what they then do. For example, the statement "I know you can do it!" is congruent with a pat on the back. All the pieces of the communication match. Satir (1972) refers to this kind of information as "leveling." When you level with someone, you are direct, clear, and honest. People send confusing messages when the communication is mixed. An example of a mixed message might be a parent who says to the child, "I am concerned about your grades," but smiles while speaking with the child and does nothing to encourage the child to improve. Mixed messages of this sort are confusing and cause misunderstanding and difficulties.

For parents to be open and supportive communicators, they need first and foremost to be good listeners. A good listener does more than hear what the other person is saying: a good listener provides the person with a sense of support and acceptance. There are two predominant listening modes. The first of these modes is called passive listening. When you listen passively, you refrain from interpreting, judging, or directing the conversation. You simply listen and provide the "uh-huhs" and the nonverbal behaviors that indicate attentiveness and support (e.g., head nods). Here's an example of passive listening:

CHILD: I had a fight with Cindy today.
PARENT: Oh?
CHILD: Yeah, she always wants her way. She never wants to do what I want.
PARENT: Hmm.
CHILD: I don't want to play with her anymore.
PARENT: I see. Certainly that's your choice.
CHILD [*a few minutes later*]: I just talked to Cindy. She wants to make-up. Can I go play outside with her?
PARENT: Sure.

Notice that the parent in this scenario did not tell the child what to do. The parent simply listened and let the child own and solve the problem. The child used the parent as a sounding board. Oftentimes, children look to their parents for this kind of support. They may not always need direction or advice; they may simply want a safe place to verbalize their feelings. Passive listening gives them the means.

Active listening calls for more action on the part of the parent. "In active listening the receiver tries to understand what it is the sender is feeling or what the message means. Then he puts his understanding into his own words (code) and feeds it back for the sender's verification. He feeds back only what he feels the sender's message meant—nothing more, nothing less" (Gordon, 1975, p. 53). Here's an example of active listening:

CHILD: I had a fight with Cindy today!
PARENT: Sounds like you and Cindy are having some troubles.
CHILD: Yeah, she always wants her way. She never wants to do what I want.
PARENT: It sounds to me like you don't like it when Cindy always wants things to go her way.

CHILD: I don't want to play with her anymore.

PARENT: I can see you're really angry with Cindy and would rather not play with her right now.

CHILD [*a few minutes later*]: I just talked to Cindy. She wants to make-up. Can I go and play with her?

PARENT: Sure.

The parent in this scenario provided verbal labels and connections for the feelings the child was having. Active listening permits children to express their concerns and feelings directly. Because parents who listen actively respond to their children in a nonjudgmental way, the children feel that their feelings are accepted and they are more likely to share their thoughts and activities with their parents in the future. And in cases of negative feelings, the children have a safe way of defusing them. Active listening, like passive listening, prompts children to take charge of their problems and solve them independent of direct parental input. This kind of nondirective but supportive communication is likely to increase the child's feelings of self-efficacy for solving interpersonal problems. This has a direct impact on the development of self-esteem and resilience by increasing the child's sense of personal control.

Is active or passive listening always appropriate for a situation? What if I don't agree with my child? Will active listening encourage negative behavior? No. Active and passive listening are ways of getting the initial information and feelings out. They are supportive strategies that promote open communication. Active listening is most effective when children are trying to communicate their problems and concerns (e.g., school, friends, fears, sports activities). It helps them identify problems and recognize probable solutions. Sometimes it is necessary to correct or instruct children. Corrections and instructions require communication that is clear, direct, and nonthreatening: "Alex, I liked that you decided to share with Nicholas"; "Jessie, I have a problem with you not being ready to go in the morning. When you're late, it makes me late for work. So you and I need to talk about how this is going to change." Gordon (1975) stresses the need for a respectful tone and manner when communicating to the child. Sometimes this is difficult to do, especially if parents are upset themselves. Communicating when you feel in control of your emotions is therefore of paramount importance. In addition to advocating the use of direct and clear statements, Gordon stresses the need to communicate in a nondefensive manner. To communicate in such a fashion, parents and teachers should avoid statements that contain "barriers" to communication. Here are a few common barriers:

1. *Ordering, directing, commanding:* "Do your homework"; "You get those dishes done right now, young lady."
2. *Warning, admonishing, threatening:* "If you put your hands on one more thing, I will cut your hands off."
3. *Preaching and moralizing:* "Good children mind their parents"; "People are starving in India, so eat your carrots."
4. *Advising, giving solutions or suggestions:* "You ought to color the dress blue." This barrier is erected by parents who give direction even though the child may not need it. Offering solutions when the child asks for them or needs them is another matter altogether.
5. *Judging, criticizing, blaming:* "Your problems have caused me to have a headache."
6. *Name-calling, ridiculing, shaming:* "You're a showoff"; "You're so self-centered, you never think of anyone but yourself."
7. *Interpreting, analyzing, diagnosing:* "You're angry with Susie because you're jealous." Of course, it's sometimes important to help children see factors that might be influencing their behavior, but the context and agenda for this kind of communication need to be clear. If a child needs to unload, it's not appropriate to interpret his or her behavior. That may discourage further communication.
8. *Questioning:* "Why do you think you failed the math test?" Again, questions can sometimes be used to help children identify features of their behavior that need modification.

An awareness of the timing of your questions and your sensitivity to your child's needs and feelings will help you determine if your questioning will be perceived as annoying or beneficial.

9. *Withdrawing, distracting, humoring:* "Don't think about it"; "You look so cute when you're angry."
10. *Sarcasm:* "And of course you're much smarter than the teacher."
11. *Flattery:* "You're the best player on the team" (when clearly the child is not). Such a statement makes the child suspect your motives or your judgment.
12. *Reassuring:* "Don't worry, it won't hurt for long." But of course the child is not thinking about tomorrow; it hurts now!

If you are to avoid all of these barriers, how do you communicate a request? A good rule of thumb is to describe what you want done and why you want it done and then give the children the information and resources they need to do it. "Anne, I see that you multiplied wrong in three of these problems. I would like for you to do them over so that you will learn from the mistakes. Here is how you do it."

Positive discipline techniques and constructive communication strategies work with most children most of the time. No one is perfect! Difficult children tax parents and techniques. I will briefly discuss the management of difficult children, but first I would like to address another major component of good parenting: the parents themselves.

Components of Good Parenting: Focus on the Parent

There's no doubt that parenting styles, techniques, and communications have a significant effect on children's development. But the styles, techniques, and communications are tied to parents themselves. What about the parents? The most obvious factor about parents is their behavior. Parents need to be good models for their children. They need to show their children by example what it means to be resilient. Parents who practice what they preach have a lot more credibility than those who don't. The parent who manages everyday stressors by confronting them directly and problem-solving them efficiently is teaching the child by example to do the same. Parents who expect others to do for them fail to teach the child one of the main components of self-esteem and resilience, namely, internal control. The parent who is over-whelmed all the time by life's trials and tribulations is modeling behavior that is antithetical to the challenge orientation. On the other hand, parents who readily admit to making mistakes and then work to rectify them teach their children by example how to make the most of a mistake. This encourages the child to see mistakes as challenges rather than threats. There are a number of other examples of how parents act as models for their children. In the studies cited in Chapter 2, resilient children had at least one resilient adult to model. In our own homes that resilient model can be ourselves.

A parent's behavior is only one facet of the situation. A parent's predominant mood or affect is also important and in many ways more basic than his or her behavior. Mood and emotions do influence behavior and attitude (Lazarus & Folkman, 1984). In perhaps one of the best articles written on the subject, Dix (1991) argues that the emotional state of the parent is the single st important factor affecting parent–child relationships. Negative parental emotions (e.g., anger, fear, anxiety, and depression) re-sult in abusive and coercive parenting (Dix, 1991; Patterson, 1982). Positive emotions (e.g., general contentment, happiness) lead to the positive bonding between parent and child. When parents have a positive bond with their children, they are far more effective as teachers and molders of their children's values and attitudes.

Several factors influence a parent's emotional state. External factors, including the parent's level of job satisfaction, financial and health concerns, and spousal issues, impact on the parent–child relationships. The stresses of these concerns quite understandably affect the parent's emotional state, which in turn influences the emotions parents have with their children. How parents handle emotions and the kinds of social supports they have serve to either mitigate or heighten the negative influence of stressors for parent and child alike. Parents going through a divorce or a job loss, for example, are less available to their children. Social supports (friends, relatives, etc.) help parents deal with their losses. Not surprisingly, parents who have social supports do better, both personally and interpersonally, with their children (Hetherington, Cox, & Cox, 1978).

Independent of these external factors, a parent's emotional state is also determined by the child's attitudes and behaviors. Parents are definitely happier when their children's attitudes and behaviors are compatible with their own expectations and concerns. In other words, our feelings as parents are largely determined by the expectations and interpretations we have of our children's abilities and behaviors. When we feel that our children are living up to our expectations and when we interpret their behavior and attitudes positively, we are generally positively affected by parenting. However, if our children fail to meet our expectations and if we also interpret their failure in a negative or threatening way, then we're likely to feel the negative emotions of anger, depression, fear, and anxiety. Part of what parents need to do in order to control their own emotions is to examine the expectations they have for their children and their own interpretations of their children's misbehavior.

There is emerging evidence to support the notion that parents who experience distress over parenting have unrealistic goals for their children (Dix, 1991). Either they overestimate the maturity of their children and expect their children to do more than they can or they misjudge the child's potential and temperament and expect things from the child that the child cannot do. Sometimes the parent's own unfulfilled aspirations get displaced onto the child. When the child fails to attain the goal set by the parent, both parent and child suffer. Setting realistic, age-appropriate goals is essential for the parent's and the child's emotional state. (Chapter

3 provides parents with information so that they can establish reasonable expectations for their children. For those parents interested in knowing what behaviors are age-appropriate for their child, a reference list of resources is provided in Appendix 1 of this book.)

Besides examining our expectations about our children, we also have to examine the interpretations we place on our children's misbehavior and our own appraisal of how well we are doing as parents. To understand our children's misbehavior, we need to examine the major motivations behind children's behavior and the principal reasons for their misbehaviors. Alfred Adler, the father of individual psychology, believed that the driving force behind all human behavior is the struggle for superiority. By superiority he meant the need to belong and contribute in a significant way to one's social community. According to Adler, children are social beings and have the same basic social needs as adults do. They need to belong and they need to feel significant in their family and school environments. The information they use to determine how well and how much they belong derives from the judgments others make of them. Misbehavior, according to Adler, is a symptom of feeling alienated and worthless.

Rudolph Dreikurs worked with Adler and further developed his psychology, applying it to children at home and at school. Dreikurs (1964) proposed four reasons for children's misbehavior:

1. *Need for attention:* If you pay attention to me, then I do belong.
2. *Power:* If I have power over you, then I belong, because I can control your interactions with me.
3. *Revenge:* I want to hurt you because I feel that I don't belong.
4. *Assumed inadequacy:* I don't belong and feel that it's hopeless to try to belong.

Jane Nelsen (1987) has a number of tips for parents so that they can identify what the goal of a given misbehavior might be. She suggests that our emotional reaction and the child's reaction when he or she is asked to stop the misbehavior provide clues for identifying the real motives behind the child's inappropriate behavior. If your reaction to your child's misconduct is irritation and annoyance, then most likely the motive for the child's misbehavior is a desire for attention. If you feel threatened or angry, the child's goal is power. If you are hurt by what your child says and does, then a possible motive is revenge. And if you find yourself extremely frustrated, the driving force behind your child's misbehavior is a feeling of inadequacy. Nelsen uses the child's reaction to a parental request that he or she stop misbehaving as a clue to the child's motives as follows: If the child first complies with your request and stops misbehaving but then resumes again, the motive is attention. If the child escalates his or her negative behavior, the goal is power. If the child responds in a hurtful way toward you, the reason is revenge. And if the child withdraws, he or she may feel inadequate and incapable of belonging.

There are, of course, other reasons why children do not comply. Sometimes they simply don't feel well or suffer from a condition that influences their impulse control. Sometimes their "tolerance barrel" is full, and the behavior is a symptom of being stressed out or angry with themselves. The point is that the reasons we assign to the child's inappropriate behavior result in our feeling a given way toward the child. If we think that our child is engaging in a power struggle with us because the child feels alienated from us, our emotional reaction to the child is markedly different than if we believe the child is just being difficult. Parents who attribute power motives to their children's misbehavior experience more negative feelings (Dix, 1991). Most of the time, the motive behind the noncompliance and limit testing of most children is the attempt to feel significant and wanted. Correcting the perceptions we have of our children's misbehaviors will help us control our own emotional response.

Parents also make evaluations about their ability to parent. These evaluations influence their emotional mood. When parents think they are effective as parents, they tend to feel good about their role. Conversely, if they perceive themselves as ineffective, they tend to feel bad about themselves as parents. The evaluations parents make of their own effectiveness as parents are influenced by several factors, including the stresses they are under, the child's response to them, and their evaluation of that response. If parents feel ineffective, they need to determine why and then correct it. Sometimes the correction involves developing better parenting skills, but sometimes it means going easier on ourselves. Most parents I know tend to believe that other parents are much more effective than they are. Sometimes this is true, but most of us struggle a lot with parenting. After all, it's the only job that requires you to be on call 24 hours a day, seven days a week, forever! Talking to other parents about parenting is often helpful, because we may find they share our troubles. In other words, chatting with other parents helps some parents keep perspective. If conversing with other parents is not your cup of tea, there are plenty of books on the market that might also help.

Components of Good Parenting: Management of the Difficult Child

The good news is that most children respond well to the principles of positive discipline and constructive communication. But there are always a few who do not. We refer to them kindly as "difficult." Difficult children require more parental effort. Even good parents are often left wondering about their effectiveness. Difficult children are at risk for poor self-esteem and coping skills because they generally receive negative feedback from others and are often treated tentatively by parents in the hope of avoiding continual conflict. The management of the difficult child is truly a challenge.

Children are difficult for a number of reasons: They may be difficult because of their temperament. They may be difficult because they have a chronic condition (e.g., allergies, diabetes, attention deficit hyperactivity disorder) that affects their behavior.

They may be difficult because they're oppositional or because they feel they don't belong and are worthless.

The first step in the process of dealing with a difficult child is to determine the reasons behind the child's contrary demeanor. Chapter 3 and the discussion provided earlier propose guidelines for making this determination. If the child has a difficult temperament, a parent needs to do the following:

1. Control the number of changes that occur at any one time, and when there are expected changes, prepare the child for them in advance. This means reviewing the rules and giving the child details about the situation. It might also involve practicing appropriate behavior for the situation.

2. Whenever possible, present requests as choices: "Sally, I need you to set the table or empty the dishwasher." Avoid continuous verbal exchanges with the child when the child is reacting in an oppositional or abusive way. If it is necessary to give the child instruction when he or she is oppositional, present the direction in a way that places the responsibility and choice on the child: "Mary, you have a choice to do as I've asked. If you do, you may go to the movies. If you choose not to, then you lose your movie privilege." If the child continues debating the issue, tell him or her that you cannot discuss the matter any further at this time.

3. Use time-out as a method of defusing high arousal. Before the child can listen or problem-solve effectively, he or she must be in a relatively calm frame of mind.

4. Redirect these children, and give them opportunities to make up for what they have done wrong.

5. Choose your battles carefully. Being on the child for everything he or she does wrong will drive you and the child wild. Often, ignoring minor inappropriate behavior is enough to bring an end to the behavior anyway.

To illustrate the management of a difficult child, let's consider the case of Dan. Dan was ten years old when I first met him. He had been placed in an experimental program for extensive intervention. Dan was temperamentally very difficult: he did not adapt well to change and was intense and negative. His negativity was expressed by oppositional behavior, which took the form of a power struggle between Dan and all authority figures. At first, the use of natural and logical consequences seemed ineffective; Dan did not take well to rewards, praise, or encouragement. He was obviously out of control. He attempted to control everything and everybody.

The first step in dealing with Dan was for his parents and teacher to recognize and accept the fact that Dan was simply a temperamentally difficult child. His behavior was not a personal attack against them, although at times it surely seemed like it. I asked the parents and teacher to set up a behavioral contract for Dan. Each person met with Dan individually (meeting with him as a group was too threatening for Dan), and he was invited to have input into the contract. At first he refused. His parents did not make a major issue of it; they simply said that that was his decision and that they would need to go ahead without him. When they presented the contract to Dan, he of course refused to read or sign it. So the contract went into effect without his endorsement. When Dan violated the contract, a consequence followed: he lost the privilege to watch TV. Because Dan continued to violate the contract, his father had to actually remove a fuse from the TV. Dan was furious. He proceeded to trash his room. Although his parents' first inclination was to physically restrain him, they removed themselves from the situation instead. Without an audience to view his behavior and to escalate his arousal, Dan calmed down. Much to the surprise of his parents, he apologized for his behavior. Because his parents did not choose to own his problem, Dan actually took responsibility for his own behavior—one of the first times he had ever done so. He decided that he wanted to negotiate, so a new contract was drawn up between him and his parents. Dan was far more compliant and pleasant. He seemed to feel more secure with the structure of the contract. Part of the problem for Dan in the past had been that his parents would often give in to avoid conflict. They also felt they were walking on eggs whenever they even talked to him. If things didn't go Dan's way, there was trouble. By taking a risk and setting limits, Dan's parents were able to help Dan structure himself.

Dan did, of course, test the limits from time to time. When he did, his parents were steadfast in their position. They allowed Dan to make choices, and they did, when appropriate, make exceptions to the rules. But they were consistent—and it wasn't easy! They discussed with Dan which issues were important to them and which were not: doing homework was not negotiable but deciding on what clothes to wear to school was open to discussion (so long as the clothes were decent and acceptable for school, Dan could choose what to wear each day).

With his parents and teacher working collaboratively, Dan's improvement generalized to the school environment. On one occasion it appeared that Dan had regressed to his old behaviors and attitudes: He was quite angry with his parents because they were not going to allow him to go to the mall with friends without some adult supervision. He took a scissors and tore up one of the seats on the bus. This, after three solid months of reasonable behavior! You can imagine how his parents and teacher felt. At first, Dan lied about the incident. Then, much to his credit, he decided to confess. He felt that he needed to speak with the principal, since he expected to be expelled from school. This, by the way, was highly upsetting to him; Dan liked his school and his teacher. The principal was so impressed with his sincerity that he was at first inclined to give him a very light punishment. But instead of letting Dan off the hook, the principal used the situation to give him an opportunity to make up for the harm he had done. It was decided that Dan would work in the cafeteria during his free time for six weeks to work off the debt for the repair of the school bus. He also had to walk to school for one week. Dan not only did his job willingly but was a big hit with the cafeteria workers and earned himself a permanent job! And because his job involved cleaning up messes, the number of food fights in the cafeteria during Dan's shift decreased. The principal's decision is an example of how one can give a child the opportunity to make up for misbehavior, but it is also an example of redirection.

Allowing Dan to become involved in responsible behavior (the job in the cafeteria) gave him the opportunity to focus his energy constructively. You might be interested to know that Dan is now a first-year college student and is doing quite well. When he graduated from high school, he thanked us all for not giving up on him. (For the reader who would like to learn more about managing the difficult child, a reading list is included in Appendix 1.)

Occasionally, children are difficult because they suffer from a chronic medical condition. These children present a somewhat different management problem. What they require is knowledge of their condition and the resources to manage it. They don't need to be pampered. Pampering impedes the development of independence and resilience. If a child has a problem, she or he has to learn to manage it and must not use it as an excuse. The adult world will expect that child to contribute fully. Parents need to learn what the child must do to manage; then they need to educate their child and provide the necessary resources. If children have the resources to manage a chronic medical condition, they can be held accountable for their behavior, like anyone else. Children with or without handicaps need to be prepared to deal with the real world. Allow me to offer two examples:

Alan is a highly allergic child whose allergies affect his mood. When he ingests milk or any food that contains milk, he becomes irritable, tearful in response to the slightest provocation, and unreasonable in his demands for attention. Once the problem behind Alan's behavior was discovered, his parents explained to him the nature of his allergy and provided substitutes for milk products. Alan's behavior improved dramatically. However, he didn't like the diet and began to again ingest milk. When Alan's negative behavior returned, his parents held him accountable. Why? Because Alan knew what he had to do to control the allergy and had the resources to manage his condition. He therefore needed to be treated like anyone else. His refusal to deal with his allergy and avoid drinking milk was irresponsible behavior and needed to be treated as such.

Because Alan is also highly allergic to mold and pollen, he

takes allergy shots, which help a little. He is expected to tolerate some of the discomfort caused by his allergies. However, when the mold and pollen are particularly bad, Alan does not have total control. During these times his stress tolerance level is very low, and he has learned to manage by reducing his schedule and taking more time-outs. In this case, time-outs are coping mechanisms, not cop-outs. His parents understand this and are supportive. They are always helping Alan problem-solve so that he can be productive and resilient despite his severe allergies.

Darrell is a child who has been diagnosed as suffering from attention deficit disorder (ADD). Darrell's ADD is severe enough to require medication. Even when he is on the medication, he must still work to maintain self-control and attention. When he's off the medication, it's very difficult for him to manage. His poor attention span and impulse control problems make appropriate behavior—especially at school—nearly impossible. Unfortunately, Darrell's father refused to give him his medication when he was visiting him, thus depriving him of the resources necessary to control his condition. In this case, Darrell's misbehavior was his father's responsibility; Darrell did not have the resources he needed to maintain control. Unfortunately, Darrell suffered. By contrast, if he misbehaves or makes poor choices when he has the resources (the proper level of medication), then Darrell must be held accountable.

Sometimes children are difficult because they feel they don't belong. Their oppositional or withdrawn behavior is in response to these feelings. If this is the case, parents need to start out slowly by spending some special time with such a child. Special time is time spent alone with the child. It need not be a lot of time; often 20 minutes will do. During this time the parent refrains from teaching or directing the child. The parent may play a game with the child or might simply watch as the child engages in an activity. With older children or highly verbal children, this special time may involve constructively listening to the child, using the active and passive listening skills discussed earlier. This special time (which, by the way, benefits all children) helps difficult children know they are loved unconditionally. The inference children draw from this kind of parental behavior is this: "If Mom or Dad is interested in what I am doing, then I must mean something to them." Often, when parents spend special time with their children, the children are more inclined to take parental direction. Maccoby (1983) and her colleagues have elegantly demonstrated that children are more likely to see a parent's point of view if the parent is sensitive and responsive to the child's point of view.

One last point needs to be made before leaving this topic. Parents are sometimes discouraged when managing difficult children. The time and effort required on a continuous basis are enough to exhaust anyone. It's necessary, therefore, that parents of difficult children do two things: take breaks from their children and set small goals for themselves and their children. Getting away from the child for a while gives you and the child an opportunity to take a break. Expecting and appreciating small successes sets both you and your child up for success. Remember, if you feel successful, you're more likely to feel better about parenting, which in turn promotes good parenting.

Chapter 5

Stories
A Natural Way to Teach Resilient Values and Attitudes

As a small child, I spent hours listening to the stories my immigrant grandparents told of their homeland and of their journey to America. I remember how enchanted and moved I was by those stories. I laughed, I cried, but, more importantly, I learned from those stories. I learned that life is good and bad and that people have to assume responsibility for their own fate if they are going to be happy and succeed. I learned what it means to work hard and to work together. I learned the value of a dream and the kind of careful thought, courage, and persistence it takes to make that dream a reality. I learned how to grow from mistakes and how to deal with disappointments. I learned when to take a risk and when not to. I learned the value of friendship and family and what is required to be a friend and to be part of a family. I learned to love and to laugh and to flow with life's ups and downs. What a gift to give a granddaughter! As a child, I was entertained and educated. As an adult, I am grateful and have the responsibility of sharing these stories, as well as my own, with my children and their children.

The Power behind Stories

Stories are the keepers of a civilization's important facts, traditions, and values. In earlier times storytellers held an esteemed position in their society. Stories teach, direct, heal, and entertain. They cost only time and serve a number of important functions.

Stories provide children and adults with an opportunity to share and relate human experiences and emotions. Bruno Bettelheim (1976), in *The Uses of Enchantment*, one of his most famous books on the topic, argues that fairy tales help children understand human problems and solutions. This is the case because a story can be read and reread and therefore looked at from different perspectives. It gives a person an opportunity to step off the stage of everyday life and look at a situation a little more objectively. We relate to stories because our lives are a kind of a story. We find that we can relate to the characters in the narratives and can therefore learn from their experiences.

Campbell and Moyers' (1988) *The Power of Myth* describes the functions that ancient myths held for cultures in the past. These stories gave people the prototypes for heroes, for good and evil, and for codes of conduct. In other words, the stories provided clues for how to conduct oneself and experience reality. Jane Yolen (1981) makes a similar case for the myths behind fairy tales. She argues that these mythical stories provide a framework for an individual's values and belief systems. Stories are inspirational and communicate important human values and morals. The appeal of the great storytellers like Jesus of Nazareth and Hans Christian Andersen is that the parables and fables they told were packed with resilient attitudes and beliefs. We remember these stories; we don't always remember facts.

Stories are also diversions. They are a kind of time-out from the stresses and strains of everyday life. Our children love to hear stories. It calms them down and develops their intellectual and creative talents. The question is, Why do people learn better from stories and why do they gravitate to them? Theodore R. Sarbin

(1986), a social psychologist, believes stories are the best means we have for understanding human behavior. He cites the work of Heider and Simmel, who found that people describe the movement of geometric figures by creating stories about human figures. The importance of this study is that it shows that people think in terms of stories. Sarbin (1986) further argues that people interpret their own lives as stories and relate their experiences in narratives.

Other evidence in support of the power behind stories comes from a related field of interest: moral development. The similarity between moral values and traits associated with resilience is that they both direct behavior. Moral values (honesty, self-control, altruism) and traits linked to resilience or hardiness (commitment, responsibility, and positive orientation) require the kind of thinking researchers have called narrative (Bruner, 1986), analog (Paivio, 1975), or syncretic (Tucker, 1981). This kind of thinking is concrete and related to interpersonal and personal situations and concerns. It is in direct contrast to the prepositional or digital thinking, which is logical, formal, and independent of context, that is characteristic of mathematicians and theoretical scientists.

It is important to keep in mind that narrative thinking requires inputs that are narrative in nature. Stories and storytelling fit the specifications for the kind of inputs we want our children to have. Hence, stories and narratives are natural ways to socialize the kinds of values and ideas we want our children to have.

Today, psychologists and educators interested in moral education are arguing for the return of the story as a teaching device. Vitz (1990) has summarized the work of a number of researchers and philosophers who have found that people develop moral values through an emotional, social, and concrete process that is best taught through stories. This means that we develop our own personal code of ethics from our experiences with family, church, friends, and school. These experiences are remembered by us as stories. It is these narratives, not a set of abstract rules and prescriptions, that determine our moral character. Indeed, Robert Coles (1986) found that resilient children facing major moral and political issues (e.g., black children who had to integrate into white schools) gathered support and inspiration from Bible and family stories. Coles presents fascinating portrayals of these children in his book *The Moral Life of Children*.

Stories, then, have impact on the development of our basic values and attitudes. Just how can we harness the natural power of a story to educate our children about the attitudes and skills necessary for resilience? Before answering this question, let us first discuss some of the important features and forms of a story.

Story Features and Forms

Two aspects of a story influence a person's thinking and attitude development. The first is the surface level, the literal interpretation of the narrative, the factual description of who the characters are and what they did and of the particulars of the situation surrounding their actions. For example, the surface meaning in Judith Viorst's (1972) book *Alexander and the Terrible, Horrible, No Good, Very Bad Day* is the description of all the things that went wrong for Alexander, from waking up with gum in his hair to his cat's preference for sleeping with his brother Anthony.

The deep level is the second aspect of a story; it is what we often refer to as the moral behind a story. It is the part of the story that touches a less conscious part of the child's mind. The deep meaning of a story is not always verbalized by children, but it affects them nonetheless. For example, the deep meaning behind *Alexander and the Terrible, Horrible, No Good, Very Bad Day* is the message that bad days are part of human experience, to be tolerated with the hope of a better tomorrow.

In addition to its surface and deep levels, a meaningful story must hold relevance for the child. That is, the child must be able to relate in some way to the story. This feature of a story is called resonance. Resonant stories have a special kind of power for a child. Jane Yolen speaks of this power as "touch magic" and "tough magic." Touch magic is gentle: it enlightens the child in some way about human experiences and values but does not elicit strong emotions from the reader or listener. For example, in Marjorie Sharmat's (1977) book *I Don't Care* a little boy loses his balloon to the wind. At first he tries to deny the sad feelings he has about this by trying to convince himself that he does not care. It is obvious, however, that he is bothered by the loss of the balloon. He has trouble playing with his friend without thinking about it; he even loses his appetite. Finally, he runs outside and just cries. After he cries, he decides to take his father up on his offer to buy him a new balloon. The story has resonance for a young child because most children can relate to the experience of watching a balloon float away and feeling melancholy about it.

Tough magic is powerful. Stories with tough magic emphasize heroic themes filled with sacrifice and hardship. The reader or listener can feel the pain and excitement of the protagonist as the story progresses. The fairy tale *Beauty and the Beast* has this kind of tough magic. The beast almost kills the father of the young maiden because he unwittingly took a rose from the beast's garden for his daughter. The daughter in turn is willing to give up her life to save her father, so she surrenders to the beast. The beast falls in love with her and is willing to let her go to visit her father, knowing that she will perhaps not return and that he might die. When Beauty returns to the castle to honor her commitment to the beast, she discovers how much she loves this grotesque creature. She kisses him, and he is transformed into a handsome-looking prince. There are a number of important messages inherent in this tale, but the point being made here is that the heroine, Beauty, was willing to sacrifice herself for someone else. She receives a lot in return, but her willingness to give of herself initially is motivated by the love she has for her father and a desire to save his life. Indeed, in many of the classical myths the heroes sacrifice themselves or face unbelievable perils for a noble purpose. These kinds of stories have tough magic. They are not always fun to read or listen to, but they offer powerful messages that nurture the critical values and attitudes of the productive and resilient personality.

Analyzing the Message in Stories

Stories are a natural means of introducing and reinforcing values and attitudes. Being responsible, goal-directed, challenged (instead of threatened) by difficulties, and appropriately other-oriented are the kinds of values at the core of the hardy and productive personality. Stories with these kinds of themes are useful starting points for teaching children about these traits. They are also useful as reinforcers and guides for the kinds of thoughts and behaviors that characterize the productive and resilient person. There are a number of stories—some old, some new—having as their theme the values of the hardy and productive personality. (Appendix 3 provides a sampling of titles and works that speak to these themes.)

While a story can have a positive impact on a child's value system, it can also have a rather negative one as well. This is because some stories relate negative messages and promote what might be considered antiresilient and antiproductive attitudes. To illustrate how one version of a story can be used to teach resilient and productive values while another version communicates quite the opposite message, I will discuss the Grimms' version of *Cinderella* and its present-day version.

In the original Grimm version, Cinderella's biological mother dies. Before she dies, she beckons her daughter to her side and says, "Dear child, continue devout and good. Then God will always help you, and I will look down upon you from heaven and watch over you." Cinderella's father then marries a woman with two beautiful daughters. These daughters have a negative disposition; they are self-centered, selfish, and outwardly aggressive and mean to Cinderella, who remains good and kind in spirit. She is robbed of her decent clothes and subjected to days of long, hard, dirty work. Faithfully, Cinderella visits the grave of her mother.

She plants a twig from a hazel tree on her mother's grave, and, as the tale goes, her tears "watered it and it took root and became a fine tree." Her spirit and disposition are so kind that birds and forest animals befriend her and assist her with her tasks. They eventually avenge her mistreatment by her stepsisters.

When the king proclaims a festival, Cinderella wants to go. She asks her stepmother's permission, and her stepmother tells her she can go if she accomplishes two tasks. When the stepmother makes the promise to Cinderella, she of course thinks that Cinderella will not be able to accomplish the tasks. But Cinderella is not immobilized by the demands of the task. Her goal is to go to the festival. So she calls upon her friends, the birds, to assist with the chores demanded by her stepmother. Cinderella completes the tasks. The stepmother is surprised, but she does not honor her promise to Cinderella. Instead, she tells her, "You can't go with us, for you've got no clothes and you can't dance. We would be quite ashamed of you."

Cinderella is determined to attend the ball. When everyone has left for the festival, she visits her mother's grave and speaks to the hazel tree: "Shiver and shake, dear little tree; gold and silver shower on me." Then a bird bestows on her a gold and silver robe and a pair of slippers embroidered with silk and silver. Cinderella goes to the festival, where she meets the prince and charms him and everyone else. At the end of the festival, she leaves the prince without identifying herself. He hosts another festival and waxes the floor, thinking that this time she will not be able to escape his company quite so fast. At the second festival Cinderella loses one of her slippers. The prince uses the slipper to identify her and goes on a quest in search of his princess. The stepsisters attempt to fit into the slipper—one by cutting off her toe, the other by trimming her heel. At first the prince is deceived, but the birds once again intervene and point out to him the blood coming from each stepsister's foot. The prince departs but later returns to the home of the stepsisters and demands to try the slipper on Cinderella. The prince recognizes Cinderella even before she puts on her slipper and even though she is dressed in rags. He takes her to be his bride. During the ceremony, a bird pokes out the eyes of the two stepsisters: "For their wickedness and falseness they were punished with blindness for the rest of their days."

Now, the actions portrayed here are violent, but what is the deep meaning in this tale? The most obvious one is that good eventually wins over evil. Children like this message. It appeals to their basic sense of justice. Unfortunately, we can't always expect that everyone and everything will be just. Justice is an important value and consciously working toward making it a reality is noble and worthwhile, but we need to help children deal with injustice as well.

Other deep meanings in this tale that are directly relevant to the themes of resilience and productivity involve Cinderella's persistence and her self-initiated actions to attain her goal. In the Grimms' version of the tale, Cinderella does not wait for her fairy godmother to make things right for her. She organizes her own resources (the hazel tree and birds) to attain her goal. *She* assumes responsibility and makes things happen, not a fairy godmother! Nor is she immobilized by the obstacles her stepmother and step-sisters put before her. She always figures a way around them. Finally, she maintains her own integrity as a kind and gentle soul despite the ill treatment from her family.

Now contrast the original tale with its modern-day version. Cinderella, disheartened because she cannot go to the ball, sits by the great fireplace and cries. Her fairy godmother appears to rescue her and directs her to collect a pumpkin, six mice, three rats, and a lizard. The fairy godmother transforms the pumpkin into a coach, the mice into horses, the rats into footmen, and the lizard into a coachman. She then waves her magic wand and transforms Cinderella into a beautiful princess. The fairy god-mother does it all! Cinderella is relatively passive. What does the child take from this story? The message is loud and clear: wait for someone more powerful than you to fix your problem. This message is antithetical to the take-charge attitude and self-initiative shown by productive individuals.

Then there is *101 Dalmatians*, a Disney favorite. The hero of the tale, a dog named Pongo, is clear about his first goal—getting his owner (affectionately called his pet) to find him a permanent female partner. He is persistent in his efforts and is quite ingenious about how he sets out to accomplish his goal. Then, when the evil Cruella DeVil kidnaps their puppies, Pongo and his mate, Perda, take matters into their own hands (paws!) and organize the rescue of the puppies themselves. They are relentless in their efforts to save their puppies and are not intimidated by the obstacles and hazards coming their way. Resilient attitudes are very clear in this tale. Taking responsibility, setting goals, facing difficulties with a sense of challenge, and looking out for the good of others are all nicely demonstrated without the violence and gore so characteristic of the Grimm fairy tales.

Thomas de Paola's (1979) *Oliver Button Is a Sissy*, Elizabeth Koda-Callan's (1989) *The Silver Slippers*, and Charlotte Zolotow's (1971) *A Father Like That* are examples of stories with resilient themes and situations familiar to children today. In de Paola's book, Oliver Button is a little boy who dislikes the more traditional male sports. His father and mother initially pressure him to participate in the more masculine activities, but Oliver resists and talks them into letting him enroll in dance classes. The other boys are merciless. They tease Oliver for his interest in dance and print a big sign on the side of the school stating OLIVER BUTTON IS A SISSY. Still, Oliver persists with his interests. He does not allow peer pressure to deter him from his goal of becoming a good dancer. He practices faithfully. He is rewarded for his efforts when he is chosen for the talent show. He dances well, and although he does not receive first prize he does manage to win over the other boys, who replace the original sign with one that says OLIVER BUTTON IS A WINNER.

In Koda-Callan's book *The Silver Slippers*, a little girl dreams of being a prima ballerina. At first she feels she will never attain her goal. Her mother presents her with a gift—a necklace with a pair of silver ballet slippers. The necklace stands as a reminder of her goal and her ability to attain it. She practices ballet every chance she gets. Her efforts pay off, and she is chosen to be the prima ballerina because she has shown the most improvement.

In *A Father Like That*, a fabulous story by Charlotte Zolotow, a mother gives her son an empowering message. The little boy describes the kind of father he would like. The mother commends the child for desiring such a fine persona of a father and tells him, "I like the kind of father you're talking about. And in case he never comes, just remember when you grow up, you can be a father like that yourself."

Oliver Button Is a Sissy and *The Silver Slippers* illustrate the worth behind setting goals and working hard to achieve them. Oliver persisted with his interest in dance despite the grief he received from his peers, and the little girl in *The Silver Slippers* gave up her playtime to practice and perfect her dance. Oliver's efforts did not result in first place, but they did win him the respect of his peers. In *The Silver Slippers* the girl did achieve her goal. In both cases the children assumed responsibility for their own actions and actively pursued their goals. They worked hard and were not discouraged by the obstacles or the amount of effort their goal required.

Oliver's story has an additional message worth discussing. Thomas de Paola does not end his story with the traditional message that everything is wonderful. Oliver did not win a prize at the talent show, but other good things resulted from his actions. The story shows him being praised by his father, mother, teacher, and peers and conveys the message that while we don't always win even when we work hard, we can still be proud of ourselves for doing our best and taking up the challenge.

Charlotte Zolotow gives children insight about how to empower themselves. The message in *A Father Like That* is that you can choose to be the person you want to be! In this story Zolotow shows how a child turned what he believed he was missing into an attainable goal instead of lamenting over what he did not have.

Biographies are another rich source of the values and attitudes associated with resilience. The *Value Tale* series by Ann

Donegan-Johnson uses biographies of famous individuals to show values such as friendship, helping, courage, and determination. Her story of Ralph Bunche, *The Value of Responsibility* (1992), speaks directly to taking charge of one's life and life situation. Ralph Bunche was born to poor black parents in Detroit, Michigan, on August 7, 1904. His parents died when Ralph was only 11 years old. He was raised by his grandmother, who was a model of resilience for him. She both valued and demonstrated the traits of a resilient personality. Despite the poverty and hardships Ralph faced in his youth, he succeeded. He succeeded because he assumed responsibility for his own fate instead of waiting to be told to do things. He assessed a situation, figured out what had to be done, and did it. He knew how to work hard and did not expect other people to cater to him. Even as a small child, Ralph understood the principles of responsibility: he sold newspapers to supplement the family's income. These values paid off for Ralph. He graduated summa cum laude from UCLA. His ability to assume responsibility and persevere benefited the whole world when he managed to negotiate a 20-year peace agreement between Israel and Palestine. This was no small task. He had to work around the clock, dealing with many frustrations, during those tense times. It would have been easy for him to give up, but he did not. For his efforts, he was awarded the Nobel Peace Prize in 1950.

I could present many more examples, but allow me instead to discuss how parents or teachers can help children extract themes of resilience from the stories they hear, read, or see.

Extracting Themes of Resilience from Stories

Charles Smith (1990) offers a number of suggestions for making story time relevant and enjoyable for children. First of all, he suggests using stories that are written in an understandable and relevant style. Stories written with a lot of unfamiliar words and complicated sentences will discourage the child and cast a negative light on story time. Stories that move along appeal to the child's imagination, and those with engaging plots are more likely to attract the child's attention and interest. Children also have their own likes and dislikes when it comes to stories. Some children have an aversion for stories portraying aggressive and dangerous behaviors, and some are adversely influenced by such stories.

To help the child extract values of resilience and productivity from a story, parents need only draw the child's attention to the themes in the story and then later use the story to help the child understand an issue she or he is facing personally. We can draw attention to particular themes in a number of different ways. The most direct way is simply to summarize the story emphasizing the theme for the child. For example, if you were reading Martha Alexander's (1983) *Move Over Twerp*, you might summarize the book for the child like this: "Jeff really handled himself well when those older boys were trying to bully him on the bus. He thought of the solution all by himself! It was a great solution too, making a big joke out of the twerp name. Those big boys really thought they were bothering Jeff, but he showed them he could make a big joke out of the teasing. He made his own shirt that said SUPERTWERP." Later, when the child is being teased by a sibling or peer, you might refer to Jeffrey's solution in *Move Over Twerp*. Stories are a source of information on how to solve problems and resolve conflicts.

Another way of drawing attention to the values expressed by a story is to ask questions that direct the child's attention to the specific value themes. The questions can then be followed up by a discussion to clarify or expand on the message contained in the story. The level of sophistication of the questions depends, of course, on the age and maturity of the child. A question that can be asked for any story for any child is "What did you like best about this story?" The child's answer to this question gives the parent or teacher an idea of what was most salient to the child. Parents and teachers could then follow the question with a discussion of what they themselves liked best about the story. This discussion would draw the child's attention to those themes that highlight the traits and values of the resilient personality. For example, I asked Nicholas, age six, what he liked best about Lis Robson's (1983) version of *Hansel and Gretel*. He responded, "When the witch got cooked in the stove." I followed his response with this: "My favorite part was when Hansel and Gretel figured out how to get out of their trouble with the witch. They must have been scared when the witch put Hansel in the cage. But Gretel did figure out what to do, and when Gretel was scared about being left in the forest, Hansel thought good thoughts and figured out how to get home." Notice that my response specifically addressed the issue of assuming responsibility and taking a challenge orientation to a problem. By emphasizing that Hansel and Gretel found a solution to their dilemma themselves, and did so even though they were scared, I communicated to Nicholas the take-charge attitude that is so important for resilience. Other values can be taken from this tale as well. Often a story contains more than one value theme. How much you draw out of a story depends on the situation and the child. For one child, talking about more than one value might cause the child confusion and therefore defeat your purpose. Another child may be able to discuss several of the themes inherent in a story. Knowing your child and working within the framework of his or her natural abilities and developmental level maximizes the probability that he or she will benefit from the story.

As the child matures and becomes more aware of the traits of resiliency, the adult can use specific questions relating to them. To illustrate, I have recorded the questions I posed and the answers received for two different stories.

Nancy Carlson's book *Loudmouth George and the Sixth-Grade Bully* (1983) is a delightful story that can be used to communicate a number of different themes and skills related to resilience. George is bothered by a sixth-grade bully called Big Mike. Big Mike intimidates George and takes his lunch each day on the way to school, leaving George with no lunch. At first, George is threatened by Big Mike. He goes without lunch and becomes so upset that he can hardly concentrate on his schoolwork. With the help of his friend Harriet, George devises a nonviolent plan to take care of

Big Mike. George and Harriet pack a lunch for Big Mike that discourages him from ever taking George's lunch again! After reading this story to a child, here are some possible questions you might ask:

1. How did George feel when Big Mike took his lunch?
2. How did George take charge of his problem with Big Mike?
3. Did George always take charge of his feelings with Big Mike?
4. What happened when he didn't take charge of his feelings or the problem with Big Mike?
5. Was Harriet a good friend?
6. How was she a good friend?
7. George and Harriet thought of a good plan to take care of the sixth-grade bully. They were much younger than the bully, but they were much smarter. How were they smarter?
8. It is easy to be afraid of a bully. At first, George was afraid of Big Mike, but did he stay afraid?
9. What did George and Harriet think they could do about the bully?

Here are the responses of Alex, age five, to the story and questions:

PARENT: Alex, how did George feel when Big Mike took his lunch?
CHILD: He was scared of Big Mike. I wouldn't be scared of Big Mike. Big Mike should get his own lunch. He's mean. He's thinking junk thoughts.
PARENT: You're right, Alex. George seemed scared of Big Mike. He was probably a little mad, too, and he is thinking junk thoughts. Big Mike should bring his own lunch or ask George politely for some of his. How did George take charge of the problem with Big Mike?
CHILD: Well, George and his friend Harriet decided to make Big Mike a really icky lunch and hide the good one. I think that was a good idea, and it worked. George was thinking with a clear mind and he really fooled Big Mike!

PARENT: What happened when George thought with a clear mind?

CHILD: Well, he took care of Big Mike. Big Mike did not steal his lunch anymore.

PARENT: Have you ever been teased by a bully?

CHILD: Yes, on the bus. There's this boy named Charlie. He calls me a kindergarten baby. He picks on the other kids, and the bus driver writes him up.

PARENT: How did you feel when Charlie called you a baby?

CHILD: I was mad at him. He's not my friend. Zack's my friend, and so me and Zack sit together and put our hands over our ears when Charlie is trying to give us cold pricklies.

PARENT: I think that's a very good way to handle the problems with Charlie, Alex. That's really good thinking.

Alex is obviously familiar with the concept of resilience. He's also a verbal child, and it's easy to elicit these kinds of answers from him. The next set of responses is from another young child, one who is not as responsive or verbal:

PARENT: Josh, how did George feel when Big Mike took his lunch?

CHILD: I don't know. Maybe he didn't want his lunch.

PARENT [*taking the book out and reviewing the pictures with Josh*]: I think maybe George was scared and mad when Big Mike took his lunch. What did George do to take charge of his problem with Big Mike?

CHILD: He made him a bad lunch.

PARENT: Do you think that was a good way for George to take care of the problem with Big Mike?

CHILD: Yes. It was funny, too.

PARENT: I agree. George did think of a good answer to his problem, even though at first he was scared and mad.

This particular story can be used to teach problem-solving and social skills. In both cases the parent emphasized the value of facing a difficult situation and doing something productive about it. If the parent's intent is to teach one of these other themes, the questions asked would be tailored to bring them out. For example, if you are interested in teaching the child some basic social skills, you might ask questions like "Do you think Big Mike can make friends by taking other people's lunches?" or "Is Harriet a good friend and why?" If the objective is to use the story to teach problem-solving skills, you might ask a question like "What other good or bad solutions did George have to deal with during his problem with Big Mike?" If the child is reluctant to answer, the parent can prompt a response by answering the question for the child, as Josh's parent did, or by asking an alternative question. The point is, brief discussions held every so often about a topic serve to acquaint the child with it and make future discussions on it more fruitful.

An older child can benefit from stories as well. *The Silent Lobby* (1990) by Mildred Pitts Waters is a fictional account about one man's fight for equality. Papa organizes efforts to win suffrage for African-American citizens during the 1960s. The opposition he and his group encounter is fierce. They lose their jobs, they are often subjected to cruel beatings, and their homes and churches are bombed in an attempt to deter them from their goal. The group remains steadfast to their commitment and efforts. Papa organizes a group to go to Washington, D.C., to lobby for their rights. They meet with a number of obstacles, including inclement weather, bus repair problems, and bureaucratic red tape. But they persevere and manage to accomplish their goals.

This story reflects a number of the themes of resilience. Papa is not satisfied with the status quo of the time, and he decides to assume the responsibility for changing it. He applies a proactive problem-solving strategy typical of people with a strong sense of control. Papa's commitment to suffrage was the goal that helped him persevere. Not only was his goal personally meaningful but it had major significance for others as well. He refused to allow problems and personal hardship to deter him from this goal, illustrating the power of a challenge orientation.

There are a number of ways these ideas can be communicated to an older child. A parent or teacher could hold a discussion about the issues addressed in the story, drawing parallels to present-day events. To initiate a discussion of this type, a parent or teacher might want to use some key questions. Here are examples of some questions appropriate for this story with the older or more sophisticated child:

1. What is Papa's goal?
2. What obstacles does he encounter?
3. How does he manage those obstacles?
4. How does he personally take responsibility for seeing that things change?
5. What do you think of Papa?
6. Do you know of any other people who stood up for what they believed in?
7. Papa stood up for the African-American person's right to vote. His decision to do so resulted in a number of personal hardships and sacrifices. Sometimes you are in a similar position. Sometimes you choose to do what you feel is right even though it may result in some problems for you. For example, you might choose to study for an exam instead of going to a party with your friends. Your friends may tease and harass you because you made this choice. Are there helpful ideas from this story you can use to deal with difficult situations?

Here's an 11-year-old child's summary of the story and responses to Questions 3, 5, and 7:

> Papa is a strong person, dedicated to his beliefs. He ignored discouraging remarks and never gave up, even when the situation seemed hopeless. He never used violence either, even though violence was used against him. I like the character of Papa, and I think that he was proud of himself. What I will remember from this story is not to give up on what I believe, especially if I know it is the right thing to do. I think Papa kept thinking about his goal—to have a Freedom party and the right to vote. I think his vision helped him through the bad times. I think that if ever I was in a similar position, I could argue for what I believe is right and remember to keep a vision in my mind.

This child understood the values communicated in the story and extracted a coping strategy from it as well. The idea of keeping a "vision" in one's mind during hard times is a useful coping tool. Not all children reading and responding to this story will articulate the ideas as well as this child did. The good news is that even if they don't, exposure to the values and discussion on any level will help them internalize those values.

In summary, questions and discussions help children tease out the values expressed in stories. A word of caution is in order: it would be totally inappropriate to do this kind of analysis with every story. Sometimes it is important to just read for the pleasure of reading. Not every story has a moral associated with it. A steady diet of moral-packed stories is overwhelming for children. They need time to assimilate the values found in stories. Likewise, a literature menu having only fun and surface meaning themes does not provide an opportunity to learn values through stories. Clearly, a balance between the two kinds of stories is desirable.

The Use of Personal Stories

Thus far in our discussion, we have focused on stories written or recorded by someone else. Personal stories, like the stories our grandparents and parents tell us, are also valuable. They're valuable for the same reasons recorded stories are important: they teach, they comfort, and they entertain. We can make use of personal stories in the same way we make use of any other story. Anne Pellowski (1987), the author of *The Family Story-Telling Handbook*, provides some guidelines for how to tell your own personal stories. Pellowski suggests that we use a variety of personal stories—stories that are entertaining, stories with a message, and stories that deal with cultural traditions and mores. When we are telling a personal story or reading a recorded story, she suggests keeping the following points in mind:

1. Tell the story with conviction. The listener needs to hear the emotion and passion behind the story.
2. Be yourself. A soft, natural voice in combination with

animated "other voices" to communicate the other characters in the story helps to make the story come alive for the
listener.

3. Pace the story appropriately. If the story is told too fast, the
child will of course miss the important points; stories
delivered in a slow and monotonous tone bore the listener
and detract from the message in the story.

4. Use gestures when appropriate. Do not use exaggeration
except when called for by the story.

5. Know your story well so that when you relate it, it flows
without unnecessary pauses.

6. When telling your story, provide enough detail to allow
the listener an opportunity to envision the context of the
story. Be careful not to provide so much detail that you lose
your listeners or distract them from the main idea of the
story.

Personal stories are fun to tell, and children love to hear them.
To illustrate how you can tell a personal story, allow me to share
one of my children's favorite stories with you:

Our second child, Jessica, was only two weeks old. Catherine,
our eldest, was almost three years old. It was early December, and
there was snow on the ground—not a lot of snow but just enough
to make the trees look like a winter wonderland. I had an important presentation to make that morning to the academic dean and
vice president of the college. But, first I had to take the children
over to the babysitter. Because it was wintertime, I had to make
sure that Catherine, known as Katie, was properly dressed. She
had to wear a snowsuit, boots, gloves, and a hat. I also had to
make sure Jessie was warmly dressed in her soft green and yellow
newborn bunting suit. Jessie was fussy that morning, and it took
longer than usual to feed her. Katie was enthralled with her little
sister but also not quite sure of the impact the newcomer might
have on her place with us. She was giving me a hard time about
getting her snowsuit on although, prior to Jessie's birth, she had
been highly independent and would insist on getting dressed
herself. This particular day she felt incapable of dressing herself

and demanded my assistance. I finally had both children dressed. I put Katie in her car seat first, and then I got Jessie in hers. I put the diaper bag and my briefcase in the back seat of the car. Finally, we were ready to go. I was now approximately 20 minutes behind schedule. I arrived at Nanny's house (that is what our children affectionately call their babysitter), took Jessie in first, and then got Katie out of her car seat and into the house. I grabbed one of the bags and left it in the corner of Nanny's kitchen where I was accustomed to leaving supplies for the children. I gave each child a quick kiss, said good-bye to Nanny, and rushed back into the car. I arrived at the college, grabbed the bag from the back seat, and raced up the stairs to the meeting room. Entering just in time to speak, I quickly took off my coat and boots and put on my shoes. Before walking to the front of the meeting room, I made a grab for my bag, but my hand reported the distinct texture of the diaper bag instead of the sleek feel of my briefcase, which no doubt was sitting idly next to my sitter's changing table. What made my confusion an event of outright embarrassment was the misfortune of my discovering the mistake at the front of the room, in full view of my colleagues. All I could do was place the diaper bag onto the conference table and register my surprise. I started to laugh, looked at the audience, and said, "I guess this is a good example of role confusion." Now everyone laughed. I proceeded with my talk, which went well, and then I hurried back to my poor baby-sitter, who was by this time desperate for the diaper bag.

Our children think this story is hilarious and they are fond of telling their friends about their college professor mom who took the diaper bag to school instead of her briefcase. They also learned something from this story: instead of construing the mistake as a disaster, I made the most of it and the presentation went well. Laughing at oneself helps a person deal productively with the distress experienced in uncomfortable situations.

Other stories we tell may be more serious in nature. Personal stories can have an especially powerful effect on children because the characters are real and the children know them personally—indeed, sometimes the characters are the children themselves. When we share our personal stories, we share part of ourselves.

Story telling is a great way to get a message across without seeming too preachy or overbearing.

Visual Media Stories:
The Impact of Television and Movies

This discussion of stories would not be complete if I did not make mention of the power behind TV, movie, and home video stories. There is absolutely no question that TV viewing has an impact on children. In 1982, the National Institute of Mental Health examined all the studies conducted on TV viewing in the 1970s and concluded that children learn from what they see on TV. What a child learns and how much she or he is actually affected by TV are determined by a number of factors, such as the level of sophistication of the TV program and the maturity of the child, the relevance of the program for the child, the kind of adult role models the child has, and the type of explanation and reinforcement an adult might give a child about the program (Liebert & Sprafkin, 1989).

What do children learn from viewing stories? They learn about attitudes and values. They learn different problem-solving strategies, and they learn to imitate the behaviors they see. Most of the research has examined the effects of TV violence on children and adults. Results are relatively consistent in showing that children and adults who watch a lot of TV violence think aggression is a good method for solving interpersonal problems and use more aggressive strategies themselves when dealing with others (Bee, 1989; Gerbner, Gross, Signorielli, & Morgan, 1980; Liebert & Sprafkin, 1988; Williams & Handford, 1986). These effects can be moderated by the home and school environment and by the explicit messages children get about what they are viewing (Collins, Sobol, & Westby, 1981). Children who see adults solving problems in nonaggressive ways and who are helped to evaluate what they see on TV are not as negatively affected by violent TV programs.

While the research on the effects of TV programs on viewers

has primarily focused on violence, other aspects of our culture—good and bad—are communicated by the content of visual media stories (Liebert & Sprafkin, 1988). Programs like "Mister Rogers' Neighborhood" or "Lassie" emphasize sharing, taking responsibility for oneself, and showing consideration for others. Some of the other popular TV programs, however, communicate attitudes that are counterproductive and promote values that inhibit resilience.

Because TV appears to be such a powerful socializer, the American Academy of Pediatrics has offered the following suggestions for parents and other caregivers (Action for Children's Television, undated; AAP, reported in Liebert & Sprafkin, 1988):

1. Limit the amount of time your children spend in front of the TV, and monitor the kind of programs they watch.
2. Watch programs with your children. Discuss what they have watched with them. You may need to help them see the unreal aspects of a story and some of the untold consequences of the behaviors and attitudes expressed. The same kinds of discussions and questions suggested earlier for oral stories can be used for visual stories as well.
3. If the characters in the visual stories use violent or nonproductive problem-solving strategies, discuss the more appropriate and productive alternatives with your children.
4. Do as you preach. If you are limiting the amount of TV watching your children are doing, limit it for yourself, too. Children will practice what they see you do.
5. Teach children to critically evaluate commercials. Talk about the foods advertised in terms of their health value. Discuss the toys in terms of their durability and worth. Commercials give children and adults a chance to develop good decision-making and consumer skills.
6. Use home videos or tapes to show children especially wholesome programs that present wholesome and productive values.

Chapter 6

Teaching Children to Cope
The Role of Relaxation, Nutrition, and Exercise

"Relax. You'll feel better, you'll think better, and you'll act better!" How often have you heard these words of advice? But why does relaxation help, and how do you relax? Stress researchers have found that relaxation helps reduce the negative effects of stress and distress. To use the barrel analogy from Chapter 3, relaxation lowers the stress level in our barrels. For these reasons, relaxation skills are resources for resiliency and productivity. To understand how relaxation works as a buffer for the destructive aspects of stress, allow me to first briefly discuss what the experts know about stress.

The Stress Response and the Relaxation Response

What is stress? Hans Selye (1956), in his now classic book *The Stress of Life*, argues that stress is change. It's anything that upsets our everyday routine or our usual physical, mental, or behavioral existence. Change in seasons, change in school or working conditions, new relationships, new circumstances that require us to develop new behaviors—all are examples of stress implied by this definition. When such changes are perceived negatively, we experience distress. Changes that are viewed positively are called eustress.

Stress is helpful at times, but it can also be quite destructive. A certain amount of stress helps us respond to physical emergencies and gives us energy. The mother who sees her child pinned under a car and all of a sudden gets the strength to lift the car and the child who is anxious about a math test and then studies hard are examples of how stress can be helpful. Distress, on the other hand, has a physical, mental, and emotional cost. For example, when you are "stressed out," you might experience any of a host of physical symptoms, like muscle tightness, headache, stomach discomfort, gastrointestinal distress, irritability, and difficulty concentrating. These can lead to a deterioration in your work output and behavior. Table 6.1 lists the most common symptoms associated with distress. But a word of caution is in order. While such physical symptoms may result from stress and not from a physical problem, consultation with your health care provider is recommended to rule out any organic difficulties. For example, if you or your child experiences persistent headaches, it's wise to check with your doctor to make sure that the headaches are not resulting from some other medical condition.

The physical aspects of the stress response are innate and common to us all. Cannon (1932) first named this response the "fight–flight" reflex. It involves two systems of the body: the autonomic nervous system (ANS), of which the sympathetic nervous system (SNS) is a part, and the endocrine system. The sympathetic nervous system acts on the major organs of the body (e.g., heart, lungs, liver, gastrointestinal system) and causes them to either speed up or slow down. The SNS also stimulates the pituitary gland, which then triggers the thyroid and the adrenal glands, which are located on top of the kidneys. The thyroid gland influences the body's metabolism. The autonomic nervous system stimulates the medulla portion of the adrenal glands, causing them to release adrenaline and noradrenaline (also known as epinephrine and norepinephrine, respectively). Adrenaline and

TABLE 6.1. Distress Signs

Physical

Cold, clammy hands	Diarrhea
Dizziness	Appetite loss
Increased pulse rate	Increased appetite
Hyperventilation	Nervous tics
Dilated pupils	Muscle aches
Stomach upset	Teeth grinding
Frequent urination	Increased sensitivity to physical
Some types of skin problems	ailments (such as allergies,
Increased vulnerability for illness	asthma)
(colds, upper respiratory	Sleep disturbances
infections)	

Behavioral

Increased irritability	Withdrawal
Hostility	Frequent bad dreams
Impatience	Difficulty concentrating
Negativism	Increased number of accidents
Tantrums	Bed-wetting
Moodiness	Loss of interest in almost all
Rigid thinking	activities
Increase in oppositional behavior	Decline in school or work
Increase in impulsive behavior	performance
Infantile or regressive behavior	Nervous mannerisms and
	laughter

noradrenaline equip the body for immediate action: they cause the heart to race and signal the rest of the body systems to mobilize against the stressor. The effects of SNS stimulation are quick and of short duration.

The endocrine system keeps the stress response going through the release of various hormones and other chemicals. These hormones and chemicals are slow-acting and stay with us longer. This is why they keep the stress response going. The posterior lobe of the pituitary gland causes the release of vasopressin, which causes the artery walls to constrict. When this happens, blood pressure increases. The anterior lobe of the pituitary releases ACTH, a hormone that acts on the cortex of the adrenal gland. When the adrenal cortex is stimulated by the chemical ACTH, it releases a number of different corticosteroids, which influence a number of important body functions. For example, the glucocorticoids trigger the pancreas to release glucagen, which increases blood sugar levels. The glucocorticoids also affect the body's immune (defense) system. Other corticosteroids, called mineralocorticoids, enhance inflammation in response to injuries. They control fluid balance in the body and, consequently, blood pressure.

The endocrine system is also responsible for the release of thyroid stimulating hormone (TSH) and somatotropin, the growth hormone. TSH stimulates the thyroid gland, which controls the body's metabolism. It has an effect on cardiac output and blood pressure. Somatotropin stimulates the growth of connective tissue, which is helpful for the healing of injuries. Somatotropin also facilitates the conversion of stored fats into energy. Too much of this hormone can result in a diabetic condition. The somatotropins, along with the mineralocorticoids, stimulate inflammation.

The involvement of the SNS and endocrine system in the stress response leads to the following:

- Tense body muscles, especially in the arms, legs, and lower back
- Increased perspiration
- Increased heart rate, experienced as pounding heart
- Tightened stomach muscles
- Shortness of breadth
- Restlessness
- Constipation
- Dry mouth
- Racing thoughts

There are a number of physically oriented coping techniques that help head off a full-blown stress response or reduce some of the negative characteristics associated with it (e.g., relaxing tense muscles). The physical mechanism behind the relaxation response is not as powerful or as well understood as the mechanism behind the stress response itself. What we do know is that relaxation tones down the action of the sympathetic nervous system and turns on the action of the parasympathetic nervous system, or PNS. When this happens, we generally get the reverse of the stress response. That is, so the person will experience slower breathing, a slower heart rate, relaxed skeletal muscles, and a lower oxygen-use rate. A more detailed list of the physical effects of the relaxation response is presented in Table 6.2. Descriptions of the more common relaxation exercises, appropriate for parents and children, are presented in the following paragraphs.

Relaxation Exercises

Breathing for Relaxation

Proper breathing is a natural antidote to stress and is the first step in most relaxation training exercises. Eastern cultures have long recognized the relaxation value of full, natural breathing. To understand how to teach children to use breathing as a relaxer, it's important to understand the mechanics of breathing.

When you inhale, you draw air into your nose (or, if you are a mouth breather, into your mouth). It's then warmed and foreign particles are filtered by the mucous membrane and cilia (bristly hairs) lining the nasal passages. The air then travels down the pharynx and the larynx into the trachea, or windpipe. From the trachea, it goes into the lungs proper. The lungs consist of a tube called a bronchus, smaller tubes called bronchioles, and small air bags, called alveoli, engulfed by small blood vessels. It's at the level of the alveoli that oxygen is exchanged for carbon dioxide. The diaphragm—a sheetlike muscle that separates the lungs from the stomach and expands and contracts autonomically (it can also be voluntarily controlled)—contracts during inspiration, allowing

TABLE 6.2. Some Physical Effects of Relaxation Response

Breathing becomes deeper and slower
Heart rate decreases
Blood pressure decreases
Sweat gland activity decreases
Saliva production increases
Blood flow to stomach and intestines increases
Muscles in the gastrointestinal tract relax and return to normal
Blood sugar decreases
Pupils of the eyes constrict to normal
Skeletal muscle tension decreases tingling sensation in hands and feet
Blood flow to kidneys increases
Stress hormone release is decreased
Feeling of calmness prevails
Heavy, sedated feeling is felt throughout body

the lungs to expand, and relaxes during expiration, causing the lungs to contract and air to be forced out. Respiratory movements are controlled by the respiratory center in the brain, the medulla.

When blood leaves the lungs, it is rich in oxygen. Oxygen provides energy the body needs to maintain itself. Without oxygen, the cells of the body die. Oxygen-rich blood from the lungs enters the left side of the heart, where it's pumped to the rest of the body via arteries and capillaries. Oxygen is exchanged for carbon dioxide in the capillaries as they bring blood to the cells of the body, and the waste-laden blood then returns to the right side of the heart, where it is pumped into the lungs for purification. The air that we breathe in during inspiration contains the oxygen needed by the lungs to purify the blood. The air that we breathe out contains the waste products, primarily carbon dioxide collected by the blood.

Shallow breathing, which causes an insufficient amount of fresh air to enter the lungs, often occurs during stressful times. When it occurs, the blood is insufficiently oxygenated and the waste products in the blood are not sufficiently eliminated. As a result, the waste products build up and poison the system. At the same time, the body is being deprived of the oxygen it needs to convert food into energy. Poorly oxygenated blood contributes to anxiety, muscle spasms, depression, fatigue, and poor digestion. Under these conditions, coping with stressful situations is compromised. Complete natural breathing provides the body with the necessary oxygen, a precondition for optimal functioning and relaxation. All physical relaxation exercises call for full breathing. In some cases, breathing exercises alone are effective in reducing anxiety, fatigue, and muscle tension. Here are some simple breathing exercises appropriate for adults and children. It's helpful to the child if you first demonstrate how to do the exercise, using yourself as the model. It's also useful to practice along with the child. Not only will your child think that it's an important thing to do (because you are doing it), but you will benefit as well.

Exercise 1: Breathing Awareness

It's important for you and your child to become acquainted with what complete natural breathing feels like and what it looks like. The following exercise, adapted from Davis and associates (1982), is designed to do just this.

Step 1: Find a comfortable spot on the floor, mat, or rug.

Step 2: Lie down with your legs slightly apart and your toes pointed slightly outward.

Step 3: Close your eyes.

Step 4: Breathe as you normally do. Place your hand on the spot that feels like it's rising and falling the most when you breathe in and out. If you are shallow breathing, that spot will be on your upper chest. This means that you are not making good use of your lower lungs and therefore not properly oxygenating your body. For complete natural breathing, you should notice the movement in your lower chest and abdomen.

Step 5: Now place both of your hands on your stomach. Take a deep breath through your nose, and then let it out through your mouth. Your stomach should rise when you inhale and fall when you exhale.

Step 6: Now place one hand on your stomach and the other on your chest. Concentrate on getting your chest to move in harmony with your stomach when you breathe. Practice this for five minutes or so.

Exercise 2: Deep Breathing

This breathing exercise is a combination of several strategies suggested by the various yoga exercises presented in *The Relaxation and Stress Reduction Workbook*, by Davis, Eshelman, and McKay (1982). Again, these exercises are useful for adults and children. They can be done in a short amount of time and require no special equipment.

Step 1: Sit up or stand up straight (be sure that you have good posture).

Step 2: Inhale deeply through your nose. As you do, fill first the lower portion, then the middle, and finally the top portion of your lungs. What happens is that the diaphragm pushes the stomach out when air flows into the lower lungs. When you fill the middle portion, both lower ribs and chest move forward. To fill the top portion of the lungs, tighten your stomach muscles to support the air in the upper lungs.

Step 3: Hold your breath to the count of 4.

Step 4: Exhale using the following procedure: Form a small hole with your mouth by imagining that you are going to blow through a straw. Exhale some of the air forcibly. Stop. Now exhale some more. Stop again. Exhale the rest of the air. When you exhale, you will be exhaling in strong, short puffs that make a "whooshing" sound.

Exercise 3: Two-Stage Breathing

Step 1: Have the child stand or sit with the spine straight.

Step 2: Have the child pretend that his or her lungs are balloons.

Step 3: Have the child inhale and imagine filling the bottom of the balloon with air.

Step 4: Have the child finish inhaling by imagining filling the top half of the balloon with air.

Step 5: Have the child exhale slowly, imagining letting all the air out of the balloon.

This exercise is a great tension breaker for home and school. It's especially useful as a stress disrupter in the early stages of the stress response. With very young children it's often helpful to first demonstrate the exercise by using a balloon, pointing out to them how the air first fills the bottom of the balloon and then the top and encouraging them to pretend that their lungs are like balloons and that when they take a deep breath the air fills the bottom of their lungs first and then goes to the top.

Meditation

Meditation has been used for centuries in the Eastern traditions and religions. In the West, meditation is a method for training concentration and focus. The basic technique involves body stretching, muscle relaxation, or diaphragmatic breathing. A comfortable sitting position in which the spine is straight and strong is assumed. The meditator focuses on a "mantra," which is an object, word, saying, or prayer. When the mind is focused on the mantra only, it does not respond to information from the five senses or to the worries and preoccupations of everyday existence. Physiologically, the meditator experiences the relaxation response. Psychologically, ardent meditators report feelings of bliss and a sense of being "one with God and the Universe."

There are various meditation exercises. None is superior to others in terms of effectiveness (Lichstein, 1988); it's truly a matter of preference and exposure. I offer Dr. Herbert Benson's (1975) exercise because it's simple and appropriate for children and adults.

Dr. Benson has designed a relaxation response technique that combines breathing exercises with a form of meditation in which attention is focused away from everyday stressors and onto a repetitive, monotonous statement. This mental exercise, along with a quiet environment, a comfortable position, and a passive attitude, prompts the relaxation response, although the mechanism involved is unclear.

Exercise 4: Dr. Herbert Benson's Relaxation Response Technique

Step 1: Find a comfortable position in a quiet place.

Step 2: Close your eyes.

Step 3: Breathe in slowly through your nose and out through your mouth.

Step 4: As you breathe out, say silently the word "one" (or any other word, saying, or prayer). If other thoughts or ideas come into your head, just let them pass and go back to concentrating on the breathing and the word or words you have chosen. For adults and older children, this exercise can be done for 5 to 10 minutes. For younger children or older children with short attention spans, a shorter interval (3 to 5 minutes) is recommended.

Step 5: When you have finished, open your eyes and sit in your chair quietly for another minute (or less) before you return to what you were doing.

Note: It's typically difficult for children and adults to concentrate fully when they first start doing this exercise. But don't despair! With practice, this is less of a problem, and most children and adults eventually do learn to concentrate quite well for the five to ten minutes required by the exercise.

The Quieting Reflex

The quieting reflex is yet another technique that can be used to induce the relaxation response. The quieting reflex was created by Dr. Charles Stroebel (1983), a psychiatrist, to deal with his own stress-related headaches. The technique itself is quick and easy. It takes a mere 10 to 15 seconds and can be done in any environment or situation. Dr. Stroebel describes the technique in detail in his book *QR: The Quieting Reflex*. He believes that it takes adults four to six months to master the technique to the point where it is automatically triggered by the early warning signs of stress.

Exercise 5: The Quieting Reflex
(adapted from Stroebel, 1983)

Step 1: Identify those situations, people, and circumstances that cause you distress.

Step 2: Smile and repeat to yourself, "Peaceful mind, calm body."

Step 3: Take a deep breath; as you inhale, count silently to 3. Exhale, counting silently to 3.

Step 4: Take another deep breath; as you exhale, allow your jaw, tongue, and shoulders to go loose and limp. Imagine a blanket of warmth and heaviness flowing down to your toes.

Elizabeth Stroebel has adapted the basic techniques of the quieting reflex for children—she calls it the "Kiddie QR"—and uses a number of metaphors to help children learn to relax.

Exercise 6: The Kiddie QR
(adapted from Stroebel & Stroebel, 1984)

Step 1: Help the child recognize the physical and behavioral signs of distress (see Chapter 3 for stress assessment strategies and stress diary).

Step 2: Have the child relax facial muscles (sometimes massaging the child's temples helps).

Step 3: Have the child form a smile.

Step 4: Have the child take two or three deep breaths, counting silently to 4 while inhaling and exhaling. For the initial training sessions, you may want to count for the child to promote an appropriate sense of tempo. **Do not have the child take more than three deep breaths** (exceeding this limit may lead to hyperventilation).

Step 5: Tell the child to open her or his mouth and relax the jaw muscles when exhaling. Instruct the child to think of something positive (image, word, place). Tell the child to let the positive, warm feelings make her or his body feel limp and loose. (If you are instructing young children, you can use expressions like "warm fuzzies," "sunshine thoughts," or "happy-face thoughts.")

Helping children identify the physical and behavioral signs of stress is critical for teaching them how to effectively cope with stressors. Children as young as three can learn to recognize the signs of stress. To help children become aware of their own stress triggers and alarms, one must first explain to them what some of the stress reactions are. Table 6.1 lists the most common signs of distress and can serve as a guide for your discussion with your child. The level of sophistication used to describe these signs will, of course, vary with the age and maturity of the child. Simply pointing out to three-year-olds that their body gets tight when they are angry or tired is perfectly appropriate. Eleven-year-olds may be able to describe a tightness in their chest and a knotted feeling in their stomach. Stress assessment strategies are presented in Chapter 3 and could be used as a method for helping parent and child identify the child's own idiosyncratic stress triggers and responses.

In addition to identifying stress triggers and responses for the child, it's helpful to prompt the child to do the quieting reflex in the context of the problem situation. To do this, it's important to catch the child "winding up" and then to redirect him or her to the quieting reflex exercise. Let me illustrate the point with a story about our youngest child, Alex, when he was five years old: Alex was attempting to put together a puzzle when his older sister Jessica decided to tell him how to do it. The unsolicited help was not received well by Alex, who was overtired. He started to whine and cry and was ready to initiate physical contact with his sister. I intervened by quietly and gently hugging him. Alex happens to be the type of child who is comforted by physical contact. I got his attention and said, "I know you're working hard on the puzzle even though you're tired. I know you feel Jessie is bothering you, and I know you're upset, because you're crying. I'm going to help you take charge of your cold, prickly feelings."

I had Alex lie down on my lap, and I massaged his temples. I asked him to smile. I then said, "Alex, pretend your lungs are balloons. When I say, 'Start,' you breathe air into your lungs as if you were going to blow up a balloon. Ready? Start: one . . . two . . . three . . . four. Okay, start letting the air out slowly: one . . . two . . . three . . . four. The air is all gone. Great, Alex! Let's try filling our balloon once more. This time when you let the air out, think of holding Cleo [our cat]. Think of the warm fuzzies she gives you. Ready? Breathe in and fill that balloon: one . . . two . . . three . . . four. Now let the air out slowly. Open your mouth and think of holding Cleo. Now let all your warm, fuzzy feelings go through your whole body, right down to your tippy toes."

After the exercise, I asked Alex if he felt better. He said that he did. I quickly reviewed what had happened, saying, "I know you were annoyed with Jessie and that you were also tired. I could tell you were feeling cold pricklies, because you looked mad and you began to cry. That was a good time for you to stop and take charge of those cold, prickly feelings. You did this by giving your body time to get rid of those cold, prickly thoughts and feelings. What did you do to get rid of those yucky feelings?" Alex was able to recollect the quieting reflex sequence. If he had said that he did not feel better, I would have repeated the exercise. If he could not remember what we had done during the exercise, I would have simply reviewed it with him like this: "You took two deep breaths and you let only warm, fuzzy thoughts and feelings come into your head and body. You did this by thinking of holding Cleo. That's how you took charge of your feelings—and you took charge even though Jessie was bothering you and even though you were tired."

By doing this kind of on-the-spot training we can help children understand their own stress triggers and reactions. We are also providing them with a method for handling stress and the expectation that they can do so successfully. These contribute to children's feelings of self-efficacy, to their repertoire of coping skills, and to their ability to be self-reliant and proactive problem solvers. All of these factors enhance resilience and self-esteem.

Imagery

Guided imagery (or relaxing imagery, as it's sometimes called) is often employed in clinical practice to help individuals deal with pain, cancer, noxious stimuli, and test anxiety (Lichstein, 1988). Maureen Murdock (1987), the author of *Spinning Inward*, has used guided imagery as a method of relaxation and as a means of enhancing learning and creativity. Her book contains a number of exercises appropriate for children ages three and up, as well as exercises for adolescents and adults. It's an excellent resource for those of you interested in using guided imagery at home or in school.

To effectively do guided imagery you will need to find a quiet place and a comfortable position. Younger children need exposure to the mental image before they actually do the exercise. One way of preparing children is to show them pictures or have them draw pictures of what they will be imaging during the exercise. It's helpful to be explicit and detailed about the image and to guide children through the exercise by speaking in a soft, calm voice.

The following exercises are examples of guided imagery that can be used with children. The exercise involving images of mountain climbing, with appropriate modifications in the instructions, has been found useful for adults and adolescents as well.

Exercise 7: Sleepy Song
(to accompany "Hush Little Baby")

Step 1: Have the child take three deep breaths (see Exercises 5 and 6 for directions).

Step 2: Have the child close his or her eyes and imagine "sleepy dust" being sprinkled all over his or her body.

Step 3: Then say, "As the sleepy dust touches your head, your head feels very, very heavy, and your forehead feels very, very heavy." Repeat for each of the following body parts: neck, shoulders, arms, hands, stomach, back, legs, feet.

Step 4: Conclude by saying, "And now your whole body feels very, very heavy and very, very sleepy."

Exercise 8: Color Exercise Procedures

Step 1: Have the child take three deep breaths (see breathing exercises for details).

Step 2: Have the child close his or her eyes and imagine a large ball. Say, "Draw a big ball in your mind. Make the ball as big as a basketball. Color the ball blue—a soft blue, like the blue in the sky. As you color the ball blue, repeat quietly to yourself the words 'blue, blue-calm, blue-heavy, blue-calm, blue-heavy.'" Repeat these words for 2 to 3 minutes.

Step 3: Now say to the child, "Give your blue ball magical powers. Each time the blue ball touches a part of your body, it will make your body feel very heavy and calm. Let the blue ball touch your head. Now your head feels heavy and calm. Let the ball touch your shoulders. Now your shoulders feel heavy and calm. The blue ball is touching your tummy, and your tummy is now heavy and calm." Continue for each part of the body.

Step 4: Say to the child, "Now it's time to let the blue ball fade. It's fading, fading, fading. And now it's gone. Open your eyes."

Exercise 9: Mountain Climbing

Recite the following instructions to the child: "Close your eyes and take three deep breaths. See yourself leaving your home. You are leaving your room, your toys, and the people who live in your house with you. [*Name them*] You are now walking down a long road. At the end of the road is a big mountain with lots and lots of trees. You are getting closer and closer to the mountain. [*Pause*] You are now at the mountain and ready to climb to the very top of it. You see yourself climbing up to the very top of the mountain.

You see all kinds of trees. You see pine trees and oak trees and maple trees. You see squirrels running up the trees and bunny rabbits running across the path. You hear the wind blowing softly on the trees, and you can smell the flowers on the path.

"You are walking and walking. You are walking right up to the top of the mountain. Your body is feeling very loose and calm. You are thinking good thoughts about yourself and the other children in your class. You are thinking good thoughts about your mom and dad and teachers. You are thinking you are a good person. You are a good friend. You are in charge of your thinking. You are in charge of how you act. You are in charge of your scared feelings. You are in charge of your happy feelings. You are in charge of your angry feelings. You are in charge of your proud feelings.

"Now you have reached the top of the mountain, and you can see all around you. It all looks very beautiful and calm. Your body feels very loose and heavy, and your mind is filled with all kinds of good thoughts:

> And you feel good
> And you feel confident
> You are as big as the mountain
> You are as big as the mountain
> You are as big as the mountain and
> When you feel scared or angry
> You will think about the mountain
> You will become as big as the mountain
>
> You will take charge of your scared feelings
> You will take charge of your angry feelings
> You are as big as the mountain

"Now it's time to come down from the mountain. You are coming down, down, down from the mountain. You are back on the long road back to your home. You are feeling calm. You are feeling confident. You see your house, and you walk into your house. You are back from your journey. You are calm. You are confident. You are in charge of your feelings and thoughts."

Exercise 10: Power Stars

Recite the following instructions to the child: "Close your eyes and take three deep breaths. Imagine yourself lying down on your bed. Your bed is warm and soft, and you can feel yourself feeling very calm and relaxed. You are looking out the window at the dark sky. The sky is filled with lots and lots of stars. Each star reminds you of a very special idea and how very special you are.

"Imagine lots and lots of stars shining right at you and reminding you of how special you are. Each star helps you think:

> I am in charge of my feelings
> I am in charge of my thoughts
> I can think good feelings
> Because I can think good thoughts.

> I have good, calm feelings
> Because I have calm thoughts
> I can have confident feelings
> Because I have confident thoughts.

> Those stars remind me
> I am in charge of my feelings
> I am in charge of my thoughts
> I can have good, calm feelings
> Because I have good thoughts.

> I am in charge of my feelings
> I am in charge of my thoughts
> I have good, calm feelings
> Because I have good, calm thoughts.

> The stars are in my mind
> The thoughts are shining in my mind
> I will remember these thoughts
> I will remember
> I am in charge of my feelings
> I am in charge of my thoughts
> I have good, calm feelings
> Because I have good, calm thoughts.

"Now the shiny stars are beginning to go away and the sun is coming up. I have all the thoughts in my brain where they will stay all day and night."

Exercise 11: Trouble Bubbles

Say to the child, "Imagine yourself making bubbles. In each bubble, put one of your negative [or cold prickly, cloudy, yucky, junk, garbage—any one of these words will do] thoughts and blow it away."

Progressive Muscle Relaxation Exercises

Progressive muscle relaxation was first proposed by Jacobsen in 1929. His basic assumptions were that the brain is influenced by the messages it receives from skeletal muscles and that the brain in turn influences the actions of these muscles. He termed this bidirectional feedback loop "reciprocal influence" and reasoned that one way of influencing the mind and the body is to consciously execute muscle relaxation exercises. In other words, by forcing the skeletal muscles to relax one can induce the mind and the body to release tension.

Other investigators have offered different explanations for how progressive muscle relaxation works as a stress management technique. Some believe that the tension–relaxation contrasts that are used in the exercise condition the person to respond differently to the early features of the stress response. That is, because the person is sensitized to the sensations of muscle tension and is conditioned to relax those muscle fibers in response to the tension, the stress response is reduced or, in some cases, avoided. This is possible because skeletal muscle tension is an important feature of the stress response (Wolpe, 1958).

The original muscle relaxation exercises designed by Jacobsen are lengthy and impractical for everyday use. A shortened version, now widely used by clinicians for the adult population, has been adapted for use with children and is presented here. While the instructions are suited for children, the basic procedure is applicable to progressive muscle relaxation exercises in general and can be used by the whole family. Table 6.3 provides a listing of relaxation resources. I should also point out that there are a number of commercially available instruction tapes (representative audio tapes and their sources are listed in Table 6.3).

Exercise 12: Progressive Muscle Relaxation

Step 1: Assume a comfortable position.

Step 2: Breathe in deeply through your nose, and breathe out slowly through your mouth.

Step 3: Close your eyes and take another deep breath through your nose and out through your mouth.

Step 4: Take your right hand and make a fist. Make the fist as tight as you can. Feel the tightness in your hand and arm. Notice that your left hand and arm feel a lot different. (Have the child hold the tension for 5 to 7 seconds.) Now relax those muscles. Open your fist and feel the tightness leaving your hand like water spilling out of a pot. (Let the child relax for about 20 seconds.) Repeat the procedure for the left hand and then for both hands at once.

Step 5: The exercise now continues with work on the arms. Make a muscle (you may need to show the child how) with your right arm. Hold that muscle as tight as you can for 5 to 7 seconds. Now let all of the tightness spill out. Relax your arm by straightening it out. Feel the difference. (Let the child relax for 20 seconds.) Repeat with the left arm.

Step 6: Proceed to the muscles of the face. Wrinkle your forehead as tight as you can. Feel the tightness. Hold the tension for 5 to 7 seconds. Now smooth the muscles out: let the tightness spill out of your head and let your head feel very, very smooth. Now make a frown. Frown as hard as you can. Feel the tight feeling in your forehead and face. Hold for 5 to 7 seconds. Now relax that frown. Stop frowning and feel thetightness in your face just going away. Relax for 20 sec-

TABLE 6.3. Relaxation Resources

Lullaby Berceuse Connie Kaldaur and Carmen Campagne (soothing music)	Music for Little People Box 1460 Redway, CA 95560
Earthmother Lullabies Pamala Ballingham (soothing music)	Music for Little People Box 1460 Redway, CA 95560
Moonbeams and Gentle Dreams Several artists (soothing music)	Music for Little People Box 1460 Redway, CA 95560
Star Dreamer Priscilla Herdman (soothing music)	Music for Little People Box 1460 Redway, CA 95560
Dulcimer Lullabies Joemy Wilsom and Friends (soothing music)	Music for Little People Box 1460 Redway, CA 95560
G'night Wolfgang Several artists (soothing music)	Music for Little People Box 1460 Redway, CA 95560
When You Wish upon a Star Daniel Kobialka (soothing music)	L. Sem Enterprises, Inc. 490 El Camino Real Suite 215 Belmont, CA 94002
Lullabies from Around the World Steve Bergman (soothing music)	Chinaberry Book Service 2780 Via Orange Way, Suite B Spring Valley, CA 91978
Relax with the Classics (all four volumes) (soothing music)	LIND Institute P.O. Box 14487 San Francisco, CA 94114
Stress Reduction Tapes Mathew McKay (taped relaxation instruction)	New Harbinger Publications, Inc. 2200 Adeline Oakland, CA 94607

(continued)

TABLE 6.3. *(Continued)*

Learning to Relax Dr. Arnold Lazarus (taped relaxation instruction)	Institute for Rational Emotive Therapy 45 East 65th St. New York, NY 10021
Self-Hypnosis Dr. William Golden (taped relaxation instruction)	Institute for Rational Emotive Therapy 45 East 65th St. New York, NY 10021
I Can Settle Down Karen Erickson and Maureen Robbey (relaxation book)	Scholastic Inc. 730 Broadway New York, NY 10003

onds. Now let your whole face feel smooth and very sleepy. Let all of the nasty, tight feelings fly right off your face. Put those tight feelings on the wall behind you. Relax for 20 seconds.

Step 7: Now work is done on the neck. Slowly press your head back. Feel the tightness in your throat. Hold the tension for 5 to 7 seconds. Now straighten your head. Feel the tightness in your throat running away. Relax for 20 seconds. Now touch your chin to your chest. Notice how tight your throat and the back of your neck feel. Hold the tension for 5 to 7 seconds. Straighten your head and feel all the tight, uncomfortable feelings leave your neck and throat. Relax for 20 seconds.

Step 8: The exercise continues with work on the shoulders. Lift your shoulders up toward your ears and bring your head down to your shoulders. (The adult may have to demonstrate this to the child the first time through.) Pretend that you are trying to touch your ears with your shoulders. Feel the tightness in your neck and in your shoulders and maybe in your throat. Hold for 5 to 7 seconds. Now let your shoulders down and straighten your head. All of the uncomfortable, tight feelings that you felt before are just going away. All of the muscles in your shoulder and throat and neck are feeling very, very tried. Relax for 20 seconds.

Step 9: Now take a deep breath. Breathe in through your nose, and blow out that air through your mouth. Repeat. Breathe in the air through your nose, and blow it out through your mouth. Pull your abdomen in and pretend that you are trying to touch your back with your abdomen. Feel the tightness in your abdomen. Hold the tension for 5 to 7 seconds. Now relax your abdomen. Imagine all those tight feelings flying out of your abdomen and into the air. Relax your abdominal muscles for 20 seconds.

Step 10: The exercise continues with work on the feet. Curl your toes down to the floor. Feel the tightness in your feet and hold for 5 to 7 seconds. Now let your toes go straight. Wiggle your toes. Now your toes feel very, very smooth and relaxed. Relax for 20 seconds. Now bend your toes up toward your face. Hold your toes tight and tense for 5 to 7 seconds. Now let your toes go straight. Wiggle your toes. Relax for 20 seconds.

Step 11: Now return to the top of your head. Make your head feel heavy and calm. Repeat slowly the words "heavy" and "calm" for 5 to 7 seconds. Repeat these instructions for the face, arms, hands, abdomen, and toes.

Quick Relaxation Exercises

Here are some other relaxation exercises you can do with children and for yourself:

Jogging in Place.   Place your arms at your sides and then run in place slowly for 1 to 2 minutes.

Shake Out the Muscle.   Start with the hands and the arms and then go to the legs and feet and shake out the tightness.

Head Roll.   In a full circular fashion, slowly (very slowly) rotate your head down, then to the right side, then up, and then to the left and down. Repeat three to four times. It's important that this be done slowly to avoid muscle strain.

Music. Music soothes the soul. The familiar old lullabies have been used for centuries to hasten the sleep of the young and the old. Research studies now show that slow, flowing music familiar to the listener induces the relaxation response. Heart rate goes down, breathing becomes slower and deeper, and skeletal muscle tension decreases, as does blood pressure (Hanser, 1985; Reynolds, 1984). Table 6.3 lists some of the commercially available tapes.

Self-Massage. Rub your temples and forehead with your fingertips.

Laughter. Humor is an ancient form of medicine. The court jesters were a welcome sight in times past because they represented an antidote to the stressors of the day. In his now famous book *Anatomy of an Illness*, Norman Cousins (1981) claims that ten minutes of hearty laughter gave him two and a half hours of pain-free bliss. Other researchers have found humor to be a marvelous stress reliever for everyday job hassles in the workplace (Davis & Kleiner, 1989); for the sometimes traumatic transitions that we have to deal with throughout adulthood (Prerost, 1989); for marital distress (Krokoff, 1991); and for police officers (Herrman, 1989), student nurses (Warner, 1991), and persons experiencing particularly difficult times in their careers or life situations (Anderson & Arnoult, 1989). Humor has also been useful to children facing the stress of hospitalization (D'Antonio, 1988) and the stresses of just growing up (Martin & Dobbin, 1988). Humor also facilitates the child's ability to be a creative problem solver and to acquire new information and skills (McGhee, 1988). Why is humor so uplifting?

Researchers have likened laughter to a form of internal jogging. It exercises the lungs and relaxes the diaphragm. It tones the cardiovascular and skeletal muscular systems and increases the level of oxygen in the blood. It may also influence our immune functioning (Martin & Dobbin, 1988). For these and other reasons, persons who laugh feel physically and mentally better. Feeling good physically optimizes our ability to deal with change and problems. It makes good sense for us to lighten up occasionally and find something to laugh about. It makes even better sense to encourage and instruct our children to use humor to relax and, when appropriate, as a method of coping with everyday hassles. Reading funny stories to our children, allowing them to watch age-appropriate humorous films, listening to our youngsters' silly jokes, and laughing at ourselves are but a few of the ways we can promote the healthy use of humor in our homes.

Nutrition and Exercise

Relaxation exercises are one way that we can physically and mentally prepare ourselves and our children to deal with the stresses and strains of everyday life. Are there other ways? The answer to this question is a strong *yes*. Good nutrition and proper exercise are very important aspects of the success-resilience formula.

Nutrition

"You are what you eat." This popular saying implies that diet affects how people look, act, and feel. But is it true? There is ample evidence to suggest that nutrients influence our brain's chemistry and, as a result, our mood, performance, sleep cycle, and level of irritability. For example, carbohydrates, which include simple and complex sugars and starches, increase the brain's level of tryptophan. Tryptophan is required for the synthesis of a very important neurotransmitter (chemical in the brain) called serotonin. Serotonin influences mood, behavior, sleep, and even our immune system. Research has shown that tryptophan may hasten sleep, dull pain, and reduce aggressiveness. However, diets that are unbalanced and too high in carbohydrates (generally found in junk foods) may cause fatigue and impair performance for both children and adults (Spring, Chiodo, & Brown, 1987). Good nutrition, then, optimizes a person's performance and productivity.

Nutrients also play an important role in stress and stress management (Adams, 1980). Poor nutritional practices cause stress to the person directly. For example, insufficient caloric intake starves the body and makes it susceptible to illness. Too many nutrients, especially for those people who are not physically active, may result in obesity. Diets deficient in vitamins and minerals cause muscle weakness and cramping, depression, anxiety, insomnia, irritability, and digestive and cardiovascular problems. Excessive consumption of the fat-soluble vitamins (A, D, E, and K) may actually make a person physically ill. Too much refined sugar causes blood sugar swings (a form of reactive hypoglycemia), causing the person to experience mood swings, headaches, and nausea. Caffeine, which is found in coffee, tea, cocoa, and chocolate, stimulates the SNS, resulting in elevated blood pressure, increased oxygen demand, increased heart rate, anxiety, insomnia, and heart arrhythmias. Foods high in salt, saturated fats, and cholesterol increase the risk of cardiovascular problems. These are just a few examples of how poor nutrition contributes to stress and detracts from a person's resilience.

In contrast, good nutritional practices contribute to physical resilience. Why? Because good nutrition is one of the ways of optimizing the efficiency and physical workings of the mind and the body. A well-functioning mind and a healthy body are assets for self-esteem and resilience. What constitutes good nutritional practices? To answer this question, it is necessary first to understand what the body needs to function properly. The body needs six different types of nutrients: carbohydrates, fats (lipids), proteins, vitamins, minerals, and water. These six nutrients are what the body needs to maintain itself and to deal with everyday and extraordinary stressors. To obtain these nutrients, a person needs to eat a variety of foods from the four basic food groups. Table 6.4 provides a general guideline to follow. In addition to providing a

TABLE 6.4. Basic Food Groupings

Food	Serving size	Nutritional benefits	Servings per day
Bread, grains, and cereal group			
breads	1 slice	Source of vitamin B_1,	Six to eleven
pasta	½ to ¾ cup	vitamin B_2, niacin,	
rice	½ to ¾ cup	iron; good source	
dry cereal	1 ounce	of complex	
		carbohydrates	
Protein group			
meats	2 to 3 ounces	Source of protein,	Two to three
fish	2 to 3 ounces	vitamin B_1, vitamin	
eggs	2 to 3 ounces	B_2, vitamin B_{12}, fat,	
dried beans	2 to 3 ounces	iron, niacin,	
peas	1 to 1½ cups	phosphorus	
nuts	½ to ¾ cup		
Dairy group			
milk	1 cup	Source of essential	Two to four
yogurt (plain)	1 cup	amino acids,	
cheese (hard)	1½ ounces	vitamin A,	
processed	2 ounces	proteins, calcium,	
cheese		phosphorus	
Vegetables			
broccoli	½ cup	Source of carbo-	Three to
asparagus	½ cup	hydrates, vitamin	five
carrots	½ cup	B_1, vitamin B_2,	
lettuce	1 cup	vitamin A,	
spinach	1 cup	calcium, folic acid,	
turnips	½ cup	iron, and fiber	
yellow squash	½ cup		
beets	½ cup		
cauliflower	½ cup		
celery	½ cup		
corn	½ cup		
beans	½ cup		
peas	½ cup		
potatoes	½ cup		

(continued)

TABLE 6.4. (Continued)

Food	Serving size	Nutritional benefits	Servings per day
		Fruits	
oranges	1 medium	Source of vitamins,	Two to four
grapefruit	1 medium	minerals, and fiber	
pineapple	½ cup		
strawberries	½ cup		
tomatoes	1 medium		
cantaloupe	½ medium		
papaya	1 large		
apples	1 medium		
bananas	1 medium		
berries	½ cup		
cherries	½ cup		
grapes	1 medium		
plums	1 medium		
prunes	1 medium		
watermelon (balls)	½ cup		

Note: Nutrient and calorie needs vary from person to person as a function of size, age, sex, and physical activity level.
Source: S. Margen and Editors of University of California at Berkeley Wellness Letter, *The Wellness Encyclopedia of Food and Nutrition* (New York: Random House, 1992).

balanced diet, parents need to encourage and instruct their children on other healthful nutritional practices. Becoming a wise consumer of food is the very first step in the process. For example, eating an occasional bag of chips or an ice cream cone is generally not a problem, but selecting a steady diet of these "bad nutrients" compromises our body's health and resilience to stress. To educate our children on these matters, we need to be educated ourselves. The resources listed in Table 6.5 will be helpful to those of you who are interested in learning more about sound nutrition. The second step in helping children develop healthful nutritional

TABLE 6.5.   Some Sources of Nutrition Information

Publication	Where to get it
Nutrition and Your Health: Dietary Guidelines for Americans. Item No. 417V. Price $5.00	Consumer Information Center Department 70 Pueblo, CO 81009
Preparing Foods and Planning Menus Using Dietary Guidelines. Item No. 172V. Price $2.50	Consumer Information Center Department 70 Pueblo, CO 81009
Dietary Guidelines and Your Health. Stock No. 001-000-04467-2. Price $4.50	Superintendent of Documents Government Printing Office Washington, DC 20402
Tufts University Diet and Nutrition Letter Price $20.00 for 12 issues	Tufts University Diet and Nutrition Letter 53 Park Place New York, NY 10007

practices is to actively plan and reinforce good nutritional choices. The child who chooses popcorn in place of a candy bar for a snack needs to be occasionally praised for the wise choice. That child also needs to see parents and other significant adults make similar good choices. Avoiding frequent visits to fast food places and minimizing our consumption of alcohol, nicotine, caffeine, and junk foods sets a good example for our children.

Carbohydrates.   Carbohydrates are the body's source of energy. There are simple carbohydrates (sugars) and complex carbohydrates (starches). The body breaks down complex carbohydrates into glucose, which is the most efficient source of energy for the body and the only source of energy for the brain. Complex carbohydrates include such foods as rice, potatoes, beans, corn, nuts, and pasta. These foods are recommended over candy bars or cake because candy bars and cake are "expensive" sources of carbohydrates, which means that while these junk foods are sources of carbohydrates, they are also high in calories, fats, sodium, and cholesterol. High levels of these nutrients are physically stressful for the body. The good old baked potato, on the other hand, is also rich in carbohydrates, is low in calories, fat, and sodium, and contains no cholesterol (Margen, S., and the Editors of the University of California at Berkeley Wellness Letter, 1992).

Fats.   Fats, or lipids, are nutrients made up of fatty acids. There are three kinds of fatty acids: saturated, monounsaturated, and polyunsaturated. Saturated fats are solid at room temperature and are found mostly in foods that come from animals (e.g., meat, milk, and butter). There are some plant sources of saturated fatty acids, for example, coconut oils and palm oils. Saturated fats increase cholesterol levels, and cholesterol levels over 240 milligrams, especially when combined with low lipoproteins (LDL), can increase a person's risk of coronary heart disease (Margen, S., and the Editors of the University of California at Berkeley Wellness Letter, 1992).

Monounsaturated and polyunsaturated fatty acids are found in plants and animals. They take on liquid form at room temperature and are considered more healthful than saturated fats. They can actually lower serum cholesterol levels (Margen, S., and the Editors of the University of California at Berkeley Wellness Letter, 1992). Cholesterol is also a fat substance. The body itself produces cholesterol, and it is also obtained from food sources. The body needs a certain amount of cholesterol to make hormones. For some people, high blood cholesterol levels represent a risk factor for coronary heart disease.

Fats serve some important functions: they help transport fat-soluble vitamins; they act as a cushion for internal organs; they store unused carbohydrate molecules for energy conversion; and they are an additional source of energy for the body. The body requires one tablespoon of fat per day to accomplish these goals (Margen, S., and the Editors of the University of California at Berkeley Wellness Letter, 1992).

Proteins. Proteins are complex nutrients made up of simpler structures called amino acids. Proteins form the tissues making up our muscles, hair, skin, nails, connective tissues, and glands. Proteins also serve as a source of energy for the body if there are insufficient amounts of carbohydrates or fats (Margen, S., and the Editors of the University of California at Berkeley Wellness Letter, 1992).

The body gets some of the amino acids it needs for the production of proteins from carbohydrates and fats. Eight of the amino acids, called essential amino acids, must be consumed because the body cannot manufacture them itself. Sources of essential amino acids are meat, milk products, and eggs. Complete proteins can be gotten from plants when a legume is combined with any grain (Brody, 1985).

Vitamins. Vitamins regulate metabolism and help in the production of hormones. Some vitamins are water-soluble, others are fat-soluble. If a vitamin is water-soluble, it means that excess amounts of it are discarded as waste and excreted in the urine. Fat-soluble vitamins dissolve in fats and are stored in a person's fatty tissue. Each vitamin has its own function and cannot take the place of another. This is one of the reasons why a balanced diet is so necessary. The vitamins B and C are especially critical during stressful times. This is the case because vitamin B complex is essential to the metabolism of carbohydrates and vitamin C plays a role in adrenaline production (Adams, 1980).

Minerals. Minerals are inorganic substances found in the earth's crust. Plants and water absorb the minerals. Minerals serve a number of important functions in the body, including bone and tissue development, nerve conduction, wound repair, hormone production, blood clotting, and red blood cell construction.

Water. Water is another essential nutrient. It is required for blood circulation, temperature control, the transporting of food nutrients to body cells, and the elimination of body wastes.

Exercise

Good nutrition goes hand and hand with physical exercise. Regular aerobic exercise lasting 15 to 30 minutes is a frequent recommendation given to people interested in achieving and maintaining good physical and mental health. Aerobic exercise refers to the kind of exercise that requires increased oxygen consumption for at least 12 minutes (preferably 30 minutes) and an elevated heart rate. Common aerobic exercises include jogging, walking, cross-country skiing, jumping rope, cycling, and dancing. Aerobic exercise performed with sufficient intensity and duration and done on a regular basis accomplishes at least two things: it heightens the body's ability to extract oxygen from the blood and it improves the body's ability to generate energy. People who are aerobically fit have good physical endurance because they use oxygen efficiently to convert fatty acids and glucose into energy. This efficient source of energy certainly helps in times of stress when the body needs more energy to deal with the stressor. The kind of aerobic program suited for you depends on your age, physical capacity, interests, and opportunities. Most proponents of aerobic exercise recommend that persons who have more sedentary life styles or health problems start out slowly and have a physical examination by their health care provider before they begin an exercise program. Aerobic programs basically consist of an hour of exercise three to four times a week. Haskell (1985) has suggested that the hour be partitioned in the following way:

1. A warm-up period consisting of stretching and strengthening exercises
2. An aerobics (20 to 40 minutes) period during which the person engages in a rhythmical set of exercises involving the large muscle groups with sufficient intensity to raise the heart (pulse) rate to a moderately high target range (The target range formula is based on a person's age and heart rate: the minimum heart rate in the target range is 160 pulse beats per minute minus the person's age, the maximum heart rate 200 pulse beats per minute minus the

person's age. So, if you are 40 years old, you would maintain a heart rate between 120 and 160 beats per minute during the aerobics period (LaPlace, 1984). There are more accurate estimates for an individual's target range, using their own resting and peak heart rates. The one offered here is quick and easy, but to be perfectly accurate consult your health care professional.)

3. A cool-down period during which the person gradually decreases the intensity of activity so that the body gradually returns to its normal state

Research has demonstrated the usefulness of a regular exercise program such as the one described here. McCann and Holmes (1984) found that a ten-week aerobic exercise program with mildly depressed college women helped to reduce their depression. Farmer and associates (1988) examined the physical activity and depressive symptoms of 1,900 physically healthy adults (ages 25 to 77); according to their findings, physically active people are less likely to have depressive symptoms. Other investigators (Long, 1985) found that aerobic exercise helps people deal with everyday stressors. Research has also addressed the question, Can aerobic exercise protect people physically and emotionally from the negative effects of a stressful event? While there are mixed results, most of the studies have shown that aerobic exercise contributes to a person's ability to withstand stress. For example, Roth and Holmes (1985) and Perkins, Dubbert, Martin, Faulstich, and Harris (1986) found that "high-stressed" adults who engaged in a regular program of aerobic exercise actually experienced fewer health-related problems than those "high-stressed" adults who were not regularly exercising. Similarly, researchers working with adolescents in stressful situations (Brown & Lawton, 1986; Brown & Siegel, 1988) found that those who engaged in regular aerobic exercise experienced fewer physical problems (i.e., sore throats, flu) than their counterparts who did not. There are of course several other physical advantages that result from aerobic exercise: physical fitness, improved cardiovascular health, and protection against osteoporosis and some other kinds of disease. For all these reasons, aerobic exercise enhances resilience. It contributes to our physical stamina and makes us better able to weather the stresses of life. The best way to encourage children to engage in physical exercise is to make it a family affair. Families who take walks together or bicycle together encourage this kind of healthy life style in their children. Children who see the adults in their life engaging in physical exercise are more likely to adopt the habit themselves. So, instead of watching TV, take a walk, go swimming, or engage in some other aerobic activity with your child. It will relax you and contribute to the development of a lifelong resilience-enhancing habit in your child.

Chapter 7

Teaching Children to Think Constructively

Imagine the following situation: You have a week's vacation. You've been looking forward to this vacation for months, you've planned a number of outdoor activities, and of course you expect the weather to cooperate. The week finally arrives, and it rains five out of the seven days. Now, there are a number of responses you could have to this situation. You might think, "This is just my luck. It's not fair! My whole vacation is ruined!" You feel miserable the whole week and return to work stressed out. On the other hand, you might say to yourself, "Well, I'm disappointed with the rain, but I'll make the most of it. What other activities can I do to make good use of my vacation time?" And despite the weather you enjoy your week off. When you return to work, you feel refreshed and ready to get back into the routine. What is the difference between these two responses? The difference is in how you choose to construe the situation.

The great Greek philosopher Epictetus said, "People are disturbed not by things but by their view of things." And Shakespeare made the very same claim in *Hamlet*: "There is nothing either good or bad, but thinking makes it so" (Act II, scene 2, line 259). The import of these famous statements is that personal control derives from the way an individual construes what's been seen, heard, or felt. In other words, it's the perspective we take and the appraisals we make of people and situations that primarily determine our emotional and behavioral reactions. The fact that you choose to look at the rainy vacation as an opportunity to do other things allows you to make the most of your time off.

Although there are a few inborn reflexes (e.g., a startle response to a sudden loud noise), there is ample evidence of a bidirectional influence between thoughts, feelings, and actions. Thoughts are in some cases the antecedents of emotions; in other cases thoughts are affected by emotions. Likewise, behavior often follows from our assessment of a situation, but sometimes our assessment of a situation is influenced by what we are doing (Lazarus & Folkman, 1984). What's important to remember is that we can consciously and deliberately alter the cycle by examining and directing our thoughts. When we do, we typically feel different and act differently.

For example, Dweck (1986) taught children who were doing poorly in math to think differently about their failure, to interpret failure as a signal to try harder: the children who were instructed in this way persisted on math tasks longer than they did before and improved their grades. And therapists who work on helping children change the way they think (cognitive behavioral therapists) have observed a decrease in anger and aggressiveness in these children (Braswell & Kendall, 1988). Learning to identify negative thought patterns and replace them with realistic, constructive thoughts and images reduces anxiety and enhances performance (Deffenbacher, 1986; Hunsley, 1987; Meichenbaum, 1985). Finally, modifying destructive beliefs has a positive effect on both physical and mental health. Constructive changes in thoughts have helped Type A personalities (Friedman & Ulmer, 1984) and cancer patients (Taylor, 1991); change to constructive thinking is also a major ingredient for mental health and good coping skills (Lazarus & Folkman, 1984). The implication of all these studies is that thoughts can be put to good use and direction, even when the objective situation is bleak.

In the scenario with which this chapter began, the two

different evaluations of the rainy vacation resulted in two very different states of mind of the vacationer returning to work. Granted, a rainy vacation is not an earth-shattering or life-threatening situation, but the kind of flexible thinking required for this irritating situation is exactly the kind of skill required for resilience in more difficult times. And it's not the case that constructive thinking eliminates the hurt. It does not. It simply allows us to channel the hurt or disappointment into constructive alternatives. Constructive thinking empowers us when mental muscle and coping skills are needed to deal effectively with a stressor. When we are able to think constructively, we are happier and better able to deal with stress and adversity.

What influences how we think about things? Researchers in the fields of cognition, social psychology, and clinical psychology have identified six major influences:

1. Language (specifically, words)
2. The opinions or beliefs we hold
3. Thinking errors (what experts call "cognitive distortions")
4. Age and maturity
5. Certain aspects of a situation or event
6. Attributions (i.e., the causes people ascribe to events)

I will discuss each one of these influences in the hope that the discussion will help parents and teachers identify and change faulty thinking and notice and reinforce constructive thinking in children.

Language, Thinking, and Your Child's Behavior

Language is the basis of thought and perception. It is the instrument we use to think about our experiences.[1] It is also used

---

[1]While most people think in terms of language, a significant number think in terms of images. If this is the case for your child, you might want to use visualization and teach him or her to think in terms of positive images.

to control behavior and communicate needs. To get a feel for how powerful language really is, consider the following statements used to describe a person who reacts in an unruffled way to a wide variety of situations: "She is even-tempered"; "She is indifferent." If we use the word "even-tempered," it results in a very different evaluation of the person than if we use the word "indifferent." An even-tempered person is viewed as calm, predictable, and in control. Someone perceived as indifferent is considered to be uncaring and unfeeling.

Our reactions to a person are guided by the labels we assign to them (Scheff, 1975). If the label is "even-tempered," we might trust, approach, and respect that person. If the label is "indifferent," we are likely to avoid or shun the person—or, at the very least, be cautious about what we disclose. Likewise, a child who is persistent in pursuit of a particular goal can be labeled as either "stubborn" or "strong-willed." The label given influences the adult's response to the child: the evaluation "stubborn" usually results in a more punitive approach to the child than does the term "strong-willed."

It is not only the evaluative label that has an impact on our reactions; word intensity does as well. The difference between "furious" and "disappointed" or "ecstatic" and "pleased" is the intensity of the emotion the words express. If I say I'm disappointed, I'm likely to react less strongly than if I say I'm furious. So not only do I have to watch the labels I use, but I also need to be cognizant of the words I use to express what I'm feeling.

Language also controls behavior directly. The Russian psychologist A. Luria (1961) and the American psychologist A. P. Copeland (1983) have discovered that people use self-talk (also called private speech, internal dialogue, and automatic self-talk) to regulate their own behavior. We literally talk to ourselves! We are not always aware of our self-talk, but it's always going on. It's particularly apparent when we are learning a new skill or engaging in a new activity of some kind. Do you remember when you were first learning to drive? Most people learning to drive think through the routine out loud: "Adjust and fasten seat belt, adjust mirror, make sure emergency brake is off" and so on. Eventually, the person does not have to repeat these steps out loud, but the self-talk continues internally.

Very young children do not use language to regulate behavior. This is because language develops over the course of the first two years and because the ability to regulate one's own behavior using language develops in three stages. In the first stage the child relies on the speech of others to control and direct behavior. Children under the age of three require this kind of intervention. They do not have the cognitive maturity to self-talk. During the next stage children begin to use language to regulate behavior, but in order to do so they have to talk aloud to themselves. When the self-talk becomes internalized, the child has reached the third and final phase of self-talk control. This third phase occurs around the age of five or six for most children. Children in this phase no longer need overt verbal guides for behavior; they can talk to themselves quietly, just as adults do (Luria, 1961).

Parents and teachers can make direct use of language to reinforce those attitudes and beliefs compatible with resilience. They can do this by using expressions that connote resilience and encouraging their children to do the same. In the following paragraphs are examples of statements that promote traits associated with resilience and productivity. Such statements serve to guide children's thinking and beliefs.

Statements That Promote Internal Control and Proactive Problem Solving

1. I can take charge of my [specific feelings].
2. It's up to me to try my best.
3. It's my responsibility to _____.
4. I can control my behavior.
5. I'm responsible for how I act and behave in a situation.
6. I may not be able to control someone or something else,

but I can always control my own reaction to whatever happens.
7. I accept responsibility for my experiences.
8. The best way to escape from a problem is to solve it.

Statements like these establish the center of control in the person, not someplace else.

Statements That Promote a Sense of Challenge

1. I can handle a little at a time.
2. Even if I feel _____, I won't feel this way forever.
3. Who knows, maybe something good will come from this.
4. I can manage.
5. I know what I can do.
6. I can stand it.
7. I may feel a little uncomfortable, but I'll survive.
8. It may hurt a little, but the hurt will go away.
9. Every experience in life is an opportunity to learn and grow.
10. Every problem is an opportunity.
11. Failure is success if we learn from it.
12. All things are difficult before they are easy.
13. When one door closes, another one opens.

Statements like these take the sting out of threats and allow the person to see change or adversity as manageable. Statements like "It's awful" or "I won't be able to stand it" serve only to exaggerate the problem and may lead to the perception that it's impossible to handle.

Statements That Promote a Sense of Commitment

1. I'm going to stick with _____ until I get it done.
2. It is my goal to _____.
3. I believe in _____.
4. I'm sticking with this so that I can accomplish my goal.

These statements clearly establish a sense of goals and direction. They also convey the notion of persistence, which is so important for commitment.

Statements That Promote an Orientation toward Others

1. I can see your point of view.
2. I want to help you.
3. I want to cooperate with you.
4. I'm not the only one who _____.
5. You see things differently from me and that's okay.
6. I'm concerned about [name of person].
7. I care about [name of person].
8. I want to help [name of person].

These statements help children become "other-oriented."

Beliefs, Thinking, and Your Child's Behavior

Researchers and clinicians in the fields of cognition and cognitive behavior modification have various ways of defining a belief. I have chosen to define a belief as an underlying assumption or opinion that people hold about themselves and their world. Beliefs filter our thoughts and form the basis for expectations. For example, if I believe all people act in a fair and just manner, then I will expect you to behave in accordance with my belief. The belief predisposes me to evaluate you positively if you act fairly. If you fail to act in a way that I perceive as fair and just, then of course I will view you negatively—unless I find good reason for why you behaved unfairly.

Beliefs are learned. Family, school, church, community, and society are the early teachers of beliefs. Personal experience influences beliefs as the child moves toward adolescence and adulthood. Because our beliefs are so fundamental to us, we are not always aware of them. And unless there is a problem, there is usually no need to question them.

Beliefs are either constructive or destructive.[2] Constructive beliefs promote constructive thinking and lead to productive emotions and behavior. Conversely, destructive beliefs produce destructive thinking, which in turn results in counterproductive feelings and actions.

Constructive Beliefs

Constructive beliefs are moderate, reasonable, and realistic. Compare the following statements: "It is my hope that people treat each other in a fair and just manner"; "People *must* treat others fairly and justly." The first statement suggests that fairness is a desirable goal but not necessarily a natural condition. The second statement sets the stage for a very different expectation, namely, that all people will act fairly and justly at all times. The first statement is a constructive belief, the second a destructive one. Why? Because the first is realistic and prepares children for the possibility that people will not always treat them or others fairly whereas the second is unrealistic and ignores the many situations when individuals are treated in an unjust fashion. Children who are prepared for the realities they are likely to experience are better able to cope with them. Unrealistic beliefs about the behavior of others do not provide children with the same kind of preparation. Generally speaking, beliefs that contain extreme and demanding language lead people to unrealistic expectations. Albert Ellis (1962) suggests that words like "should," "ought," and "must"

[2]Rational emotive therapists and researchers (e.g., Bernard & Joyce, 1984) use certain criteria to classify beliefs as either rational or irrational. Cognitive behavior therapists have offered different criteria for identifying rational and irrational beliefs. However, everyone agrees that an irrational belief leads to destructive evaluations whereas a rational belief results in constructive judgments. For pragmatic reasons, I have chosen to refer to rational beliefs as constructive beliefs and to irrational beliefs as destructive beliefs. The criteria for differentiating between the two kinds of beliefs represent a combination of the criteria offered by the different cognitive behavior modification schools.

lead people to think destructively. He calls the persistent use of this language "musterbation."

Constructive beliefs fit the objective qualities of the situation. What this means is that what I hold to be true needs to be verifiable—unless the belief is a matter of faith. (And when it's a matter of faith, an individual needs to realize that the belief is an opinion, not a fact, and that it is true for some people but certainly not for all people.) Beliefs that are not a matter of faith can also be opinions, but they have some objective reality. For example, a child's belief that she or he is the best math student in the class is constructive if the objective evidence supports it (e.g., the child has the highest math average in the class). Similarly, the belief that Susie loves chocolate ice cream is also verifiable, by means of her response to chocolate ice cream. But the belief that chocolate ice cream is the only flavor worth eating (and that all individuals holding a contrary opinion share a defective belief) is destructive. There clearly is no objective base for such a position. The person who holds this belief has transformed an opinion with no reality base into a dogmatic doctrine.

Constructive beliefs promote goals and behaviors that are healthy for the individual and society. The belief that it's important to try to reach one's goals is a constructive belief because it prompts resilient attitudes and behaviors. The belief that it's easier not to even try is destructive because it supports the hopeless, helpless attitudes and behaviors that are observed in nonresilient individuals.

Destructive Beliefs

Destructive beliefs, like constructive beliefs, have certain characteristics. There is, for example, a demanding quality to them. They are filled with "shoulds," "can'ts," "musts," "have to's," and other extreme language. Destructive beliefs communicate the idea that people or situations need to be a particular way or need to be different from the way they are. Demanding beliefs are destructive because they often seek to change other people or situations. Other people and situations are not always influenced by what we have to say or by what we do. Besides, other people respond rather poorly to demands; they do better with requests.

Destructive beliefs are often cop-outs (Anderson, 1981), which place the responsibility for change on someone else. A cop-out is the belief that someone else is responsible for why I feel the way I do or why something did not get done. "He made me angry"; "It's her fault that I failed"; "He makes me feel so good!"— these are all examples of cop-outs. Others cannot make us feel this way or that; they do not control how we interpret or evaluate a situation. Someone else's actions may have prompted me to think a particular way, but ultimately I have control over the way I think, and therefore the way I feel. Cop-outs are destructive because they encourage people to think and behave as though they are externally controlled. In other words, cop-outs discourage people from assuming control for themselves.

Destructive beliefs have catastrophic themes (Ellis, 1962). Destructive beliefs often paint a "doom and gloom" picture of reality when things do not go quite the way we would like: "When I don't get an A, it is awful"; "When John calls me a name, it is terrible"; "I'll just die if I don't get first place." These are all examples of beliefs that distort a person's perspective and lead to negative feelings and behaviors. The catastrophic self-talk makes a challenge orientation nearly impossible because it discourages a person from coping with the situation. When we evaluate a situation in extreme negative terms, we may actually create a scenario that is worse than the reality of the situation.

Destructive Beliefs of Children and Adolescents.   There appear to be three major categories of destructive beliefs that affect children and adolescents. The destructive beliefs discussed in the following paragraphs were identified through interviews with children and adolescents (Ellis & Bernard, 1983; Waters, 1982).

"I must excel in everything I do and get the approval of everybody all the time or else I am worthless."   This is a destructive belief because

it promotes an unrealistic set of expectations. It also leads the child to believe that all mistakes are awful things with irreversible consequences. In reality, people can learn and perfect their skills through mistakes. The difference between winners and losers is not that winners win; many winners were losers in past competitions. Rather, it's that winners learn from mistakes and losers don't. Losers are immobilized by mistakes and tend to give up when they make mistakes. This belief is destructive to the positive challenge orientation and willingness to persist that are so important to resilient children and adults. Moreover, a person may not excel in every area. Very few people do. Believing that you are worthy only if you excel at everything you do is destructive. Your natural abilities may vary across areas, making you more or less proficient in those areas. For example, your athletic ability may be far less than your intellectual abilities. Believing that you are a worthwhile individual only if you are good in sports and academically inclined is unrealistic and likely to result in a negative self-evaluation.

Negative self-evaluations reduce our sense of self-efficacy and compromise our ability to hold resilient and productive attitudes. Likewise, the belief that we need the love and approval of everybody all the time is equally destructive. It is the unusual person who is approved of by everyone all the time. Believing that this kind of continuous approval is a prerequisite for self-worth is therefore unrealistic and unnecessary. Besides, one has to differentiate between approval and unconditional love and respect. I may not approve of your behavior, but that does not necessarily mean that I don't love or value you as a person. For example, there are plenty of occasions when I disapprove of my children's inappropriate behavior, but this does not mean that I don't love or respect them as individuals. In a similar vein, adolescents and some adults often interpret disagreement as rejection. I may not agree with your opinion, but it does not automatically mean that I don't respect and care for you as a person.

Finally, there may be occasions when others do reject you as a person. While this may be disappointing and perhaps hurtful, it doesn't mean that you are worthless. People dislike others for a multitude of reasons. You may be rejected for the color of your skin or the religion you choose to practice. Or you may be rejected because your interests and values are incompatible with those of others. Whatever the reason, rejection from some people some of the time is inevitable for most of us. The good news is that we need unconditional love from just a few people for a positive self-concept. Teaching children to understand that occasional rejection from others is common and to be expected helps them maintain a healthy sense of self when encountering negative responses from others.

"I must have and acquire what I want or else I will be miserable." How many times have you heard this one? Plenty, I'm sure. Children who believe that they *have to* get their own way are vulnerable because such a belief sets up unrealistic expectations in them. Again, the real world cannot always assure that they will get what they want all the time. If they truly believe that this is the only way they can be happy, they are bound to be miserable, as it's impossible to always get what one wants. Besides, sometimes what children think they want is not at all what they want.

"I must always feel happy and life should be easy and fun." Again, the expectation implied by this belief does not correlate well with what happens in real life. To expect no discomfort in life and to expect that things will be fun and easy all of the time is to expect too much. Discomfort and sadness are just as much a part of the human condition as comfort and joy. We have to be prepared to accept the range of life's conditions if we want to be happy, productive, and resilient.

Thinking Errors and Your Child's Behavior

Destructive beliefs and language are not the only reason people come up with faulty evaluations. People also make errors in the way they process the information they receive. Researchers refer to these errors as cognitive distortions. Let's examine what they are and how they influence the way an individual thinks. Aaron Beck, a well-known American psychiatrist, has identified seven kinds of thinking errors, or "cognitive distortions." These distortions create problems because they result in faulty and maladaptive evaluations, which are threats both to self-esteem and to resilience. Let's look at and examine the common kinds of errors that both children and adults make.

Overgeneralization

When people overgeneralize, they draw a conclusion based on one event and assume that it will be true for all other similar (and sometimes dissimilar) circumstances. Children who believe that because they have failed one spelling test they will fail all other spelling tests, and perhaps all other school tests, are demonstrating overgeneralization.

Selective Abstraction

When a person takes something out of context and at the same time ignores all other pieces of information, he or she is committing the error of selective abstraction. Here's an example of selective abstraction, which is a little like selective attention: Suzie gets her report card. She receives all A's and one B. The B is in gym. Suzie concludes that she is a poor student. When she talks to her parents about the report card, she reports only the B. She has ignored the rest of the grades and has also failed to tell her parents that the gym teacher gave only one A and two B's. You can see the havoc that this kind of distortion has for self-esteem and resilience.

Arbitrary Inference

When a person comes up with an evaluation that is not supported by fact and acts upon it as if it were true, he or she has made an arbitrary inference. Some of the destructive beliefs that we discussed earlier provide the basis for arbitrary inferences. Consider this example: Jill concludes that her father does not love her anymore because he does not kiss her as he enters the house (he happened to be sneaking in her birthday gift). Jill's conclusion is based on her father's failing to kiss her this one time. An obvious example of arbitrary inference! There are less exaggerated examples as well: "I don't like you because you play the piano and I don't like the piano." Another person's piano playing is an arbitrary piece of information on which to base an evaluation of his or her character.

Magnification

Magnification happens when a person exaggerates one aspect of an event. A child who reports, "The teacher yelled at me all day," when the teacher simply pointed out an error on an arithmetic paper is guilty of magnification.

Minimization

A person who plays down the importance of a positive event, for example, the teen who believes that the A on the chemistry final was a fluke, is demonstrating minimization.

Dichotomous Thinking

One of the most common thinking errors stems from the belief that people and things are either good or bad, black or white, right or wrong. People and situations don't always fit in one or the other category. Most of us are good *and* bad, smart *and* dumb, pleasant *and* unpleasant, and so on. To categorize ourselves or others in a restrictive one-category box is to miss *at least half* of the full picture! Thinking in a dichotomous fashion restricts flexibility. Flexibility is a must for problem solving and for a challenge perspective.

Personalization

The thinking error of personalization involves the tendency to assume personal responsibility for things and events in your environment that go wrong when there is no rational base for doing so. For example, the child who believes that she caused the teacher to get a headache because she happened to disobey her by talking in the library is guilty of personalization.

Thinking Errors of Young Children

Another common error that children make is to believe that everyone else thinks as they do. A corollary to this error is the belief that others should "know" what's on their mind and what they need. Young children are more likely to think like this because they have not yet developed the ability to see things from another's perspective. They are egocentric by nature and frequently process information about others falsely because of this bias. For example, Mary is upset with her big sister Jane because Jane didn't ask her if she wanted to go ice-skating. Mary believes that Jane knew she wanted to go ice-skating! This is a perfect example of an egocentric processing error. Children, of course, are not the only ones who make this error. This kind of processing error interferes directly with social skills and interpersonal relationships.

Age, Maturity, and Thinking

The egocentric processing error in particular draws attention to the necessity of looking at the effect maturity has on thinking, especially as it relates to thinking constructively. Developmental psychologists study how people change as they age and mature. They have identified changes in almost every area of development. The areas that are of most concern to our discussion are the changes in language and intellectual abilities. These changes are important to know because they set the outer limits on how people—and children specifically—come to understand their world.

Newborns are limited in terms of what they can say and think. That picture changes rapidly over the course of the first two years of life. Moving into toddlerhood, a child becomes increasingly able to understand simple language. In fact, children understand language before actually producing it. Between 10 and 15 months, the child begins to use single words to communicate a number of different things. The two-word sentence emerges around the age of 18 months. These two-word sentences are telegraphic in nature and contain content words only. Descriptors like "in" or "mad" are missing from the child's vocabulary. As the child approaches the preschool years, there is a dramatic increase in vocabulary and in the ability to use and understand grammar. By the time children are five or six, their speech and language approximates that of adults. However, there are still important differences in language capacity between young school-age children and older children (ten and eleven) and adults (Hetherington & Parke, 1986).

Young children have difficulty communicating about absent objects and about feelings (Shatz, 1983). This does not mean that they can't; it simply means that we cannot take this ability for granted when dealing with young children. They also have difficulty with semantically complex sentences. For example, the sentences "Jane likes to please" and "Jane is easy to please" have two very different meanings, but the word "Jane" is in exactly the same spot in each sentence. In one case Jane is the doer of the action, and in the other case she is the recipient, or is what linguists call the logical object (Chomsky, 1969). Young children get confused by sentences like the second one. Similarly, young children have difficulty picking up on subtle feedback (e.g., sarcasm, slight changes in nonverbal expression); by age seven, they are much better at this, although clear, direct communication is superior in every case. The ability to use and analyze language improves with age. Four-year-olds have difficulty understanding that sounds make up words. They also have trouble analyzing their own language for clarity and meaning. Seven-year-olds are much better, and ten-year-olds are better yet (Hetherington & Parke, 1986).

Closely tied to language proficiency are cognitive, or intellectual, abilities. As with language, there are definite developmental changes that occur in the child's ability to understand and reason, changes that impact on the way children think.

Preschool children engage in what psychologist Jean Piaget called "preoperational thought." The major accomplishment of the preoperational child is the development of language. Preoperational children use language to represent objects and to control and regulate behavior, but they have a number of limitations. For one thing, children of this age have difficulty reasoning and concentrating on more than one aspect of an object or situation at a time. For example, if you have two glasses filled with milk and one of those glasses is tall and thin while the other is short and fat, though each contains the same volume, preoperational children generally perceive the tall, thin glass as bigger. They do this because of an inability to focus on the height and the width of the glass at the same time. This inability to "decenter" contributes to the preoperational child's egocentricity. Children are egocentric when they have difficulty seeing a situation from other than their own perspective. This does not mean that they are selfish or inconsiderate. Piaget's writing is very clear about this point. Children of this age have difficulties thinking about more than one aspect of any situation at the same time; they have trouble decentering in the social area just as they do in nonsocial areas. The older preoperational child (three or four years old) can be taught to think in a less egocentric way.

Preoperational children are also animistic; that is, they attribute humanlike qualities to inanimate objects. For example, our son Alex had to make sure that his stuffed Dalmatian dogs were snug and warm at night before he would even consider falling asleep. Other children attempt to feed their pet rocks or favorite stuffed animals, believing that they have human needs. And, of course, stories and cartoons reinforce the child's animism when they portray animals and objects with humanlike characteristics.

Preoperational children have difficulty thinking about how they think (Flavell, 1979). Unlike older children, they do not ask the question, "Now, how did I figure that out?" or "What was I thinking when I did that?" The implication of this for the discussion at hand is that one has to present errors in thinking in a different way to young children. The implication of this limitation is that younger children have to be directed by adults to think about what they need to think about. I will be discussing just how to do this shortly.

At about the age of seven or eight children move into what Piaget called the "concrete operational" period. During this time children develop the ability to reason. They can process more than one piece of information at a time, and they can reflect on how they are thinking. Their major limitation is that the kind of reasoning they do has to do with concrete topics. For most children it's not until the age of 11 or 12 that they can reason in abstract terms. By the time children reach adolescence, their thinking is quite similar to that of adults. They lack the experience and the knowledge, but the basic cognitive structures are in place and ready to be used.

In summary, children's cognitive maturity determines the kinds of thinking they do and how they evaluate the world. The maturity of the child will also determine the way parents and teachers instruct him or her on the techniques of constructive thinking.

The Influence of the Situation on Thinking and Behavior

Certain aspects of the situation interact with a person's temperament and influence how that person thinks and reacts. Stress researchers Richard Lazarus and Susan Folkman (1984) examined a number of studies and concluded that the following features exert the most influence:

1. *Event uncertainty,* or the extent to which you know if something will take place and when
2. *Event novelty,* or the extent to which a situation is a familiar one
3. *Event ambiguity,* or the extent to which you know what is expected of you in a situation
4. *Number of event changes,* or the extent to which change has taken place over a given period of time
5. *Event severity,* or the extent to which harm has been done

For some people, knowing whether and when something is going to happen is far less stressful than being unsure whether it's going to happen. Thus, a scheduled test, no matter how unwelcome, may arouse less anxiety in some people than the possibility of a pop quiz. Recall the two brothers, George and Alex, introduced in Chapter 3. George would perceive a pop quiz negatively, at least initially, whereas Alex would be less inclined to think of it this way. Similarly, some students may prefer to know their test results, even if those results are disappointing, than to remain in a state of uncertainty. Not knowing leaves some people wondering and perhaps imagining the worst possible scenario; knowing mobilizes them to think of solutions for the problem. In other words, the reason George and others are bothered by event uncertainty is that it interferes with their ability to predict and prepare for the stressor. This need for predictability also explains why event novelty and event ambiguity may also be distressing.

When a situation is novel or when the rules and expectations are unclear, you don't know what is or will be expected of you. The newness and ambiguity make adapting to the change difficult. A person who has trouble adapting to change has to use purposeful effort to think positively about a novel situation. On the other hand, for a person like Alex, the novel situation represents a challenge instead of a threat. New situations temperamentally fit Alex, who likes change and novelty; novel situations seem to occupy his thoughts whereas familiar and routine events are sometimes perceived as distressing because they don't hold his interest or attention.

A similar set of circumstances exists when there are a number of event changes in a short span of time. Let's use George and Alex as examples again, and let's assume that they have just moved to another state. The move necessitated a change in school districts, a change in their living environment, and a change in friends. By nature, George would find it difficult to accommodate to so many changes in a short period of time. But Alex would perceive the events as exciting. Why? George needs time to adapt and Alex does not. The essence of what I'm saying is this: differences in temperament influence the way we think about the situations we experience.

Finally, the severity or negativity of a situation influences how we think and react. The death of a parent, grandparent, or favorite person is distressing to anyone. People react differently to these stressors, but there is no doubt that losses such as these affect everybody in some way. Children or adults who are subjected to a number of negative events may begin to think in a rather depressed and negative fashion. This is certainly understandable. This does not mean that they have lost all resilience. They may require support and help from others in order to maintain a reasonable perspective. In fact, resilient people recognize when they need help, and they take the necessary steps to get it.

Attributions, Thinking, and Behavior

When people achieve a goal—for example, when a child learns to read or when a parent receives a promotion at work or when 16-year-old Shannon Miller earns several medals at the 1992 Olympics—what do you think they are thinking? Social psychologists have studied this question and have discovered that people automatically think, "Why? Why did I do well?" In fact, people question all sorts of actions and outcomes: "Why did he lose his temper?"; "Why did she do that?"; and so on. Attributions are the names given to the reasons ascribed to actions and outcomes (Heider, 1958). When Suzie believes that the A on the reading test is because she is a good reader, she has made a personal attribution. She sees herself as the cause of her success. But Suzie could make a different attribution: she could think that she got the A because the reading test was simple. In this case, Suzie has made an external attribution; that is, she perceives the situation, or some factor external to herself, as the cause of her success.

As you can imagine, the kind of attribution Suzie makes will influence what she thinks of herself as a reader and what she might do in the future about reading. If she thinks she has the ability to read, she is unlikely to shy away from reading assignments. But if she thinks she is a poor reader and can do well only if the test is easy or if someone helps her, then she will give up on a reading test that challenges her even a little.

There are four basic causal attributions (Heider, 1958). That is, we can attribute the outcome of an event to (1) some trait or ability in the person, (2) the effort the person extends, (3) the situation or someone else, or (4) luck or chance. Suzie, for example, can attribute her success to her ability only or to her ability, her effort, and the situation. If there is more than one cause assigned to an outcome, the observer (in this case, Suzie herself) has to decide the importance of each factor. Is it more ability than effort, or is it a little ability and a lot of effort? The end result is a weighted causal attribution, which then leads to a host of other judgments and behaviors.

Children (and adults) are observers of themselves as well as of other people. Often the attributions we make of ourselves are different from the ones we make of others (Jones & Nisbett, 1972). The difference in attributions sometimes contributes to communication difficulties. It's therefore necessary to make our thinking clear to others and to not assume other persons view situations as we do.

Thus far, I have discussed the factors that influence thoughts, feelings, and actions. This information provides a base for understanding how to teach children to think constructively. The pragmatics of constructive thinking come largely from the field of cognitive behavior modification. They involve teaching children the dynamics behind the thinking-feeling-behaving connection.

The Pragmatics of Constructive Thinking

The pragmatics behind constructive thinking are largely geared to instructing children how to be mentally resilient. There are two major objectives associated with this goal: (1) understanding how thoughts, feelings, and behaviors influence each other and (2) taking charge of a destructive thought-feeling-behavior cycle by changing thoughts.

For children to understand the thought-feeling-behavior connection, they need to be able to recognize feelings, recognize thoughts, and see the connection between thoughts, feelings, and behavior. To break a destructive thought-feeling-behavior cycle, children need to be able to

1. identify destructive thoughts
2. redefine situations by modifying verbal labels
3. redefine situations by modifying destructive beliefs
4. redefine situations by generating solutions
5. redefine situations by generating alternative perspectives. (e.g., "How can I get something from this situation?" or "How can I time-limit the pain?")

Because children vary in maturity and because developmental maturity influences how they think, it's necessary to adapt the instructions to the child.

Instructing Young Children (Ages 3 to 6)

Young children first need to learn how to recognize and correctly label feelings in themselves and others. They need to know the external and internal indicators of emotions. External indicators are those things that show "on the outside." A smile, a scream, a cry, a stern tone of voice, sagging shoulders, and a straight, open posture are all examples of external indicators. Internal indicators, or "inside clues," indicate physiological arousal (see Chapter 6). A queasy stomach, clammy hands, and shakiness are some of the physical symptoms experienced by the individual.

There are a number of ways a young child can learn the ABCs of feelings. A good way to start is to use stories and pictures. By pointing out different emotions and the different ways they are expressed by the various characters in a story, we can help the child learn the basic components of an emotional experience. There are other equally good avenues a parent might use to help children become aware of feelings, for example, playing a game of emotional charades or constructing a collage of magazine pictures depicting people expressing different emotions. Once the basics have been mastered, parents and teachers can help children understand how others might be feeling or how the children themselves are feeling. Helping children understand that they have feelings and that those feelings get communicated to others in certain ways enhances their social skills and their ability to think constructively.

The second step in the process of helping young children understand the thought-feeling-behavior connection is teaching the child the various labels that can be used to describe an emotion. Giving children an emotional vocabulary will ultimately help them learn to direct emotions appropriately. So, for example, describing feelings as "disappointed" or "a little upset" gives children some verbal leverage to use when they need to cope with a negative situation.

Teaching young children about feelings is only part of what's needed to think constructively. Children need to know what thinking is all about and how it's connected to feelings. Since children are such concrete thinkers at this age, it's helpful to give them concrete definitions and examples of what constitutes constructive and destructive thoughts. I often use the TA for Kids program and vocabulary to introduce the notion of constructive and destructive thoughts and the connection between thoughts and feelings (Freed & Freed, 1977). TA for Tots uses "warm fuzzies" to describe good feelings that come from thoughts like "I like you," "I can do it," and "I'm proud." "Cold pricklies" are bad feelings that come from thoughts like "I can't do this," "It's not fair," and "I want my way." I find that younger children can easily understand these terms and can then use them to describe other thoughts and feelings they experience or read about in stories.

To help them think constructively the adult must supply children with appropriate self-statements and effective problem-solving strategies, because children at this age are not capable of generating them themselves. I will illustrate how this might be done with an example involving five-year-old Jane, who is most reluctant to attend the first day of school. Jane wakes up the day before school starts with a stomachache, which intensifies throughout the day. Jane does not want to go to school, and when her mother insists, she begins to cry hysterically. Jane is obviously fearful about going to school. To help her deal with this new situation, it will be necessary to teach her how to think constructively about the first day of school. To do this her mother would take the following steps:

1. Help Jane identify fearful feelings.
2. Help her understand that the fearful feelings are the reason why she has a stomachache.
3. Normalize her feelings about the first day of school.
4. Help her understand that her thoughts are connected to her feelings.
5. Help her think differently about the first day of school.

The dialogue might go something like this:

MOTHER: Jane, I think you're a little scared about going to school tomorrow. Sometimes when we're scared we get stomachaches and our faces look very worried.
JANE: I'm not scared. I don't want to go to school.
MOTHER: You know, I was scared the first day I went to kindergarten. Yup, I remember I had a funny feeling in my stomach. It was like having

butterflies in my stomach. I remember telling Grandma that I did not want to go to school. I told her I'd go next year!

JANE: What did Grandma say?

MOTHER: She said I had to go to school and that those butterflies would go away. And they did.

JANE: I don't want to go to school. I'm scared.

MOTHER: I know you are, honey. Maybe we can put our thinking caps on and figure out how to take the scared feelings and turn them into warm, fuzzy feelings.

JANE [crying]: I don't want to go to school.

MOTHER: Cold prickly alert! I heard a cold prickly. I heard you say, "I don't want to go to school." [Mother says this in a gentle, lighthearted way so that the child understands its supportive nature.] Now, Jane, tell me what you think kindergarten is going to be like.

JANE: I don't know, Mommy, I just don't want to go.

MOTHER: Some people are scared of kindergarten because it's new and they don't know what happens. That's a scary feeling. That's why I was scared of kindergarten. Other people are scared because they'll miss their moms or dads when they are in school. There is good news, though!

JANE: What is it?

MOTHER: You can help yourself feel better. Do you know how?

JANE: No. How?

MOTHER: You can put warm, fuzzy thoughts in your head, and then do you know what will happen?

JANE [smiling]: I'll have warm, fuzzy feelings?

MOTHER: Right, right, right. So let's think of some warm, fuzzy thoughts in place of the cold, prickly thoughts.

JANE: Okay, Mom. This is going to be fun.

MOTHER: Good. I just heard a warm, fuzzy thought—"This is going to be fun!"

The parent then helps the child replace the worrisome thoughts with positive thoughts and gives the child other strategies to use. In Jane's case the dialogue continues as follows, with Jane's mother helping her generate positive thoughts and images:

MOTHER: Let's draw a fun picture of kindergarten.

JANE: Okay, Mom. I'll draw my teacher.

MOTHER: Super thinking! I love it. She looks like a nice teacher.

MOTHER: Jane, there are a few other tricks you can do to help yourself. You know the butterflies you feel in your stomach?

JANE: Yeah?

MOTHER: Well, tell yourself, "The funny feelings I have in my stomach are because I am excited." And now let's think of all the fun things you can do in kindergarten.

Jane's mother helped her identify the feelings and thoughts behind her fear of kindergarten, something Jane was unable to do by herself. Most children her age have the same difficulties. In fact, untrained older children and adults have similar troubles. They are not consciously aware of their destructive thought patterns. Jane's mom needed to help her identify what those thoughts and feelings were; then she helped Jane change the pattern by giving her alternative statements and images (the pictures Jane drew) to concentrate on. Jane's mom also helped her see that her feelings were shared by others and were therefore normal. This is sometimes very reassuring. If Jane's mom suspects that Jane is having difficulty the next morning before going to school, she can help her by repeating the positive thoughts out loud with her. She might also send the pictures Jane drew to school with her to give to the teacher. Sometimes a plan of action makes a child better able to deal with the ambiguity of a new situation. Giving the teacher the pictures might help Jane feel more comfortable with the new teacher.

Parents can reinforce this coping strategy by using guided imagery or any of the other techniques mentioned in Chapter 6 to deal with physiological arousal. They may also want to give the child the opportunity to visit the school and meet the teacher. These are all problem-solving strategies that are useful to the child and that build on constructive thinking strategies.

Instructing Older Children (Ages 7 to 10)

The strategies discussed for young children apply to older ones as well. Children aged seven to ten need to understand the language of emotions and the relationship emotions have to thoughts and behaviors. What is different is how these are explained and the kinds of verbal handles used by the child. For example, instead of "warm fuzzies" and "cold pricklies," you might use terms like "positive," and "productive" to describe helpful thoughts and "negative" or "hurtful" to describe destructive thoughts. In addition to using a more sophisticated vocabulary, children of this age are also capable of identifying positive and negative thoughts in themselves and in others. They can come up with positive thought substitutes themselves, but they occasionally require some prodding and direction from adults. The oldest children in this age range become somewhat capable of disputing their own erroneous beliefs and ideas. This is because they are beginning to develop the capacity to reflect on their own thinking (metacognition).

Stories are a great vehicle for teaching children the process of constructive thinking, especially those stories that address the influence of destructive and constructive thoughts on behavior. For example, in the story entitled *The Recital*, by J. Joseph and E. Short (1992), a young boy, Oliver, attempts to master a piece of piano music for an upcoming recital. He becomes quickly frustrated when he finds himself making numerous mistakes. Instead of persisting, Oliver wants to give up and quit the piano altogether. His grandmother intervenes by helping him think differently about the mistakes. Oliver decides to continue with the piano and finally masters the piece of music. The message in this story is very explicit: Winners think about mistakes as opportunities to improve, as challenges.

Once children have the basic idea that destructive thinking is associated with negative feelings and behaviors, adults can help them apply the process of rethinking to their own problems and lives. To do this a parent can follow these steps:

1. Help the child identify positive and negative feelings.
2. Help the child identify the positive and negative thoughts that are connected to feelings.

3. Identify features of the situation that are important and/or troublesome to the child.
4. Help the child take a constructive perspective by helping him or her modify destructive beliefs and ideas.
5. Identify and apply constructive self-statements to the situation (words that communicate resilient attitudes and ideas are particularly important here).

To illustrate how these steps are applied, I will use a scenario involving competition and disappointment, issues that are especially troublesome for today's youth.

Angie, age eight, wants to compete for a particular role in the annual *Nutcracker* production. The number of roles available for children is limited, and the competition is fierce. Angie is at first reluctant even to try because she feels that she will "never get the part." Her parents take this opportunity to teach her about dealing with competition. Here is the verbal exchange that takes place between Angie and her father:

FATHER: I think that you're hesitant about trying out for the *Nutcracker*. I'm glad to talk to you about it because I know how hard it is sometimes to try out for something you want when there are a number of other good, talented kids trying out at the same time.

ANGIE: Thanks, Dad, but I don't want to talk about it. I don't think I want to try out, okay?

FATHER: Do you want to be in the production, Angie?

ANGIE: I really want to, but I'm scared that I won't get a good part. Maybe I won't get a part at all. There are a lot of girls trying out.

FATHER: The only person you need to compete with is yourself. What counts is trying. If you don't try, you'll never know whether you can do it or not. Trying to do your best is the real challenge, Angie. It's hard, I know. But that's what all the famous actors, actresses, athletes, and dancers did. By trying, they gave themselves the chance. They took charge of their feelings. If you don't try, what happens is that your negative thoughts take charge of you.

ANGIE: But what if I don't get a role? Or what if I get a stupid part? I'll feel awful and stupid, I just know it.

FATHER: Yes, Angie, you'll surely feel awful and stupid, but not because you don't get the part. No, Angie, that's not why. It will be because you think that not getting the part makes you look stupid. And that's not true. There are other reasons why people don't get parts. And those reasons don't necessarily have anything to do with a person's talent.

ANGIE: Like what, Dad?

FATHER: Like size or color of hair—sometimes people get parts for reasons we don't know. Sometimes it seems so unfair, and sometimes it is. The point here, Angie, is that thinking "I'm dumb if I don't get the part" just makes you feel bad.

ANGIE: Okay, Dad, I'll try out, but if I don't get the part, don't expect me to be happy about it.

FATHER: I think you're making a good decision to try. If you don't get the part, I surely would expect you'd feel disappointed. I certainly would. But, honey, that disappointment will go away because you can make it go away.

ANGIE: Okay, Dad.

Angie did try out but she did not get the role she wanted, although she did get a role. At first, Angie seemed devastated, but again her parents took the opportunity to teach her how to constructively manage an emotion:

ANGIE [*sobbing*]: I don't want to be in the *Nutcracker*. I don't want to dance. I hate everyone.

FATHER [*after letting Angie cry for a while*]: I know. We know you're very disappointed, but we're proud of you and we're glad to sit down and talk about this.

ANGIE: I don't want to talk. I should never have auditioned. I knew it. I got a stupid part, a part for kids that can't dance.

FATHER: Angie, you think the part you got was for kids who can't dance?

ANGIE: Yes, that's what I said!

FATHER: But you *can* dance. Maybe there's some different way of thinking about this.

ANGIE: I said I didn't want to talk about it!

FATHER: Understood. We'll leave you be. If you want us, we're right here.

[*Angie goes up to her room and comes down five minutes later.*]

ANGIE: It's just not fair. I worked hard and I got the worst part.

MOTHER: Listen, honey, I know you're disappointed, and I know that if I were in your position, I'd be just as disappointed. But maybe we can talk about it. Sometimes talking about it gives you a different way of looking at it. First of all, I found out that there were twice as many children trying out this year than there were parts. Is that true?

ANGIE: Well, yes.

MOTHER: And I understand that the little girl chosen to be Clara is older than you and had your part last year.

ANGIE: Well, yes.

MOTHER: Then one thing you can do right now is give yourself some credit for getting the role. The second thing that would be helpful is to stop saying you got a stupid part—because it looks like you did very well—and the third thing you need to do is see how much fun you can make this part. Sometimes we can make something that looks uninteresting really exciting just by having a positive attitude. Angie, put your positive thoughts to work.

ANGIE: Okay, Mom, I'm feeling a little better.

Angie goes to rehearsal. She takes on a positive attitude and finds that the role is not as bad as she had first imagined. In fact, she likes the role now and enjoys herself. Her parents take the opportunity to reinforce how she chose to deal with her disappointment:

MOTHER: Angie, Dad and I are very proud of the way you chose to think about your role in the *Nutcracker*. I know you were initially very upset, thinking that it was a bad part and that you must be a bad dancer to get such a part. But you did think about it for a while, and you were able to see things differently. You took on a positive attitude, and now you're doing a great job.

If you were to analyze what Angie's parents did, you would find that they helped Angie label and relabel her feelings. Using a combination of active listening and constructive communication, the parents were able to direct Angie to think differently about the situation. They helped her identify the errors she was making in sizing up the situation and provided an alternative interpretation for her. They were very careful to allow Angie to defuse first, always respecting her feelings. As a result, Angie was able to rethink the situation and handle it quite well.

There are a number of ways parents and teachers can prompt children to think about their thinking (Waters, 1982). Here are some of the more common strategies:

1. Direct questioning (e.g., "What did you say to yourself when that happened?")
2. Situational charades (a game in which the child is asked to guess what kind of thoughts people are having in the situation being pantomimed)
3. Thought bubbles (Bernard & Joyce, 1984) (a technique in which the child indicates what the characters in a story are thinking and saying by drawing them with "bubbles" of dialogue above them)
4. Story-telling technique (Elkins, 1983) (in which the parent makes up a story or uses an existing story and asks the child to think about all the things that the characters might be thinking or children are asked to tell their own personal stories and explain what they are thinking)

Once parents determine what their child's pattern of destructive thinking is, they can proceed to help the child learn to think constructively by using these very same techniques. For example, the parent can use the story-telling or thought bubble technique to illustrate positive thoughts and to communicate resilient ideas. In addition, there are existing stories that address these issues quite directly. A number of stories that lend themselves to a discussion of thoughts are listed in Appendix 3 in Sections 3.2, 3.10, and 3.11. Publishers who address the issue of constructive thinking for children are as follows:

1. Stories designed to help children deal with destructive beliefs and ideas associated with competition, peer relationships, and academic problems are published by

Young Set Learning Associates
45 Fountain Street
Clinton, NY 13323.

2. The adventures of Pumpsey the dragon, and how she uses her clear mind to think about any number of situations common to school-age children, are offered by

Timberline Press, Inc.
Box 70187
Eugene, OR 97401.

3. *Color Us Rational*, by V. Waters (1979), is a series of pamphlets for parents, designed to help them teach their children to think constructively, and stories about constructive thinking for children that is published by

Institute for Rational Living
45 East 65th Street
New York, NY 10021.

Instructing Preadolescent and Adolescent Children

Generally speaking, children as young as ten or eleven have the cognitive capacity to think about what they are thinking and to reason in a way that goes beyond the grasp of younger children. When children reach this stage of development, they are able to rationally debate and analyze their thoughts.

Parents of preadolescent and adolescent youngsters can approach the topic of constructive thinking in a more sophisticated fashion. Here are the steps suggested by clinicians who work to correct faulty thinking in adolescents (Bernard & Joyce, 1984): Instruct adolescents on the relationship between thoughts, feelings, and actions (if such instruction has not yet been provided). Explain that one way to control oneself (internal control) comes from directing one's thoughts in a constructive way. This entails the following: (1) recognizing destructive thought patterns in oneself, (2) recognizing the situational cues that prompt them, (3) understanding the underlying beliefs that support them, (4) understanding the errors in thinking that support them, (5) disputing destructive thoughts, and (6) generating realistic and constructive thoughts and self-statements. Teach adolescents to assume a balanced perspective by helping them learn to (1) focus on a small aspect of the problem at a time, (2) find information that will give them the most objective view possible of the problem, (3) think about the "worst thing that could happen" as a way of objectively rating the negative impact of the situation, and (4) think of how the negative situation can be used to their benefit.

To help adolescents recognize and change destructive thought patterns parents can have them ask themselves, "What am I thinking?" and then have them say or list any of the thoughts that come to mind. Parents can encourage adolescents to consider each thought and ask, "Is this constructive?" (using the criteria for constructive beliefs) or "Is this destructive?" (using the criteria for destructive beliefs). If a thought is recognized as a destructive one, the adolescent should be encouraged to identify which beliefs or errors need to be corrected. Finally, parents can have adolescents ask themselves, "What constructive thoughts can I think that will help me handle this situation?"

To illustrate how these steps might apply, I will discuss a situation involving a 15-year-old. Carol is bright and very responsible. Her day-to-day performance is outstanding. She participates in class discussions and is always well prepared, and her assignments are always well done. Her problem is that she cannot take tests. She seems to freeze even during tests in her favorite subjects, and her anxiety about a test starts the day before. Carol can feel her heart pounding; sometimes she actually feels nauseous and gets a headache. Carol's parents can help her. They can explain that the physical symptoms she is having are a sign of destructive thinking and that the destructive thinking might in fact be a major reason for why she freezes on tests. The dialogue might go something like this:

MOTHER: Carol, are you feeling anxious about the biology test tomorrow?
CAROL: Yes, Mom. It's already started. I feel shaky and nauseous I'm scared to death that I'm going to bomb out on this test. It seems there's nothing I can do. I study and study. But when it comes to taking the test, I just freeze.

MOTHER: Yes, I get the picture. It's clear to me that you have worked very hard this year and that you actually know the material. I have an idea about how you can change the outcomes here [internal control message]. I've been reading that people can help themselves by systematically changing the way they think about situations. Now, you're feeling anxious because you're thinking you're going to bomb another test.

CAROL: Well, Mom, that's been my pattern.

MOTHER: I know, Carol. Would you like to change it?

CAROL: Sure, I'd do anything!

MOTHER: Okay. Let's start with listing all of the thoughts you have about the upcoming test.

CAROL: Okay, but what do you mean?

MOTHER: Just stop and think about what is now going through your mind. What thoughts do you have about the test?

CAROL: Well, I think I'm going to fail. I think that I won't be able to remember anything tomorrow. If I don't get an A on this test, I'll never get into a good college and I know how stupid I'm going to feel!

[*At this point Carol is visibly upset.*]

MOTHER: Why do you think you're going to fail?

CAROL: Because I traditionally screw up on tests.

MOTHER: Why do you think you have trouble with the tests?

CAROL: Because I freeze and then I can't remember anything!

[*Carol's mother now attempts to help Carol correctly identify the nature of the problem and the connection between her thoughts and both her anxiety and her performance.*]

MOTHER: Think about what you just said. What's the reason for your poor performance on the test?

CAROL: I said that I freeze on tests because I get so anxious. [*Carol is suddenly struck with insight about the problem with her performance.*] Oh, I see what you're getting at, Mom! My anxiety is my problem.

MOTHER: Right! The real problem is not the test but your anxiety.

[*Here her mother helps Carol put the problem in the right perspective.*]

CAROL: But what can I do about the anxiety?

[*Carol's mother can now help her problem-solve by encouraging her to find an alternative label for her arousal feelings and adopt an alternative strategy for reducing the arousal, identify the destructive self-statements feeding the anxiety, generate more constructive self-statements.*]

MOTHER: Two things. You need to address the physical aspects of the anxiety and you need to take care of what is causing the anxiety. To take care of the physical part of the problem, remember that anxiety is excitement that gets labeled negatively. To reduce the excitement, you can start now by doing some of the relaxation exercises on the tape I have in my room. You listened to them the other day and thought they were pretty good. Once you feel more relaxed, you can start desensitizing yourself by actually forcing yourself to do the exercise to reduce the anxious feelings. I'll show you how to do it in just a few minutes. But remember, Carol, the excitement you feel is a sign that your body is preparing for the test. Think about the physical sensations you feel as excitement. Talk about them as excitement instead of anxiety. To determine what's causing the anxiety, think about the thoughts you told me before. Remember you said, "I'm scared, I'm going to fail, I won't be able to remember, I will feel like a fool if I fail, I'll never get into a good college."

CAROL: Yes, I remember.

MOTHER: These are what the experts call irrational beliefs. They are destructive. Do you see why they might be destructive?

CAROL: Sort of.

MOTHER: Well, first of all, assuming that you're going to do poorly tomorrow because you have done poorly in the past is not necessarily true. It's an overgeneralization. [*Mother is helping Carol identify irrational beliefs and errors in thinking.*]

CAROL: But I've had trouble on every single biology test.

MOTHER: Tomorrow is another day. Remember, it's not the test that's the problem, it's the anxiety. And you can do something about that. [*Mother is empowering Carol by again helping her keep the problem in perspective, she is providing her with a constructive way to view the problem and reminding her that she can make efforts to solve her problem.*] You have more control than you think.

CAROL: I can say that I'll do great, but I don't believe it!

MOTHER: Right, in which case it won't work. Besides, you also think that if you don't get an A on this test, you won't get into a good school. That's not exactly true; it's another good example of those errors in thinking we talked about earlier. Now what can you think and say that is believable and at the same time helpful?

[*Here Carol's mother is helping her identify her destructive beliefs and replace them with more constructive self-statements.*]

CAROL: Well, for starters, I could say I may not do as well as I would like, but I'm not going to fail. I'll just do a little better this time and a little better the time after that so I can eventually get my A. Getting a B is not going to stop me from getting into a good college. I can live with it. The real test is dealing with the anxiety.

[*Carol is now generating her own constructive statements.*]

MOTHER: Well done. Let's go work on your anxiety.

Carol's mother then helps her desensitize herself to the physical aspects of the arousal. She does this by having Carol relax away the tension caused by just thinking about the biology test. Every time Carol thinks about the test and begins to feel any of the physical discomforts associated with anxiety, she is instructed to take a deep breath and do any one of the short relaxation exercises described in Chapter 6. In addition, she is taught to remember and rehearse the constructive self-statements that she and her mother generated.

Summary

To a very large degree we are what we think. When we think constructively, we make better decisions and, consequently, are more productive. Constructive thinking contributes to the effective management of change and adversity. It is an important component of effective problem solving, a topic that is discussed in the next chapter. Conversely, destructive thoughts result in poor decisions, unproductive and frustrating attempts to accomplish tasks, and poor problem solving. Because thought affects these critical areas, it impacts on our self-esteem and coping skills. Constructive thought contributes to positive self-esteem and resilience whereas destructive thought erodes the self-concept and makes the person more vulnerable to change and adversity. Age, maturity, situational factors, and attributions influence thought. Parents and teachers can help children of all ages learn to think constructively.

Chapter 8

Teaching Children to Make Good Decisions

Ann decides to save the five dollars she earned, Rachel decides to spend hers. Julia decides to cheat on a math test, Maria decides against it. Sherrie decides to give in to peer pressure and stay out all night to party, Justine decides to keep her curfew and come home. Decisions, decisions, decisions! We make them all the time. Some decisions involve choosing between innocuous options, and some have to do with selecting the best solution for a personal, moral, or interpersonal dilemma. Sometimes the decisions we make have a major impact on our lives, sometimes they don't. Being able to make good decisions is a must for productivity and resilience (Spivack & Shure, 1974). Why? Because good decisions lead to success and effective coping.

The Decision-Making Process

The way we make decisions can vary, depending on the kinds of choices we have to make. To simplify matters I am going to discuss the decision-making process for three different kinds situations: (1) practical personal situations (e.g., how to spend an allowance, what courses to take in school); (2) problem situations

involving moral and interpersonal issues; and (3) self-control issues involving delay of gratification, impulse control, resisting
temptation, and low frustration tolerance.

Practical Personal Situations

Learning to make good choices begins with deciding between options that affect us personally. Practical personal decisions require the child to make a choice between two or more
alternatives, and sometimes between alternatives that have different long- and short-term gains. Deciding how to spend an allowance, whether to study for a test or visit a friend, whether or not to
do what a parent has asked, or what to do about a poor grade—
these are the kinds of practical decisions I am talking about. The
steps involved in practical decision making include the following:

1. Determining the nature of the need, want, or problem
2. Determining the options available
3. Determining how the options fit with one's resources,
   interests, personal characteristics, temperament, learning
   style, and physical makeup
4. Determining the costs and benefits associated with each of
   the options
5. Making a choice
6. Implementing the choice
7. Evaluating the choice

Here is an example: John, age ten, is having difficulties in
school with English and social studies. He has never had difficulties in the past with these subjects and has no known learning
disability or problem. John's parents sit down with him to explore
the problem and some possible solutions. John willingly sits down
with them to problem-solve. His parents explore with him the
reasons for his difficulties in these subject areas, and together they
determine that John has trouble fitting study time into his busy
schedule. The problem is defined as a busy schedule that pre-
cludes study time. The next step is to determine John's options.

During the evaluation of John's options, several factors are considered, including the relative pleasure his activities give him, the possibility of pursuing some activities at alternative times, and the relative drain on John of doing the various activities. Dropping study time from the schedule is not an option because academic performance is highly valued. The following is a written summary of the decision-making process conducted by John and his parents:

1. *Problem*: Failing English and social studies
2. *Reason for problem*: Insufficient time to study
3. *Options*: Drop piano lessons; drop football; drop paper route
4. *Analysis of options*: Piano lessons and football are good stress relievers for John and a good balance to the stresses and strains of school. The paper route provides an additional source of revenue for John but takes a large chunk of time out of his schedule.
5. *Choice*: John determines that while he would miss the revenue of the newspaper route, the time it requires is too costly. He figures he can reduce his extracurricular expenses and manage with his weekly allowance. The time saved would result in additional time for study.
6. *Implementation*: John arranges for his friend and neighbor to assume his paper route.
7. *Outcome*: Three weeks after the new schedule change, when John evaluates his decision to drop the paper route, he feels that it was a good decision because his grades have improved and he is feeling a lot better.

The scenario presented is an example of what can and often times does happen in homes. However, not every situation is so easy to solve. For one, children may not perceive the problem, or they may not perceive the problem in the same way their parents do. If this is the case, the first step is to find a way to define the problem so that both child and parent can agree. For example, if John had not been bothered by his poor grades in English and social studies, his parents would have had to make them a problem for John either by making involvement in sports and piano contingent upon academic performance or by finding an alternative incentive for good grades. When there is a good relationship between parent and child, often (not always) a conversation is sufficient to establish a mutual agreement about the nature of the problem. Sometimes parents have to reevaluate their own view of the problem and accept the child's perception of it. For example, the parents of a child who is being excluded from an activity of his or her peer group may find this a very distressing situation. However, the child may not be motivated to change the situation, because he or she is not concerned about being excluded. In this case, the parents have the problem, not the child, and they would do well to reconsider their perception of the situation.

How do parents know when to redefine their own perspective of a situation and when to encourage their children to adopt their view? The answer to this question is not simple or straightforward, but the rule of thumb is to ask themselves the following questions:

1. Does the problem represent a major threat to my child's life or well-being?
2. Does the problem represent a major threat to my child's sense of values?
3. Does the problem represent a major threat to other people?
4. Will my child be harmed permanently if he or she refuses to accept the view that there is a problem?

If the answer to any of these questions is yes, the parent needs to proceed with efforts to have the child view the problem as a problem. If the answer to all of these questions is no, then the parent may want to reconsider or back off. As hard as it is, it is sometimes necessary to let children err so that the resulting situation will motivate them to problem-solve. For example, Mrs. Smith is bothered by the fact that her 14-year-old daughter, Jamie, leaves assigned projects to the last minute. Mrs. Smith attempts to get Jamie to deal with her procrastination, but Jamie refuses. Mrs. Smith decides, quite prudently, that she will allow Jamie to find out for herself the consequences of procrastination. She tells Jamie that it is up to her to decide when to do her school projects but that if she receives less than a B on a project, she will need to agree to work on other assigned projects in a more timely fashion. Jamie agrees. She does poorly on her next project because of her procrastination and decides to work out a different schedule for doing the remaining projects of the year.

In addition to a possible disagreement between parent and child on the definition of a problem, there is also the question of partially effective alternatives and of how much help the parent should give to the child during the problem-solving process. Sometimes the available alternatives will not completely solve the problem for the child. For example, suppose dropping the paper route results in only a partial solution to John's problem. Then John would need to pursue additional alternatives. As for the question "How involved should a parent be in the child's attempt to problem-solve?" the answer is, it depends. It depends on the cognitive and emotional maturity of the child (I will address this issue shortly) and on the nature of the problem and how skilled the child is at problem solving. Initially, children and adolescents may need assistance. As they become more proficient at problem solving, they require less direct intervention and more moral support. Complex or difficult problems may require more direct input. Including the child in decisions that affect the family, whenever possible, is good problem-solving training. If you recall, this is what democratic parents do; it gives children the opportunity to learn how to make good decisions and it gives them practice making decisions.

Not all practical decisions involve problems. John, for example, could follow the same steps in deciding what to do with his allowance. The decision process might look something like this:

1. *Issue:* Should I use my whole allowance to purchase an arcade game video tape?

2. *Options:* I could spend my whole allowance and purchase the tape, or I could forgo purchasing the tape and save my allowance.
3. *Analysis:* I would like to purchase the tape, but I don't absolutely need it; I would need to use my whole allowance if I decide to purchase it.
4. *Cost–gain analysis:* If I purchase the tape, I will not have the money I need to go on the class trip, and I really want to go on the class trip.
5. *Decision:* I will forgo the home video arcade game tape for now and buy it later.
6. *Implementation:* I will put the allowance away for use on the class trip.

This scenario is also a good example of self-control. In this case the self-control involves choosing a long-term goal (class trip) over an immediate goal (videotape). Children who lack self-control require specific instruction (procedures developed by Meichenbaum are discussed later in this chapter) on how to delay gratification.

Moral and Interpersonal Situations

Decision making is also required in situations that involve basic moral dilemmas, for example, keeping rules, telling the truth, keeping promises, and honoring friendships, and in situations that involve interpersonal dilemmas, such as deciding what to do when you don't agree with a friend and managing conflict with others. The skills necessary to deal with moral and interpersonal problems develop over time and involve the following steps (D'Zurilla, 1988):

1. Problem orientation
2. Problem definition and formulation
3. Generating alternatives (brainstorming)
4. Evaluating alternatives
5. Choosing an alternative

6. Implementing the chosen alternative
7. Evaluating the outcome
8. Changing or reinforcing the plan

During the problem-solving orientation stage, the emphasis is on getting the child (or adult) to have a positive mental set about solving the problem. This means recognizing that there is a problem, viewing the problem as solvable, holding realistic expectations about the amount of effort and time needed to solve the problem, and believing that you can do something about either solving the problem or managing your reaction to the problem.

To define the problem, children must be able to understand the situation not only from their own perspective but, when appropriate, from another person's perspective (social perspective taking). They are taught to think constructively about the problem (see Chapter 7) when conceptualizing it. They are also taught to view the problem as the discrepancy between what currently exists and what realistically might exist. Children also need to learn how to make a distinction between problems they can fix directly (problem-focused formulation) and problems that require an emotional adaptation to a situation (emotion-focused formulation; see D'Zurilla, 1988). (This relates to the distinction I made in Chapter 2 between problem-focused coping and emotion-focused coping.) A problem-focused formulation means that the problem can be resolved. For example, homework is a solvable problem because one can re-arrange one's schedule or do whatever else is necessary to handle the problem directly. On the other hand, if the problem is parental divorce or death of a loved one, then the best one can do is learn to live with the situation by constructively thinking about the problem (see Chapter 7). To sum up, if a problem situation is changeable, then a problem-focused formulation is in order. If the problem is perceived as unchangeable, then an emotion-focused formulation is required. In many cases, both problem- and emotion-focused formulations are required.

Another important part of the problem formulation is what

psychologists call "social perspective taking" (Selman, 1980). Social perspective taking is, basically, seeing the problem from someone else's point of view. It is being able to understand how another person thinks and feels in a given situation. Understanding that another person's perception may be different from our own has important implications for solving interpersonal conflict. Conflict management and negotiation skills require social-perspective-taking skills.

Problem definition is also influenced by moral beliefs and cause–effect reasoning. Small children who believe that getting what they want is fair and right, independent of any other factors, think that not getting their way is a problem. Conversely, an older child or adult is inclined to consider a number of factors before concluding that a situation represents a problem. Younger children also differ from older children and adults in how they view moral situations. For example, younger children view any kind of rule breaking as a moral problem. Older children and adults are inclined to consider other factors, such as the rule breaker's intent, before they make a judgment about the behavior. Identifying the antecedents of a problem is important for problem formulation. This is especially true in situations that involve strong emotions because feelings influence problem perception and solution choices. How we reason about a situation will influence the problem perception, the problem formulation, and the kinds of solution alternatives that are generated.

Once the problem has been defined, it is necessary for the child or adult to generate alternative solutions to the problem. These need to be concrete and realistic. D'Zurilla (1988) suggests generating as many relevant solutions as possible (the quantity principle) without initially judging appropriateness, feasibility, or utility (the "deferment of judgment" principle). He also suggests considering different kinds of alternatives (the variety principle). The ability to generate alternative solutions is positively correlated to social adjustment and can even be found in young children (Spivack & Shure, 1974).

Once the list of alternatives is generated, it is necessary to evaluate each one. Consequential thinking (Spivack & Shure, 1974) is used to determine what the consequences of choosing a particular alternative might be for oneself and for others. Children are encouraged to judge each alternative in terms of (1) the anticipated benefits; (2) the resources, actions, and plans necessary to carry out the alternative; (3) the possible obstacles; (4) how well it fixes the problem; and (5) how many other problems it is likely to cause.

The problem solver is then in a position to plan out the solution and actually execute it. Once the solution has been executed, the child needs to evaluate the solution and make the necessary changes. At this point, parents can help children by encouraging them to reinforce themselves for a job well done. I'm sure that by now you may be thinking that problem solving is time consuming. You are of course right. But some of the most significant problems children and adults face are around for a long while and require this kind of careful consideration. Besides, once children get into the habit of approaching dilemmas in this way, they become efficient problem solvers.

To illustrate the process of problem solving, I would like to use a scenario that involves both a moral and an interpersonal issue: resisting negative peer pressure. Andrew, age 12, has been getting into trouble at school; he has had five detentions in school in the past two weeks. At home Andrew is very irritable and oppositional. His parents decide to sit down and discuss the situation with him. Utilizing some of the constructive communication techniques discussed in Chapter 4, Andrew's dad learns that Andrew feels torn between his friends and his own moral standards. He is particularly bothered by the fact that his friends have recently found great sport in tormenting John, one of the unpopular boys in the class. They push John into mud puddles, call him unkind names, destroy his homework, steal his lunch or lunch money, and "rough him up." Andrew is a sensitive and caring person. He himself was harassed by the same group of boys the year before, and John was one of the few kids who refused to join in. Instead, John befriended Andrew and even helped him with homework assignments. And now Andrew feels he has turned on John. Andrew is truly in a bind. He is going along with the group because he fears that if he doesn't they will resume their attacks against him. Andrew feels that he is "between a rock and a hard place"; he does not know what to do.

The first step in the problem-solving process is to help Andrew see that he can choose differently. The dialogue between Andrew and his dad might go something like this:

DAD: Andrew, I feel there is something bothering you. I need to talk to you about the school detentions and what I feel the problems are at home.

[*The message is direct and constructive. The parent then discusses the school detention and specific examples of problems he perceives at home.*]

DAD: The detention notices the school sent home indicate that there is a problem with John. I am interested in hearing your side of the story.

[*Andrew proceeds to relate the story to his father. His father listens passively and then summarizes what he has heard.*]

DAD: I get the feeling you want to support John but feel that if you do, the group might once again torment you. I guess if I were in your situation, I would feel pretty trapped, too. The question is, do you have alternatives?

ANDREW: I don't know, Dad. I don't think that I have very good choices.

DAD: I think you have more choices than you think. I would be glad to help you brainstorm if you would like.

ANDREW: Okay, Dad.

Andrew and his dad sit down and brainstorm some alternatives. Here is a summary of the whole problem-solving process:

Step 1: Andrew recognizes the problem and comes to see that he can choose to behave differently.

Step 2: Andrew recognizes his need to
   a. resist peer pressure,
   b. deal with the negative feedback received from his peers for taking a stand,
   c. give John some support while at the same time minimizing the costs of such action to himself.

Step 3: Andrew generates the following alternatives:

ALTERNATIVE 1: Seek out Peter, leader of the peer group, and talk to him privately about how John is being treated.

ALTERNATIVE 2: Leave situation alone and continue as is.

ALTERNATIVE 3: Redirect group when they begin to badger John.

ALTERNATIVE 4: Walk away from group when they begin to badger John.

ALTERNATIVE 5: Publicly state disapproval of the group's action and offer John an opportunity to engage in an alternative activity.

ALTERNATIVE 6: Choose a few other kids in the peer group who may feel the same way about the situation and devise a plan with them to redirect the group when it begins to badger John.

ALTERNATIVE 7: Choose a few other kids in the peer group who feel the same way about the situation and plan an activity that includes John.

ALTERNATIVE 8: Walk away quietly when the group is badgering John and seek John out later to plan an activity with him. At the same time, look for other more socially appropriate friends.

Step 4: The alternatives are evaluated:

ALTERNATIVE 1: Andrew feels uncomfortable with this alternative, believing that Peter is likely to badger him as well as John.

ALTERNATIVE 2: Andrew (much to the relief of his parents) does not feel comfortable with this alternative. He is bothered a lot about how John is being treated and is not pleased with his own behavior or the resulting consequences.

ALTERNATIVE 3: Andrew is not sure he has the skills or confidence to redirect the whole group, especially with Peter as the leader. Andrew feels that Peter has a strong influence on the group and that his influence could not easily be diminished.

ALTERNATIVE 4: Andrew feels that he could quietly walk away when the group badgers John. He sees that walking away would certainly address the first problem, since it would provide an avenue for resisting peer pressure, and would also reduce the probability of negative feedback, although it certainly would not eliminate the risk altogether. He recognizes that the one drawback to this alternative is that it is not visibly supportive of John.

ALTERNATIVE 5: This alternative represents a mixed bag of costs and benefits. Publicly stating his disapproval of the group's behavior toward John is supportive of John, which is clearly a benefit, but the potential costs are great. Andrew feels that Peter would certainly be angered and would retaliate with a vengeance.

ALTERNATIVE 6: Andrew can identify two other kids in the group who he thinks might feel as he does. But he is not sure and feels that if he is wrong, this approach would not solve any of the problems.

ALTERNATIVE 7: The same drawbacks identified for Alternative 6 are true for Alternative 7.

ALTERNATIVE 8: This alternative has all the advantages of Alternative 4 and would give John some support, too. There is still the chance that Peter might find out and badger Andrew again.

Step 5: Andrew chooses an alternative. He decides on Alternative 8. He then has to figure out what he needs to do in order to execute the alternative. He contacts John and makes plans to play chess at his house. He also explains to John his dilemma and tells him that for now he is going to walk away if the group starts bothering him. Andrew's father congratulates him on his analysis of the situation and takes the opportunity to suggest a few other more emotion-focused solutions as well. He shares with his son some personal stories of similar situations and what he learned from them. He also suggests that Andrew prepare for attacks from Peter, since Peter is very likely to find out that

Andrew is not going along with the crowd. He recommends establishing a new group of friends and encourages Andrew to use constructive thinking to deal with peer rejection and harassment. (Constructive statements and strategies are detailed in Chapter 7.)

Andrew's father was hoping that Andrew would choose Alternative 5 and stand up to Peter on principle. Andrew was clearly not ready to do this. The alternative chosen was, from the father's point of view, a good compromise and a good start toward a more assertive stand against social bullying. What happened in the end was that Peter did notice that Andrew was not joining in with the group when they were attacking John. He also found out that Andrew had befriended John. Peter, as you might have expected, started to attack Andrew once again. This time Andrew was prepared. He was able to stand up to Peter assertively and, as a result, won the support of the other group members. Andrew's father reviewed the whole situation with him, praising him for his choices and highlighting the aspects of problem solving that were useful to him. If the scenario had not turned out as well as it did, Andrew would have had to either generate more problem-focused alternatives or move to an emotion-focused perspective that would make use of constructive thinking strategies.

Self-Control

A dollar today, or do I wait and get five dollars tomorrow? Do I take the five dollars out of Mom's purse, or do I wait to ask her? Do I jump at the first answer on the arithmetic test, or do I carefully think through all of the choices? Do I give up when I encounter an obstacle, or do I persevere? Self-control is the ability to make the better choice in situations such as these. It involves being able to delay gratification; resist temptation; and respond in a reflective, rather than impulsive, way to situations or choices.

Donald Meichenbaum (1985) is a researcher-clinician who has investigated ways of teaching children self-control. He used Luria's findings, showing the influence of internal language on behavior, and those of Walter Mischel (1983), who studied delay of gratification, to formulate his strategies. There are various self-control training techniques. Most of them include the following steps (Hinshaw & Erhardt, 1991):

1. The parent demonstrates the decision-making process or behavior by verbalizing out loud the strategies he or she is using.
2. Verbalizing the steps for the child, the parent then has the child go through the task.
3. The child then performs the task while verbalizing the steps out loud in the presence of the parent.
4. The child performs the task again, this time whispering the instructions.
5. The child then performs the task, verbalizing the steps internally.

To illustrate this strategy, I will apply the steps to a situation where a parent is teaching an impulsive child to think before acting: Brenda, age 12, does poorly in school. Brenda's parents are quite concerned and seek out a professional evaluation. The evaluation reveals that Brenda's poor performance is due entirely to her impulsive response style to multiple choice questions. Brenda's mother then obtains a copy of a social studies exam. She goes through the exam with Brenda, telling her exactly how to think about the problem:

> Brenda, listen to how I think about the problem. I'll read the first question and then I need to read each of the possible answers. [*She goes through and reads each alternative out loud.*] Next, I ask myself, Which of these answers is the best right answer for the question? [*She then thinks out loud about each alternative.*] Now, Brenda, you do the next question. Read the question out loud and then read each possible answer.

Brenda reads the next question and each of the possible answers. Then her mother instructs her to think out loud as she evaluates each alternative. Brenda's mother has her repeat the process for the next five questions. After that she instructs Brenda to whisper her thoughts as she attempts to answer the question. Then Brenda practices the strategy several times while verbalizing all her thoughts internally.

This same self-control strategy can be used for other kinds of impulsive behavior. For example, in the scenario used to illustrate a practical personal situation, John had to delay gratification in order to save enough money for a class trip. If John were an impulsive spender, his parents might help him by discussing with him how to think through his choices. They could do this by verbally modeling the decision-making process described under "Practical Personal Situations." They could have John list his alternatives and verbalize reasons for holding off on his purchase. They could brainstorm with him to determine other strategies that might help him delay gratification. For example, they might suggest that he keep the announcement of the class trip on his desk as a reminder of what he is working for. John could rehearse out loud why he decided to hold off on buying the home video arcade game tape and to save the money for the class trip. He could then review his decision steps, this time whispering them to himself. Finally, he could review the decision-making process by verbalizing each step internally.

Self-control training of this sort can also be used to deal with aggressive behavior and low frustration tolerance. Children are taught to identify their own physical cues of arousal (a knotlike feeling in the stomach and sweaty palms are examples of physiological arousal; other common indicators are discussed in Chapter 6). A good strategy for teaching children to do this is to point out indicators of arousal in yourself and others, as well as in the child; for example: "I know that I am getting angry or frustrated because my stomach gets to feeling really tight and my hands and arms feel the very same way." Discussing the physical aspects of arousal sensitizes the child to cues that are associated with destructive thoughts and feelings. Catching ourselves early in the arousal cycle increases the probability that we will maintain control. Once people are highly aroused or upset, it is much more difficult for them to maintain self-control or to problem-solve effectively. In situations where children or adults are highly aroused, it is better to allow them to cool off before attempting to deal rationally with the problem.

Children can be taught to identify the kinds of thoughts that are associated with anger or frustration; for example: "Anger is the way I feel when I feel scared" or "I feel like giving up when something looks hard." The parent who is teaching this skill to a child would first model it out loud for the child. The parent might say, "I get angry when I think you aren't listening. When do you think you get angry?" Or: "I feel like giving up when I have to do something that I don't know how to do. When do you feel like giving up?" Children can also be taught to identify the situations that tend to induce the anger or frustration response in them. The parent might start out by disclosing to the child their own situational triggers: "I find myself getting angry whenever Mr. Adams blames me for his own mistakes. What kind of things do you get angry about?"

Once children have learned to identify the thoughts, physical body sensations, and situations that are associated with their feelings of aggression or frustration, they are then taught to use these cues as signals to stop, think, evaluate, and act:

1. *Stop:* Parents can teach children to use some verbalization or visual image that signals them to calm down and reflect before acting. "I need to calm down" or "Freeze!" or simply "Stop!" are appropriate verbal cues; visualizing a red light is equally appropriate for children who think more in terms of images.

2. *Think:* Parents can teach children to think about what's happening and to determine what they need to do to think constructively and act appropriately. "What's happening here?"; "What am I thinking?"; "Let me think about this in another way"; "What can I do?"—these are all examples of sentences that can prompt children to think.

3. *Evaluate:* Parents can help children think about the consequences of selecting various alternatives and decide on one that is

socially appropriate. "What will happen if . . . ?" and "If I do this, then this is likely to happen" are examples of the internal monologue a parent can encourage.

4. *Act:* Parents can help children learn to evaluate the efficacy of their actions: "All right, did my plan work the way that I thought it was going to?"

To show you how such instruction might work, I will describe a situation with a 13-year-old girl who has a quick temper and a short fuse. Karen is an attractive adolescent with many fine qualities. Her one major problem is that she tends to get very angry when a situation fails to go her way or when she feels her rights have been violated. Recently, Karen has had difficulties with her cheerleading coach. Karen feels that the coach does not particularly like her and that she blames her for everything that goes wrong. Karen's immediate response is to mouth off to the coach, which of course only hurts Karen. Karen's parents would be wise to help her learn techniques of self-control. They might, for example, help Karen recognize and channel her angry feelings:

MOTHER: Karen, I know that you have some difficulties with the coach.
KAREN: Well, the coach is always picking on me. She hates my guts and treats me poorly. If she is going to treat me that way, she deserves what she gets.
MOTHER: I know that you feel the coach treats you poorly, and, quite frankly, Karen, I have seen her treat you unfairly on occasion. I don't blame you for being upset with her. I know I felt angry with her as well. What concerns me is how you choose to deal with your feelings. The coach is in a position to kick you off the team. What I am willing to do is to brainstorm with you on ways to express your frustration to the coach so that you don't get into trouble. Are you interested?
KAREN: No, I don't think so, Mom, but thanks anyway.

After another practice in which Karen has a run-in with the coach, the coach gives her a warning and tells her that if she does not shape up, she is off the team.

MOTHER: My offer, Karen, is still available if you want to talk.

KAREN: I'm ready. I really can't stand the coach.

MOTHER: Okay, what about the coach triggers your anger?

KAREN: It's the way she looks at me and the way she talks to me. She always claims I'm not paying attention when that is not true. If something goes wrong, she blames me. If I make a mistake and someone else makes the same mistake, she picks on me only.

MOTHER: How do you physically feel when you get angry? Can you feel your stomach muscles tightening up or your heart pounding?

KAREN: Well, I'm not sure, maybe both of those.

MOTHER: Good enough. It might be helpful in the future to pay attention when you are getting upset.

Karen and her mother then brainstorm on ways that Karen can "stop, think, evaluate, and act" when she feels herself getting angry with the coach. Karen decides that she will think of a brick wall that separates her from the coach and she also decides on the statement "Chill out, Karen, she can't get to you." With some help from her mother, Karen figures out the following strategy for accepting negative feedback from the coach:

1. Face the coach.
2. Maintain eye contact.
3. Say nothing while the coach is talking.
4. Reflect back, as accurately as possible, what the coach has said; for example: "Excuse me, coach, let me make sure I understand what you said. You think I was . . ."
5. State own side of the story if it is different from the coach's.
6. Apologize to the coach, if warranted.
7. If an apology is unwarranted, go along with the coach and see her later about the disagreement.

With encouragement from her mother, Karen reviews the plan. They role-play it several times before the next cheerleading practice. As expected, the coach does reprimand Karen for not paying attention. To her credit, Karen follows through with the plan. The coach is very surprised and refrains from criticizing Karen for the rest of the practice. The assistant coach observes the entire episode and makes a point of talking with Karen after the practice. She congratulates Karen for controlling herself and admits that the coach was unfair in her accusations. Since Karen responded so well, the assistant coach offers to talk to the coach on Karen's behalf. Karen has no other problems with the coach, and the rest of the season goes well.

Karen was fortunate to have an assistant coach willing to stand up for her. But this happened only after the assistant coach saw that Karen was making a concerted effort to control herself. Karen's mother also handled the situation well. She used a constructive parenting approach with Karen: she validated her feelings about the coach without condoning her behavior or solving the problem for her. As a result, Karen learned a valuable lesson in self-control.

Developmental Changes in Decision-Making Capabilities

For children to make good choices they have to be able to generate alternative solutions to problems, think about the consequences of those alternatives (consequential thinking), view the situation from another's perspective (social perspective taking), and think about how to implement the alternatives to effect a solution (means–end reasoning).

Researchers George Spivack, Jerome Platt, and Myrna Shure (1976) have found that young children (ages four and five) can (1) generate alternative solutions for age-appropriate problems (e.g., wanting something someone else has); (2) verbalize the potential consequence of various alternatives (e.g., asking for a toy versus grabbing for it); and (3) predict what will happen to a child who engages in a particular alternative. As a general rule, children of this age are unlikely to take the perspective of another (although there is evidence that they can be taught to), nor are they proficient with means–end reasoning. However, the general predictor of overall adjustment for children this young is their ability to generate alternative solutions. Parents and teachers need to help most young children understand the other person's perspective and identify the plan and steps required to realize the solution to a problem. Most young children, then, require assistance to solve problems in moral, interpersonal, and self-control situations.

As the child matures and enters middle childhood, existing skills are refined and new ones are added. Four interpersonal thinking skills have been identified by Spivack and his group: the ability to conceptualize alternative solutions, means–end planning (cause–effect thinking), consequential thinking, and social perspective thinking (i.e., the ability to take in the perspective of others and to recognize that a situation can be interpreted differently by different observers or participants). Social perspective taking allows children to infer motives and to explain their own behavior and the behavior of others in terms of those attributed motives.

Children in middle childhood are generally capable of generating alternative solutions to problems and articulating the sequence of steps necessary to carry out solutions. Children who have these skills are better problem solvers and are judged to be better adjusted than those who don't (Spivack et al., 1976). But one has to remember that means–end reasoning, consequential thinking, and social-perspective-taking skills are just beginning to emerge; parents may have to help the child with these skills initially.

By the time children reach adolescence, they are able to generate alternatives, specify plans to execute them, conceptualize the consequences associated with various alternatives, spontaneously link cause and effect, and see the situation from another's vantage point. In the work done by Spivack and associates, the generation of alternatives, means–end thinking, consequential thinking, and social perspective taking best predict social adjustment. In contrast to younger children, older children and adolescents are developmentally capable of learning all the problem-solving subskills and of applying them to social situations.

Social perspective taking, the ability to imagine oneself in another's position and understand how that person might think, feel, and react, is such an important skill that it requires further discussion. Robert Selman (1980), a psychologist, has studied how children develop social-perspective-taking skills. Selman found that children pass through specific stages as they acquire this skill. In the first stage, called egocentric role taking, children aged three to four fail to see the difference between their own view of a social situation and the view that others hold of that situation, believing that others see things the same way they do. Around the age of five, children move into the subjective or differentiated perspective stage. Children in this stage do acknowledge the point of view of others, but they cannot consider their own viewpoint and the viewpoint of another at the same time. Nor can they accurately judge the other's perspective. As a result, children still appear egocentric, placing their own viewpoint above others without clearly thinking about the consequences of such actions.

At around age six, children move into Stage 2, the self-reflective or reciprocal perspective stage. At this point children understand that others may have a different perspective and realize that other people have the same level of understanding about them. Such an understanding allows the child to consider the thoughts and feelings of others. However, children of this age have a difficult time considering the perspective of a third party; for example, they have difficulty understanding how a parent can view their perspective and a sibling's perspective of the same situation at the same time.

The ability to assume a third-party perspective (mutual perspective taking), which emerges around the age of ten, characterizes the mutual perspective stage. Children can now conceptualize how a third person might see their point of view and the point of view of the others involved in a situation. For example, Louisa may now be able to imagine what Mom might think about her reaction to her little sister as well as understand her little sister's perspective.

The fourth and final stage is characterized by a societal or in-depth perspective. This perspective refers to the ability to conceptualize a social group's perspective, for example, the point of view of women or of Native Americans. This ability emerges during adolescence and continues to develop during adulthood.

Perspective taking impacts on decision making because it influences how the person weighs various alternatives. For example, if the only perspective that I can imagine is my own, then all the alternatives I consider favor only my desires and goals. If, however, I can also take the other person's perspective, then I not only will come up with other alternatives but will consider the impact of those alternatives on others when I weigh the costs and benefits of a given alternative.

Perspective taking is not the only factor that influences the kinds of decisions made. Moral judgments often come into play for those decisions requiring moral choices and actions. Like perspective taking, moral reasoning has distinct features at different stages of development. Jean Piaget and Lawrence Kohlberg studied moral reasoning during childhood using situations that involved rule keeping and transgressions. While both theorists have their critics, their theories are consistent with empirical findings.

According to these theorists, younger children are generally motivated to avoid punishment and gain tangible rewards. They use moral absolutism to make judgments, meaning that everything is perceived as right or wrong, with nothing in between. The implication of this kind of reasoning for problem solving is that younger children's choices of alternatives are restricted. As a result, they may require assistance seeing the worth of choices that are not clearly black or white.

As they mature, children become more flexible in their judgments and are able to consider such things as a person's intent. Their choices of behavioral alternatives are now influenced by the approval value of such alternatives; that is, children at this stage (eight to ten years old) are concerned about how others will view them should they engage in a particular behavior.

The most advanced stage of moral reasoning is one marked by flexibility. Moral judgments are now based on norms that are democratically decided upon or that relate to some higher-order principle. William Damon (1977) has looked at how children think about positive justice. Positive justice has to do with the distribution of resources and fairness. During the preschool years children equate fairness with getting what they want ("I should get it because I want it"). Older preschoolers may offer external justification for their claims ("I should get it because I am bigger" or "I should get it because I am smaller"). These hedonistic notions gradually give way to positive justice determined by strict equality. Now justice means that everyone should get the same, no matter what. Around the age of six or seven, children start using the principle of reciprocity to make judgments about what is fair and what isn't: "He helped me, so I will help him" or "If I work hard, I should get the reward, too." During middle childhood (ages eight to ten) and into adolescence children become more sophisticated about their social justice reasoning. They become sensitive to the equity principle, believing that people should receive in proportion to what they give: "Mary should get four and Susie one because Mary did more of the work." And at around the age of ten, children are able to consider extenuating circumstances and balance equity, equality, and reciprocity principles: "John should get a little more than Bill, even though they did the same amount of work, because John had less to start with and needs more right now."

Social justice norms impact on decision making in several ways: For one, they influence whether or not an action will be perceived as a problem. Secondly, perceptions of social justice influence the alternatives that are considered. Finally, social justice norms affect how alternatives are weighed and which ones are ultimately chosen.

I hope that the developmental information presented here prepares readers for what they can reasonably expect of children of different ages in terms of decision making. The ages are meant only as approximate guides. The important point is to understand how children at different stages of development reason about problems and alternatives. With this information in hand, let us now consider how parents can promote good problem-solving skills in their children.

Parents as Promoters of Good Decision Making

Parents can facilitate good decision making in their children by modeling it for them. Children learn from what they see and hear. Parents who make good decisions provide good models for their children. To get the most mileage out of good decision making, parents are advised to occasionally share their decision-making steps with their children: "Hey, Alex, let me tell you how I decided to wait and buy this car instead of the first one I saw." (The explanation not only helps Alex understand the steps involved in decision making, but it also shows him the benefits of delaying immediate gratification for a better option in the future.)

Parents can facilitate good decision making in their children by pointing out the steps involved in the decision-making process used by characters in stories. Stories are a great way to introduce children to the process of decision making. Appendix 3, Section 3.6, lists some children's books that deal with decision making. Parents can use stories as an introduction to actually instructing children on the steps of problem solving. For example, in Martha Alexander's book *Move Over Twerp* young Robert decides on an excellent solution to the bully problem on the school bus. A parent can use this story with young children and literally detail the steps, including the alternatives considered, that Robert took to deal with the problem. It can then be followed up with a discussion about a problem or decision the child has to make.

Parents should give children the opportunity to make choices. The major rule to follow here is to avoid solving those problems that children can solve for themselves. Even young children need to be encouraged to problem-solve and to choose solutions whenever possible. The opportunities can be as simple as deciding between nutritious snacks and as sophisticated as being included in a discussion of some family problem. When children have the opportunity to choose, they learn to choose. As with any other skill, practice and exposure to decision making promote proficiency. Parents who decide everything for their children or who attempt to shelter them from all problems are pampering their children. Pampering is one of the major obstacles to the development of good problem-solving skills.

Is helping children problem-solve the same as pampering them? The answer to this question is, it depends. Initially, children require instruction. Young children require adult guidance. If they need help, it should be given to them. If you don't know how much help a child requires, ask him or her to talk through the problem. Sometimes in hearing a child talk through a problem, the parent can determine the child's deficiencies and help him or her make up for them. And sometimes verbalizing the problem can help a child become aware of missing links in his or her understanding and can enable the child to correct these on his or her own. In any case, the child's attempt to make a good decision needs to be encouraged and fostered.

Parents can practice problem-solving strategies with their children. Role playing provides a good opportunity for children to try out problem-solving strategies. In role play children can experience the perspective of another person by pretending to be that person, and they can practice what to say or do in a given situation. (Recall Karen's use of role play to help her deal with the difficult coach.) By practicing beforehand, children become more familiar with and adept at problem solving. As a result, they are more likely to be successful in the actual situation.

Chapter 9

Cultivating Social Skills in Your Child

There is one thing we know; that man is here for the sake of other men. . . . Many times a day I realize how much my own outer and inner life is built upon the labors of my fellow men, both living and dead, and how earnestly I must exert myself in order to give in return as much as I received.

—ALBERT EINSTEIN

Our relationships with others pervade almost every aspect of our lives. People who have good social skills and strong interpersonal connections are more positive about themselves, more productive and successful on the job, better adjusted, and physically healthier than those who do not (Johnson, 1990). Why? Because feedback from others is one of the pieces of information people use to establish their self-esteem. Also, researchers have discovered that healthy interpersonal relationships protect people from the negative effects of stress. Good interpersonal skills, then, are self-esteem builders and resilience boosters.

Technically speaking, social skills are socially acceptable behaviors that are used by people when they interact with each other. Children and adults are considered socially skilled when their

253

interactions are "personally beneficial, mutually beneficial, or beneficial primarily to others" (Combs & Slaby, 1977, p. 162). Trower (1980) makes a distinction between skill components and the social skill process. Skill components are the individual behaviors that are socially appropriate and valued. Greeting someone with a "Hello" or "How do you do?" is an example of a social skill. The skill process refers to the application of an appropriate set of skills to a situation initially and a following through with the "right" kind of responses for the social situation. Examples of children successfully engaged in a social process are those who know how and when to respond to another child who has asked them to do something they can't do and those who know how and when to make a request of a parent or teacher.

Types of Social Skills

There are a number of taxonomies or inventories of social skills. Table 9.1 presents one such list. I will discuss each of the skill areas in that table separately.

Self-Awareness Skills

While a feeling or emotion is a private affair, the manifestation of the emotion has social consequences. For example, an expression of anger needs to be appropriately vented or it is likely to result in negative social consequences.

The first step in teaching self-awareness to children is encouraging them to recognize their own feeling states and how those feelings influence behavior (see Chapter 8). Because young children have less trouble identifying positive emotions than recognizing negative and surprise feelings (Moyer, 1974), parents and teachers may need to spend more time helping them identify the latter. Moreover, because young children tend to center on one aspect of the situation only, they sometimes miss important information that could help them decode feeling states and may need

TABLE 9.1. Types of Social Skills

Self-awareness skills

Awareness of one's own feeling states and how they affect one's behavior

Acceptance of one's own strengths and weaknesses (and consequent tolerance for the strengths and weaknesses of others)

Awareness of how one communicates feelings and attitudes to others

Interpersonal skills

Communication skills

Ability to identify and respond appropriately to nonverbal cues of others

Ability to appropriately express positive and negative feelings and attitudes

Ability to actively listen, including making eye contact and refraining from distracting the other

Ability to accept positive and negative sentiments from others

Ability to initiate and sustain conversations with others

Role-taking skills

Ability to recognize how feeling states in others affect their behavior

Ability to express empathy

Ability to recognize how situations affect others' behavior

General ability to engage in prosocial, cooperative, and other-directed behavior (e.g., sharing, taking turns, helping out)

Problem-solving skills

Ability to generate alternative solutions

Ability to evaluate alternatives and react appropriately

Ability to maintain self-control

Ability to avoid confrontation

Ability to size up situation (i.e., to view it objectively, to conceptualize the effects of various behaviors on it, and to know the required behaviors and actions)

Ability to manage conflicts amicably (conflict management skills)

---

help from time to time recognizing the emotions and situations that influence their behavior.

Self-understanding and self-acceptance are valuable assets. People feel better about themselves when they accept their personal strengths and weaknesses. This positive attitude is reflected in their behavior and demeanor and results in positive feedback from others. Moreover, people are more likely to accept others' strengths and weaknesses when they have accepted their own. Self-acceptance does not necessarily assure acceptance of others, but it does contribute to it. If you truly accept the fact that you are poor at a particular activity, you are less likely to negatively evaluate someone else who is equally poor at the same activity.

Acceptance of self and other starts with a descriptive evaluation of oneself and others. Very young preschool children describe themselves only in terms of their physical characteristics ("I have brown hair") or in terms of their abilities and traits ("I am good at running"; Harris & Liebert, 1984). Self-acceptance starts out with an awareness and acceptance of one's basic physical characteristics and later extends to intellectual and psychological traits as well.

To help children develop self-acceptance and tolerance toward others, parents need to evaluate children realistically, communicate to them the value of their unique talents, and help them put their weaknesses in perspective. Let your child know that everyone has weaknesses, and share with your child your own strengths and shortcomings. Being realistic about your own strengths and weaknesses and liking yourself are behaviors that set a good example for your child and encourage her or him to do the same. Communicate to your child the value of accepting other people for their strengths and weaknesses. Acceptance of others can be taught by example, as when a parent congratulates another person or shows good sportsmanship. Praising children for accepting and valuing differences found in others and praising them for being good sports are other methods that help them learn to accept others. An unhealthy attitude toward self or other people results in destructive competition, which has the potential for creating a state of chronic distress and promoting defensive social interchanges.

There are children's books that deal with the issue of acceptance of self and others. For example, in *Mr. Tall and Mr. Small* by B. J. Brenner (1966) a giraffe and a mouse meet in the forest. At first, each thinks the other looks peculiar. They engage in a series of arguments, each attempting to convince the other of his own superiority. Then a forest fire breaks out, and the two must combine their individual strengths to save themselves. C. S. Zolotow (1968) develops a similar theme in her book entitled *My Friend John*. In this book two boys respect each other's strengths and weaknesses, and each uses his strength to compensate for the other's weakness.

Reading stories of this kind to your child and drawing attention to the need for individual differences will help your child learn self-acceptance and tolerance for others. For example, you might read *Mr. Tall and Mr. Small* and ask the following questions:

1. What were Mr. Giraffe's strengths?
2. What were Mr. Mouse's strengths?
3. What was Mr. Giraffe unable to do?
4. What was Mr. Mouse unable to do?
5. How did Mr. Giraffe and Mr. Mouse think about each other before the fire?
6. What did they learn about each other when the fire broke out?

You could then follow up the discussion with questions like these:

1. What are you good at?
2. What is your (sister, brother, friend) good at?
3. How can you and your (sister, brother, friend) work together?

The final self-awareness skill to discuss involves presenting a positive image to others. How you appear to others affects how they evaluate and react to you, and how you in turn respond to them. This is the kind of social feedback that impacts on self-esteem directly. Presenting a positive image requires that children have some understanding that others might view them differently from the way they view themselves. According to Selman and

Jasquatte (1978), this third-party perspective develops around the age of eight. Adults cannot assume that children are automatically concerned about how others see them; young children need to be enlightened about the impressions they leave with others. A good way for parents to teach this skill is to give children direct, concrete feedback about what they are projecting. For example, in a positive situation the comment from the parent might go something like this: "Mary, when you smile and volunteer to do the dishes, I think you are being very cooperative." To help the child identify negative nonverbal communication, the parent might say, "Mary, when you pout, I get the impression that you are angry because you did not get your own way. I prefer for you to tell me you are angry." Parents have to be careful to be specific and concrete if the child is going to benefit. Furthermore, this kind of feedback is best given when you and your child have the time to discuss the issues and when the atmosphere is positive or neutral.

It is helpful to point out to children the verbal and nonverbal behavior in others, explaining the impressions such behaviors create. The models of these behaviors can be people seen on TV or those familiar to the child.

Communication Skills

Interpersonal communication is all of the verbal and nonverbal messages that pass between two people. When people communicate, they receive, send, interpret, and infer information from the messages they exchange with each other. These messages have meanings attached to them that influence the quality, kind, and duration of the interaction.

It is essential that children understand nonverbal language, since this is the most frequent kind of communication. Nonverbal information provides the cues for how and when to communicate with others. A child needs to know, for example, that a worried look on Mom's face means that this is not a good time to ask her for a new bike. To teach children how to accurately interpret nonverbal language, Minskoff (1980a) suggests focusing on five different kinds of nonverbal communication:

1. Body language such as posture, facial expressions, and gestures
2. Spatial relationships between people (e.g., if two people are standing far apart, as they converse, what does this mean about their relationship?)
3. Loudness and different kinds of intonations
4. Paralanguage (such as yawns and interruptions)
5. Artifactual cues, badges, uniforms, clothing, jewelry, and the specifics of a situation (e.g., everyone is quiet or busy)

There are several ways that parents can teach their children the skills necessary for understanding nonverbal language. For very young children, a game of nonverbal charades is a possibility. Making a game out of what people look and sound like when they're feeling different ways helps children become sensitive to important nonverbal communications. For older children and adolescents, analyzing the nonverbal content in movies or magazine pictures serves a similar function. For example, sometimes it's fun to shut off the sound track of a movie and infer what is going on solely on the basis of nonverbal cues. Talking about nonverbal behavior in yourself and others is the most direct way of educating children about nonverbal communication. This instruction needs to take place using the constructive communication techniques discussed in Chapter 4; it should also take place during a calm or neutral time. Discussing how your child or another person sends nonverbal messages when you and your child are engaged in a disagreement or are in an emotion-charged situation is not appropriate or useful. The child will most likely discount what you are saying and interpret your attempts to instruct defensively.

A word of caution is in order. Sometimes nonverbal messages are ambiguous. For example, joy can be expressed through laughter or tears, and a blush may be a sign of embarrassment, pleasure, or anger. Cultural differences also play a part in determining the meaning of a nonverbal message. Standing close to another while conversing is a sign of warmth in one culture but an indication of a power difference or hostile exchange in another (Johnson, 1990). The best we can do is to help our children understand that nonverbal messages may mean different things to different people.

In addition to teaching children how to interpret nonverbal communication, social skills training also teaches the art of constructive verbal communication. Teaching constructive communication begins with instructing children to be good listeners, which involves maintaining eye contact and refraining from verbal and behavioral distractions when others are communicating. Instruction then focuses on helping children identify the kinds of verbal statements they like and don't like to hear from others. Positive statements include compliments, expressions of appreciation, and positive salutations; negative statements are criticisms, expressions of blame, and demands. Next, children are taught how to give and respond to both positive and negative comments. Role play is the best vehicle for accomplishing this task. In role play parents might, for example, focus on instructing children to smile and say "Thank you" when receiving a compliment from another. Or they might help their children practice receiving negative feedback by having them role-play the following behaviors:

1. Keeping a serious face when receiving negative feedback
2. Maintaining eye contact
3. Keeping calm (the strategies discussed in Chapters 6 and 8 are useful here)
4. Repeating back the concern expressed by the other person ("What you are saying is that you don't like it when I . . .")
5. Thinking constructively about the negative comment or request (Chapter 7 has details about how to do this; admittedly, this is quite difficult to do, but this ability is a valuable social skill)
6. Choosing the best alternative to deal with the situation (problem-solving strategies are discussed later in this chapter)

Here is an example of a situation where the child accepts negative feedback from a teacher in a socially skillful way: Jeremy has a difficult time keeping his desk organized. As a result, he often loses important papers and assignments. One day his teacher confronts him: "Jeremy, your desk is a mess! Look at it! How can you keep anything straight? You will need to stay in during recess and clean it out." Jeremy looks directly at his teacher and nods his head in agreement. Now, Jeremy does not like to stay in at recess. He is not happy with the teacher's form of discipline, but he keeps his composure by telling himself to keep calm. In the past Jeremy argued with his teacher, a response that resulted in a week's restriction from recess. Now he takes the opportunity to think about the teacher's negative feedback. He realizes that what she is saying is true, but he wishes that she would not yell at him in front of the whole class! He decides not to say anything to her until recess time, when he is alone with her. At recess time Jeremy approaches the teacher and says, "Ms. Smith, I know that my desk is a mess and that's why I have trouble finding papers. Maybe I can think about a way to keep my desk clean. But could you please not yell at me in front of the other kids? They make fun of me when you do this."

Jeremy discusses the problem with his mother. He proposes keeping in his desk a folder with different pockets for organizing his papers. His mother commends him for his solution and for how he managed the negative feedback from the teacher. The teacher is also impressed with Jeremy's acceptance of her criticism and with his solution to the problem. She apologizes to him for reprimanding him in front of the other children and promises not to do it again.

This example demonstrates all the principles of accepting negative feedback cited earlier: Jeremy maintained eye contact. He remained calm, even though he was angry with the teacher for yelling at him in front of the whole class. He generated a solution to the problem and addressed the teacher in an assertive way about his concerns. Jeremy, who is nine years old, was not always able to do this, but with some help and encouragement from his parents he now is much better at accepting negative feedback from others.

Parents can also help children learn how to give both positive and negative messages to others. Role play is an ideal technique to use in instructing children in this social skill. Through role play children can practice using the following rules when giving a positive or negative message to another:

1. Use "I" statements: "I like your . . ." or, in the case of a negative comment, "I feel bad when you . . ."

2. Use clear and specific statements: "I like the way you share your crayons with me" or "I don't like it when you interrupt me." Younger children have difficulty being specific, but with practice and good examples they can learn.

3. Use consistent verbal and nonverbal messages. If you are giving another person a compliment, smile; if you're expressing a concern, keep a serious face. When verbal and nonverbal communications are incongruent, people become suspicious of the verbal message and question your credibility.

4. Use clear descriptors for your feelings. There are three main ways that feelings are expressed verbally: with a label ("I am happy"), in terms of an action ("I could jump for joy"), or with a figure of speech ("I'm flying!").

5. Use words that describe the other person's actions. A mistake most people make is to place an evaluation or interpretation on the behavior of others. Instead of just saying, "I don't like it when you won't share your cars," a child might say, "You are selfish because you won't share your cars." The use of the evaluator "selfish" automatically increases the likelihood of a conflict.

Handling negative feedback from others is the ultimate challenge for social skills training. Training that focuses on behavioral control over negative emotions must take into consideration the points made in this chapter and in Chapters 6, 7, and 8. Obtaining physical control over emotions and thinking in a constructive way about negative feedback increases the likelihood of responding in a socially appropriate way. Cartledge and Milburn (1986) cite the work of Fagan and associates, who suggest that parents and teachers convey to children the following truths:

1. The way we think and feel is our own private business. We have a right to feel or think angry or sad thoughts.
2. All actions are not okay. Some behaviors are illegal and harmful.
3. You can think and feel differently from how you behave. You can think and feel angry without having to hurt someone or get into trouble yourself. There is a right way to get your feelings out and a way that will just get you into trouble.

When children and adults are able to control their feelings and thoughts, they are in a much better position to problem-solve. Problem solving means venting our feelings appropriately as well as finding a reasonable resolution to the negative situation.

Finally, good communication requires good conversational skills. These skills, which are indispensable to initiating and maintaining friendships, include the following:

1. Taking the initiative and getting involved in an activity.
2. Introducing oneself to the other.
3. Showing interest by paying attention and asking relevant questions.
4. Showing interest in the other person or activity.
5. Giving accurate positive feedback. (Be careful not to overdo the compliment; people who give too many compliments are sometimes perceived negatively, that is, as insincere or as ingratiating themselves in order to get something from others.)

Role-Taking Skills

Role taking is the ability to see a situation from another's perspective. It is a vital social skill because it facilitates communication, interpersonal problem solving, and interpersonal relations. Role taking or perspective taking involves first recognizing feeling states in others and then understanding how those feeling states affect their behavior. There are developmental differences in children's ability to take the perspective of another person. While experts disagree as to when most children are capable of taking another's perspective, they all agree that the very young child (five and younger) has to be instructed to do so. In other words, the child has to be taught to consider another person's point of view. As the child matures, perspective taking develops naturally.

In addition to recognizing and understanding how another might feel, role-taking skills also involve responding appropriately to the feelings and needs of others. In Chapter 2, I referred to this aspect of role taking as "other-orientedness." Appropriate responding includes empathetic responses, cooperative behavior, and sharing.

Parents can promote role-taking skills in a number of different ways. They can teach children to be sensitive to the feelings of others by encouraging children to think about others. For example, praising the child on an outing who wants to bring something home for a sibling is reinforcing the child to think about others. Commending the child who volunteers to share and encouraging the child who responds to another person's distress in a helpful and appropriate way are other ways parents can encourage children to be "other-directed." Stories and naturally occurring events are good ways to introduce the skill of role taking. By highlighting for a child how a particular character in a story interpreted and then responded to the needs and feelings of another, the parent is instructing the child in the subskills that go into role taking. The parent can then identify opportunities for the child to do the same. Giving children the opportunity to learn about different people and cultures exposes them to other perspectives and viewpoints. Experiences of this sort also encourage and perfect role-taking skills. Of course, parents who show consideration for others, act in cooperative ways, and verbalize their understanding of how others feel are teaching perspective taking by example.

Sometimes children who are having difficulty seeing a situation from the other's perspective require direct instruction: "Yes, John, I understand that you were only joking when you called Susie a dork, but Susie did not think it was a joke. You will need to think about how Susie feels the next time you want to joke with her." Instruction of this nature, given in a neutral, calm, and nonevaluative way, effectively communicates the other person's perspective.

Teaching children to cooperate is one of the more important ways that parents and teachers educate children to be other-oriented. Cooperation is a mind-set as well as a set of specific skills: to be cooperative, you have to "want to" in addition to knowing how. The "knowing how" includes listening to what another has to say, coordinating one's own activities and efforts with those of other people, and engaging in behaviors that are inclusive of others (Sapon-Shevin, 1986). Cooperative games are a good way to promote this cooperative mind-set. Sapon-Shevin (1986) offers four criteria for judging a game as cooperative: (1) the game directs children to include, rather than exclude, others; (2) the game requires turn taking and sharing; (3) the game requires participants to help each other out; and (4) the game requires participants to focus on each other's strengths. Although some games promote cooperation, others do just the opposite. Games like "king of the castle" encourage name calling, and musical chairs and "steal the bacon" foster exclusion. These kinds of games need to be discouraged and replaced with games that are more cooperative in nature. Cooperation can also be taught through stories and actions. Stories like *Two Good Friends* (Dalton, 1974) and *The Blind Man and the Elephant: An Old Tale from the Land of India* (Quigley, 1959) emphasize the value and necessity of working together.

Problem-Solving Skills

Every relationship contains the potential for conflict and disagreement. Even healthy relationships have their share of conflict. Resilient personalities employ good problem-solving skills to resolve conflict in productive ways. Chapter 8 contains a number of those strategies. What I will elaborate on now is conflict management skills.

Confronting a conflict and negotiating a resolution generally involve the following steps (Johnson, 1990): (1) addressing the person directly about the conflict, (2) expressing your perspective on the problem, (3) taking the perspective of the other person, (4) expressing cooperative intent, and (5) developing a plan. Conflict management is no easy task. Most children require some level of assistance. If children are exposed to these skills early in life, there is a greater probability that they will master them by the time they reach adulthood.

What do children need to know in order to be successful at conflict management? First of all, they need to know when and how to confront the problem situation or person. Self-awareness and communication and role-taking skills play a major role in conflict management and negotiations. Children need to know, for example, that if the nonverbal and verbal cues of others indicate high arousal, it is not a good time to confront them. Confronting others when you or they are upset only serves to escalate the conflict. Expressing a desire to resolve the conflict and setting up a time to talk about the problem are good conflict management responses. Children need to be instructed to express their perceptions of the problem in an objective, nonthreatening way when confronting another person. One way to ensure such a delivery is to use "I" statements and to focus the anger one has on the other person's behavior, not his or her character: "Amy, I have a problem with the kinds of names you call me on the bus."

After expressing one's perspective on the problem, the next step is to try to understand the other's point of view. This requires active listening skills and is difficult for adults as well as children when they are emotionally charged. This is why it is better to manage the conflict when tempers and anxieties are under physical and mental control. Children need to be instructed to check out their interpretation of the other person's perspective by paraphrasing his or her statement: "Sue, let me see if I got this right You called me a dork because you thought I took your notebook?" This is a good example of a paraphrase statement that clarifies the nature of the problem.

Finally, expressing an openness to cooperate and resolve the conflict sets the stage for negotiating a resolution. The resolution plan might involve a compromise, or it might involve some other resolution or agreement—including an agreement to disagree. Ideally, it involves (Johnson, 1990) (1) a negotiated understanding of the problem, (2) an agreement on how the parties will act differently in the future, (3) an agreement on what to do if one of the parties deviates from the agreement, and (4) a time the opposing parties will meet to review the plan.

Here is an example of a dialogue between two ten-year-old girls as they attempt to manage a conflict:

SUE: What a jerk you are, Amy! Can't you keep your hands off my stuff?
AMY: Look, Sue, you always blame me when you are careless and lose your own things.
SUE: Yeah, well everyone knows you are the biggest thief in the whole class!
AMY: And everyone knows that you are the biggest liar, too!

At this point the argument escalates, and the two girls actually become physically involved. This scenario is a good example of poor conflict management. Allow me to replay the dialogue, this time with Amy using an appropriate conflict management strategy:

SUE: What a jerk you are, Amy! Can't you keep your hands off my stuff?
AMY: Excuse me, Sue, but I don't have your notebook. Maybe you forgot it at home or something!
SUE: No, I didn't. You took it. Everyone knows that you are the biggest thief in the class.
AMY: Listen, Sue, I don't like to be called a thief, and I didn't take your notebook. If you want, I'll help you find it.
SUE: I know you took it. Don't try to cover it up!
AMY: Listen, Sue, I think we'd better talk about this later. I am too mad at you to do it now.

SUE: I don't want to. I want to settle it now.

AMY: I can't. I need to cool down.

[*Amy walks away and Sue follows, harassing her all the way. Amy keeps herself under control by thinking constructive thoughts: "I am not going to let Sue get to me. She can't get me to start this fight. I will get to class, and she will have to stop." When the girls reach their classroom, Sue proceeds to tell the teacher that Amy stole her notebook. The teacher calls Amy up to her desk and asks her about the incident.*]

AMY: Mrs. Smith, I told Sue that I did not take her notebook. I even offered to help her find it. She kept saying that I took the notebook and even called me a thief. I walked away from her because I was getting mad. I did not want to get into trouble like I did before, so I came right to class.

MS. SMITH: Okay, Amy. I am pleased that you decided to do what you did. Sue, you and Amy need to work this out after math class.

[*Amy approaches Sue after math class.*]

AMY: Look, Sue, I know you think I took your notebook. But I didn't. I would be upset too if I thought you took my notebook. I will help you find it. But I cannot help you if you keep saying that I took the notebook or if you call me names. If you think I took the notebook, ask me first; don't accuse me. I promised you the last time that I would not take anything that belongs to you—and I haven't.

[*Sue finally accepts Amy's offer. They find the notebook—in Sue's desk. While the girls are not the best of friends, they have managed to reduce the conflict between them.*]

In this scenario Amy used all the right steps to solve the conflict. She told Sue directly and clearly what she did not like about what was happening, and she did so in a nonjudgmental way. She expressed an understanding of Sue's problem and communicated a cooperative intent. She ended the conversation by offering Sue a conflict management approach should another disagreement arise between them.

Parents can teach children conflict management skills in much the same way they teach any other social skill. Reading and discussing stories that show different conflict management strategies is a good way to introduce the relevant ideas and skills. Role-playing particularly difficult situations, while practicing constructive communication, constructive thinking, and good problem-solving strategies, is an excellent way to prepare children for problem situations. And, finally, engaging in good conflict management strategies yourself encourages your child to do the same.

Chapter 10

Summing It All Up

Children are the lifeline of our society and our world. They are the greatest natural resource a country has. For our world to be safe and productive, our children must be self-accepting, tolerant of other people's differences, and resilient. Parents and teachers have the responsibility for nurturing the kinds of healthy attitudes and skills that children require in order to develop these attributes. The skills and attitudes required have been discussed in preceding chapters and are summarized in figures. Figure 10.1 highlights the inputs to self-esteem and resilience. Figure 10.2 summarizes the methods parents and teachers can use to teach children the important attitudes and skills. Figure 10.3 depicts the outcomes of positive self-esteem and resilience.

For children to like themselves and develop good coping skills, they first need to feel accepted for their own qualities and characteristics and to accept these themselves. Chapter 3 discusses how a parent or teacher might assess and work with a child's own individual characteristics. When people close to children accept and love them for who they are, the children are more likely to develop a positive sense of self. Children also need to learn to be constructive thinkers and good problem solvers. Those who can maintain a positive perspective on change and a challenge perspective toward adversity are better able to deal with distress. Likewise, children who are good decision makers not

FIGURE 10.1. Inputs to children's self-esteem and resilience.

only avoid the consequences of poor decisions but also are able to effectively deal with life's everyday stressors. Chapters 7 and 8 describe how parents and teachers can promote these kinds of skills in children.

Good nutrition, proper exercise, and stress-coping strategies are prerequisites for maintaining good physical and mental

Teaching methods →	Child's skills →	Results
Modeling of attitudes and skills	Self-evaluation	Self-esteem
General feedback	Constructive thinking	Resilience
Democratic discipline styles	Problem-solving strategies	
Personal stories	Social skills	
Literature	Coping skills	
Mass media	Life style habits	

FIGURE 10.2. Teaching methods leading to self-esteem and resilience.

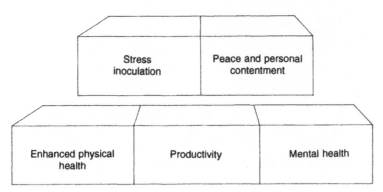

FIGURE 10.3. Outcomes of positive self-esteem and resilience.

health. Children who feel better act better, and children who can manage the physical characteristics of distress deal better with life's challenges. Chapter 6 details the kinds of life style habits children need to adopt in order to maintain a good sense of self and a resilient outlook on life.

Finally, people do better when they have a strong sense of purpose, which comes from the ability to set reasonable goals, and good social supports, which is enhanced by good social skills. Chapter 9 addresses the cultivation of social skills, and several of the chapters describe the ingredients necessary for establishing reasonable goals.

Parents and teachers are the best source of information and instruction for their children. Children learn from what they see. Parents and teachers can model the kinds of skills and attitudes that are presented in this book. When they do, their children are more likely to learn and internalize these skills and values. In addition, the resilient attitudes and behaviors can be communicated through personal stories, literature, and the mass media and reinforced through parental discipline techniques and communication. The end result is a child who is more likely to be productive, resilient, and healthy.

The skills and attitudes discussed in the chapters of this book are applicable to a range of problems children and adults face in today's world. A number of examples were used to show how particular skills could be applied to deal with problems in a productive and resilient way. Now I would like to apply the techniques and attitudes to two important areas: competition and loss. At some point in our life all of us face the stresses and strains that come from competition and from the loss of someone or something near and dear to us. The skills and attitudes discussed in the preceding chapters can be applied to these situations.

A Resilient Approach to Competition and Mistakes

Healthy competition is useful and mistakes are inevitable. Successful and resilient children deal with competition constructively and grow from their mistakes. You can help your child manage competition and mistakes by implementing the following suggestions: Talk openly with your child about problems. Here is an example of how a parent might initiate a conversation: "Kate, I sense that the competition on the soccer team is fierce. I can imagine that it is difficult to play under those circumstances." Give your child a way to manage the physical symptoms associated with competitive anxiety. The strategies mentioned in Chapter 6 are useful for teaching children to recognize and manage those symptoms. Help your child take a constructive perspective on competition. The general ideas covered in Chapter 7 are helpful here. Specifically, parents can help children put competition in perspective by making the following points:

1. The best kind of competition is competition that leads to self-improvement.

2. The greatest athletes, dancers, musicians, and intellectuals did not always come out first. They viewed competition as a challenge and a way to find out just how far they could push

themselves. They competed more with themselves than they did with other people. When we compete only with others, we are limited by them; when we compete with ourselves, we are limited only by our own capacity and attitudes.

3. Mistakes and failures are opportunities to learn. The most productive individuals made their share of mistakes. The difference between them and their less productive counterparts is that they learned from their mistakes.

4. Sometimes we have to accept the fact that someone else is smarter, faster, or more talented. But another person's talent does not render one incompetent and worthless. It takes all kinds of people to make this world work efficiently. In fact, more often than not, people excel in some areas but not in others. Even people who are seemingly multitalented are not able to master all of the tasks necessary to keep the world going.

Admittedly, these ideas are difficult notions to communicate to a child who wants to be on top. Here is what one father told his daughter on the subject of competition:

> Kate, a good way to look at competition is as an opportunity to improve your skills. Think about each soccer game as a personal challenge to do just a little better than you did before. Some of the greatest athletes did not always come out first. They made their share of mistakes. The difference between a real winner and a loser is that winners learn from their mistakes. They also understand they can't always be on top in everything they do. All they do is their best—each and every time.

Parents can help children do their best. If your child can honestly do better at a particular task, help him or her generate strategies for perfecting the necessary skills. Such strategies involve the following:

1. Determining what the deficits (problems) are for optimal performance

2. Generating solutions for those problems (the solutions might be specific actions, or they might involve additional practice and skills training)
3. Evaluating the strategies (i.e., determining if they helped improve the performance)
4. Refining the strategies, if necessary

Finally, it is important to provide children with feedback. If your child has done a good job dealing with competition or mistakes, let her or him know you think so. If your child is having difficulties, provide her or him with the guidance to manage the distress more constructively.

A Resilient Approach for Dealing with Loss or Disaster

Living through the loss of a parent, grandparent, sibling, close friend, or even a pet influences the behaviors and thoughts of children and adults. Furthermore, seeing or hearing about the losses that result from a disaster affects the psyche even of those not personally involved, although in a less intense way. The guidelines that follow provide parents with a strategy for helping children deal with and grow from experiences of loss or disaster.

Pay Attention to Your Child's Behavior

Children, like adults, do not always react immediately to the stress of a loss or disaster. The distress often shows up later as separation anxiety, sleep and eating problems, regression to more infantile behavior, or a sudden change in normal behavioral style (i.e., a kind, even-tempered child may suddenly become aggressive and ill-tempered). Age influences the way a child responds to a loss or disaster: Young children (under age five) may not be able to express their anxieties verbally and are more likely to act them out in play or in their everyday behaviors. Older children are better equipped to verbalize their feelings but may still act them out first.

Respond to Your Child's Behavior in a Nurturing and Supportive Way

Children may need some additional time and attention following a loss or disaster. It is very difficult for parents or guardians to supply this if they have experienced the same loss or disaster. Sometimes a teacher, neighbor, or another relative can help supplement parental support in such cases. And sometimes it is important for parents themselves to obtain the necessary help from others so that they can nurture and support their child. The kind of support a child requires varies from individual to individual. Some children need help interpreting their feelings, others need to be encouraged (but not forced) to express their feelings, and still others may require concrete supports like night-lights or extra time with a parent. Anticipate separation concerns and fears and provide reassurance. For example, a child may revert back to being afraid of the dark and may need a night-light on for a short time while adjusting to the loss or trauma. A parent who responds with "Don't be scared of the dark" or "You are acting like a baby" is not being supportive. A response like "Sure, we can keep the night-light on tonight" is reassuring and supportive for the child.

Validate Your Child's Feelings

Let children know it is okay and normal to feel sad, angry, or even afraid. These emotions are normal and typical for situations involving loss. To deny them or discourage their appropriate expression simply adds to the distress load of the situation.

Share Your Feelings with Your Child

When you share your feelings with your child, you validate your child's right to his or her own feelings and you clarify for your child the reasons for your behavior and moods. Sometimes children misinterpret parental distress. For example, children who see a parent grieving the loss of a spouse might think that something is wrong with the parent and may fear that that parent might die, too. By indicating the reasons for their tearfulness, parents spare the child from having to conjure up a reason for their distress.

Provide Your Child with a Resilient Perspective

Helping children put a loss or disaster in perspective is no easy task. The constructive thinking strategies discussed in Chapter 7 are directly applicable to this task. To begin, a parent needs to find out what the child is thinking. Sometimes children blame themselves for the loss or disaster. I once had a five-year-old child in my practice who felt that her baby sister died because she had been angry with her. In reality, her sister died in the hospital from a congenital heart defect. The parents spent a great deal of time with the dying child, leaving my patient, Angela, in the care of her grandparents. Angela missed her parents and blamed her sister for their absence. Helping Angela see that she was not responsible for her sister's death was the first step in putting the loss into perspective for her.

Another perspective-taking step includes making the loss or trauma count in a positive way. Admittedly, there may be no perceivable gains in a disaster, but sometimes good can come from the hurtful situation. For example, when a tornado destroyed their home in Xenia, Ohio, little Jackie thought her family would never have the home they had before. She was right; they never did. Instead, the neighborhood was greatly improved, with the neighbors now realizing the worth and strength of friendship. Most of us know of situations where the crisis itself becomes the motivation for a major goal. Angela, who is now 17, expects to become a neonatologist, an ambition that resulted from the death of her infant sister some 12 years ago. Remember also the case of Terry Fox. He made his personal crisis count in a positive way by raising money for cancer research. These are all examples of individuals who directed their personal pain in a fruitful direction.

Help your child understand that in time the uncomfortable

feelings he or she is now experiencing will wane. Personal stories or literature can be used to communicate this message: "You know, George, I felt terrible when my best friend moved away. I felt bad for two months. After a while, I began to feel better. Now I don't feel bad at all."

Help your child understand the objective facts. Children, like adults, misrepresent the facts when they are in a crisis situation. As a result, they draw erroneous conclusions. Angela is a case in point: when her sister died, not only did she believe that it was her fault but she also feared the same thing would happen to her. By explaining the facts to children in terms they can understand, parents can resolve some of their confusion. And remember to use the language of resilience. Statements like "We will get through this difficult time" or "We feel bad now, but we will feel better tomorrow" are good examples of resilient talk.

Normalize Your Child's Routine

The predictability that comes from a routine helps stabilize the chaos that so often follows a loss or crisis. In other words, routine is the one thing that is the same at a time where everything else seems to be changing; routine offers people security in times of crisis.

Let Your Child Participate in Crisis Resolution

Allow your child to become involved in efforts to resolve the problem. When children are allowed to participate in the resolution of a crisis, they are better able to bring closure to the traumatic experience. The degree of involvement is, of course, dependent upon the age and maturity of the child. It can include such things as helping in the cleanup after a natural disaster, participating in religious rituals, and joining discussions about plans for the future. To illustrate how this might be done, consider this example: The father of David, age 11, and Patricia, age six, recently died after a long battle with leukemia. Their mother included the children in the funeral arrangements. David wanted to lead a prayer group at his father's wake, and Patricia drew pictures for Daddy "to take to heaven." In the months that followed the father's death, the family became involved in putting together a "memory album" in his honor.

Conclusion

The challenge we have as parents is greater than it has ever been before. The problems of our society and our world demand the foresight, determination, commitment, and cooperation of responsible individuals who are willing to solve problems in a productive and peaceful way. When we contribute to our child's self-esteem and resilience, we are investing in the development of such individuals and thus in the future, and we are bestowing upon our children a legacy that optimizes their life, their health, and their world.

Bibliography

Adams, J. D. (1980). *Understanding and managing stress: A book of readings*. San Diego: University Associates.

Alexander, M. (1983). *Move over twerp*. New York: Dial.

American Academy of Pediatrics (1986). *Television and the family*. Elk Grove Village, IL: Author.

Anderson, G. A., & Arnoult, L. K. (1989). An examination of perceived control, humor, irrational beliefs, and positive stress as moderators of the relation between negative stress and health. *Basic and Applied Social Psychology, 10,* 101–117.

Anderson, J. (1981). *Thinking, changing, and rearranging*. Eugene, OR: Timberline Press.

Anthony, E. J. (1974). The syndrome of the psychologically invulnerable child. In E. J. Anthony & C. Koupernik (Eds.), *The child in his family: Children at psychiatric risk*. New York: Wiley.

Antonovsky, A. (1979). *Health, stress and coping: New perspectives on mental and physical well-being*. San Francisco: Jossey-Bass.

Arnold, L. (1990). *Childhood stress*. New York: Wiley.

Austin, G. (1988). *Love and power, parent and child: How to raise competent, confident children*. Rolling Hills Estates, CA: Robert Erlmann.

Bandura, A. (1977). *Social learning theory*. Englewood Cliffs, NJ: Prentice-Hall.

Bandura, A. (1982). Self-efficacy mechanism in human agency. *American Psychologist, 37,* 122–147.

Baumrind, D. (1970). Socialization and instrumental competence in young children. *Young Children, 26*(2), 104–119.

Baumrind, D. (1977). Current patterns of parental authority. *Developmental Monographs, 4,* pt. 2.

Baumrind, D. (1983). Rejoinder to Lewis' reinterpretation of parental firm control effects. *Psychological Bulletin, 94,* 101–104.

Becker, W. C. (1964). Consequences of different kinds of parental discipline. In M. L. Hoffman & L. W. Hoffman (Eds.), *Review of child development research* (Vol. 1). New York: Russell Sage.

Bee, H. B. (1989). *The developing child*. New York: Harper & Row.

Benson, H. (1975). *The relaxation response*. New York: Morrow.

Bernard, M. E., & Joyce, M. R. (1984). *Rational emotive therapy with children and adolescents*. New York: Wiley.

Bettelheim, B. (1976). *The uses of enchantment: The meaning and importance of fairy tales*. New York: Knopf.

Block, J. (1981). Growing up vulnerable and growing up resistant: Preschool personality and intervening family stresses. In C. D. Moore (Ed.), *Adolescence and stress* (pp. 42–57). Washington, DC: U.S. Government Printing Office.

Block, J. H., & Block, J. (1980). The role of ego-control and ego-resiliency in the organization of behavior. In W. A. Collins (Ed.), *The Minnesota Symposium on Child Psychology 13: Development of cognition, affect and social relations* (pp. 68–72). Hillside, NJ: Erlbaum.

Braswell, L., & Kendall, P. C. (1988). Cognitive–behavioral methods with children. In K. S. Dobson (Ed.), *Handbook of cognitive behavioral therapies* (pp. 167–214). New York: Guilford Press.

Brenner, B. J. (1966). *Mr. Tall and Mr. Small*. Reading, MA: Addison-Wesley.

Brody, J. (1985). *Good food book*. New York: Bantam Books.

Brown, J. D., & Lawton, M. (1986). Stress and well-being in adolescence: The moderating role of physical exercise. *Journal of Human Stress, 12*, 125–131.

Brown, J. P., & Siegel, J. M. (1988). Exercise as a buffer of life stress: A prospective study of adolescent health. *Health Psychology, 7*, 341–353.

Bruner, J. (1986). *Actual minds, possible worlds*. Cambridge, MA: Harvard University Press.

Campbell, J., & Moyers, B. (1988). *The power of myth*. New York: Doubleday.

Cannon, W. B. (1932). *The wisdom of the body*. New York: Norton.

Carlson, N. (1983). *Loudmouth George and the sixth-grade bully*. New York: Puffin.

Cartledge, G., & Milburn, J. (1986). *Teaching social skills to children* (2nd ed.). Needham Heights, MA: Allyn and Bacon.

Catell, R. B. (1971). *Abilities: Their structure, growth and action*. Boston: Houghton Mifflin.

Chomsky, C. (1969). *The acquisition of syntax in children from 5 to 10*. Cambridge, MA: MIT Press.

Clark, R. M. (1983). *Family life and school achievement: Why poor black children succeed or fail*. Chicago: University of Chicago Press.

Coles, R. (1986). *The moral life of children*. New York: Atlantic Monthly Press.

Collins, W. A., Sobol, B. L., & Westby, S. (1981). Effects of adult commentary on children's comprehension and inferences about a televised aggressive portrayal. *Child Development, 52*, 158–163.

Combs, M. L., & Slaby, D. A. (1977). Social skills training with children. In B. B.

Lahey & A. E. Kazdin (Eds.), *Advances in clinical child psychology* (Vol. 1, pp. 52–68). New York: Plenum.

Cook, B. W. (1992). *Eleanor Roosevelt.* New York: Viking Press.

Cooley, C. H. (1909). *Social organization.* New York: Charles Scribner's Sons.

Coopersmith, S. (1967). *The antecedents of self-esteem.* San Francisco: Freeman.

Copeland, A. P. (1983). Children's talking to themselves: Its developmental significance and therapeutic promise. In P. Kendall (Ed.), *Advances in cognitive behavioral research and therapy* (Vol. 2, pp. 181–213). New York: Academic Press.

Cousins, N. (1981). *Anatomy of an illness as perceived by the patient: Reflections on healing and regeneration.* New York: Bantam.

Dalton, J. (1974). *Two good friends.* New York: Crown.

Damon, W. (1977). *The social world of the child.* San Francisco: Jossey-Bass.

D'Antonio, I. J. (1988). The use of humor with children in hospital settings. *Journal of Children in Contemporary Society, 20,* 157–169.

Davis, A., & Kleiner, B. H. (1989). The value of humor in effective leadership. *Leadership and Organizational Development Journal, 10,* 1–111.

Davis, K., Eshelman, D., & McKay, D. (1982). *The relaxation and stress reduction workbook* (2d ed.). Oakland, CA: New Harbinger Press.

Deci, L. L. (1975). *Intrinsic motivation.* New York: Plenum.

Deffenbacher, J. (1986). Cognitive and physiological components of test anxiety in real-life exams. *Cognitive Therapy and Research, 10,* 635–644.

de Paola, T. (1979). *Oliver Button is a sissy.* New York: Harcourt, Brace, Jovanovich.

Dix, T. (1991). The affective organization of parenting: Adaptive and maladaptive processes. *Psychological Bulletin, 110,* 3–25.

Donegan-Johnson, A. (1992). *The value of responsibility.* Los Angeles: Value Tales.

Dreikurs, R. (1964). *Children: The challenge.* New York: Hawthorn.

Dunn, R., & Dunn, K. (1977). *How to raise independent and professionally successful daughters.* Englewood Cliffs, NJ: Prentice-Hall.

Dweck, C. S. (1986). Motivational processes affecting learning. *American Psychologist, 41,* 1040–1048.

D'Zurilla, T. J. (1988). Problem-solving therapies. In K. S. Dobson (Ed.), *Handbook of cognitive behavioral therapies* (pp. 85–136). New York: Guilford Press.

Elkins, A. (1983). Working with children in groups. In A. Ellis & M. E. Bernard (Eds.), *Rational-emotive approaches to the problems of childhood.* New York: Plenum.

Ellis, A. (1962). *Reason and emotion in psychotherapy.* New York: Stuart.

Ellis, A., & Bernard, M. E. (1983). Rational-emotive approaches to the problems of childhood. In A. Ellis & M. E. Bernard (Eds.), *Rational-emotive approaches to the problems of childhood* (pp. 435–473). New York: Plenum.

Eysenck, H. J. (1982). Development of a theory. In C. S. Spielberger (Ed.), *Personality, genetics and behavior.* New York: Praeger.

Farmer, M. E., Locke, B. Z., Mosciki, E. K., Donnenberg, A. L., Larson, D. B., & Radloff, L. S. (1988). Physical activity and depressive symptoms: The

HNANES I Epidemiologic Follow-Up Study. *American Journal of Epidemiology, 128,* 1340–1351.

Flavell, J. H. (1979). Metacognition and cognitive monitoring: A new area of cognitive development inquiry. *American Psychologist, 34,* 906–911.

Freed, A., & Freed, M. (1977). *TA for kids.* Sacramento, CA: Jalmar Press.

Friedman, M., & Ulmer, D. (1984). *Treating Type A behavior and your heart.* New York: Knopf.

Funk, S. C., & Houston, B. K. (1987). A critical analysis of the hardiness scale's validity and utility. *Journal of Personality and Social Psychology, 5,* 572–578.

Gardner, H. (1983). *Frames of mind: The theory of multiple intelligence.* New York: Basic Books.

Garmezy, N. (1983). Stressors of childhood. In N. Garmezy & M. Rutter (Eds.), *Stress, coping and development.* New York: McGraw-Hill.

Gerbner, G., Gross, L., Signorielli, N., & Morgan, M. (1980). Aging with television: Images on television drama and conceptions of social reality. *Journal of Communication, 30,* 37–47.

Gilmore, J. (1974). *The productive personality.* San Francisco: Albion.

Gordon, T. (1975). Parent effectiveness training. New York: New American Library.

Hanser, S. B. (1985). Music therapy and stress reduction research. *Journal of Music Therapy, 22,* 193–206.

Harris, J. R., & Liebert, R. M. (1984). *The child.* Englewood Cliffs, NJ: Prentice-Hall.

Harter, M. (1983). Developmental perspectives on the self-system. In P. H. Mussen (Ed.), *Handbook of child psychology* (4th ed.), New York: Wiley.

Haskell, W. L. (1985). Exercise programs for health promotion. In J. C. Rosen & L. J. Solomon (Eds.), *Prevention in health psychology.* Hanover, NH: University Press of New England.

Heider, F. (1958). *The psychology of interpersonal relations.* New York: Wiley.

Herrman, J. D. (1989). Sudden death and the police officer. Special issue: The death of a child. *Issues in Comprehensive Pediatric Nursing, 4,* 327–332.

Hetherington, E. M., Cox, M., & Cox, L. (1978). The aftermath of divorce. In J. H. Stevens & M. Mathews (Eds.), *Mother–child and father–child relations.* Washington, DC: National Association for Education of Young Children.

Hetherington, E. M., & Parke, R. (1986). *Child development: A contemporary viewpoint.* New York: McGraw-Hill.

Hinshaw, S. P., & Erhardt, D. (1991). Attention deficit hyperactivity disorder. In P. C. Kendall (Ed.), *Child and adolescent therapy* (pp. 98–123). New York: Guilford Press.

Hoffman, L. W. (1991). The influence of the family environment on personality: Accounting for sibling differences. *Psychological Bulletin, 110,* 187–203.

Holt, P., Fine, M. J., & Tollefson, N. (1987). Mediating stress: Survival of the hardy. *Psychology in the Schools, 24,* 51–58.

Hull, J. G., Van Treuven, R. R., & Virnelli, S. (1987). Hardiness and health: A critique and alternative approach. *Journal of Personality and Social Psychology, 53,* 518–530.

Hunsley, J. (1987). Internal dialogue during academic examinations. *Cognitive Therapy and Research, 11,* 653–664.

Jacobsen, E. (1929). *Progressive relaxation.* Chicago: University of Chicago Press.

James, W. (1950). *The principles of psychology.* New York: Dover. (Original work published in 1890)

Johnson, D. W. (1990). *Reaching out: Interpersonal effectiveness and self-actualization* (4th ed.). Englewood Cliffs, NJ: Prentice-Hall.

Jones, E. L., & Nisbett, R. L. (1971). The actor and the observer: Divergent perceptions of the causes of behavior. In E. E. Jones, D. Kanouse, H. H. Kelley, R. E. Nisbett, S. Valins, & B. Weiner (Eds.), *Attribution: Perceiving the causes of behavior* (pp. 79–95). Morristown, NJ: General Learning Press.

Joseph, J. M., & Short, E. (1992). *The recital.* Clinton, NY: Young Set Learning Associates.

Kagan, J. (1985). Temperamental contributions to social behavior. *American Psychologist, 44,* 668–674.

Kagan, J., & Snidman, N. (1991). Temperamental factors in human development. *American Psychologist, 46,* 856–862.

Kimchi, J., & Schaffner, B. (1991). Childhood protective factors and stress risk. In E. Arnold (Ed.), *Childhood stress* (pp. 475–495). New York: Wiley.

Kobasa, S. C. (1979). Stressful life events, personality and health: An inquiry into hardiness. *Journal of Personality and Social Psychology, 37,* 1–11.

Kobasa, S. C. (1982). The hardy personality: Toward a social psychology of stress and health. In G. S. Sanders & J. Suls (Eds.), *Social psychology of health and illness* (pp. 3–28). Hillsdale, NJ: Erlbaum.

Kobasa, S. C., Maddi, S. R., & Courington, S. (1981). Personality and constitution as mediators in the stress–illness relationship. *Journal of Health and Social Behavior, 22,* 368–378.

Kobasa, S. C., Maddi, S. R., & Kahn, S. (1982). Hardiness and health: A perspective inquiry. *Journal of Personality and Social Psychology, 42,* 168–177.

Koda-Callan, E. (1989). *The silver slippers.* New York: Workman Publishing.

Kohlberg, L. (1968). The child as a moral philosopher. *Psychology Today, 2,* 25–30.

Krokoff, L. J. (1991). Job distress is no laughing matter in marriage or is it? *Journal of Social and Personal Relationships, 8,* 5–25.

Kuczen, B. (1987). *Childhood stress: How to raise a healthier, happier child.* New York: Delta Books.

LaPlace, J. (1984). *Health* (4th ed.). Englewood Cliffs, NJ: Prentice-Hall.

Lazarus, R. S., & Folkman, S. (1984). *Stress, appraisal and coping.* New York: Springer-Verlag.

Lichstein, K. L. (1988). *Clinical relaxation strategies.* New York: Wiley.

Liebert, R. M., & Sprafkin, J. (1988). *The early window* (3d ed.). New York: Pergamon Press.

Long, B. C. (1985). Stress-management interventions: A 15-month follow-up of aerobic conditioning and stress inoculation training. *Cognitive Therapy and Research, 9*, 471–478.

Luria, A. (1961). *The role of speech in the regulation of normal and abnormal behaviors.* New York: Liveright.

Maccoby, E. E., & Martin, J. A. (1983). Socialization in the context of the family: Parent–child interaction, In P. H. Mussen (Series Ed.) & E. M. Hetherington (Vol. Ed.), *Handbook of child psychology: Vol. 4. Socialization, personality and social development.* New York: Wiley.

Margen, S., and the Editors of the University of California at Berkeley Wellness Letter (1992). *The wellness encyclopedia of food and nutrition.* New York: Random House.

Martin, R. A., & Dobbin, J. P. (1988). Sense of humor, hassles and immunoglobulin A: Evidence for a stress-moderating effect of humor. *International Journal of Psychiatry, 18*, 93–105.

Maslow, A. H. (1964). *Religions, values, and peak experiences.* Columbus, OH: Ohio State University Press.

McCann, I. L., & Holmes, D. S. (1984). Influence of aerobic exercise on depression. *Journal of Personality and Social Psychology, 46*, 1142–1147.

McCarthy, B. (1987). *The 4MAT system: Teaching to learning styles with right/left mode techniques.* Barrington, IL: Excel.

McCranie, E. W., Lambert, V., & Lambert, C. (1987). Work stress, hardiness, and burnout among hospital staff nurses. *Nursing Research, 36*, 374–378.

McGhee, P. E. (1988). The role of humor in enhancing children's development and adjustment: Chapter commentary. *Journal of Children in Contemporary Society, 20*, 249–274.

Meichenbaum, D. (1985). *Stress inoculation training.* New York: Pergamon Press.

Miller, S. M. (1991). *The school book.* New York: St. Martin's Press.

Minskoff, E. H. (1980a). Teaching approach for developing nonverbal communication skills in students with social deficits: Part I. *Journal of Learning Disabilities, 13*, 118–124.

Minskoff, E. H. (1980b). Teaching approach for developing nonverbal communication skills in students with social deficits: Part II. *Journal of Learning Disabilities, 13*, 203–208.

Mischel, W. (1983). Delay of gratification as process and as person variable in development. In D. Magnusson & V. L. Allen (Eds.), *Human development: An interactional perspective.* New York: Academic Press.

Moskovitz, S. (1983). *Love despite hate: Child survivors of the Holocaust and their adult lives.* New York: Schocken Books.

Moyer, D. M. (1974). The development of children's ability to recognize and express facially posed emotions. Unpublished doctoral dissertation, Ohio State University.

Murdock, M. (1987). *Spinning inward.* New York: Shambhala.

Murphy, L., & Moriarty, A. (1976). *Vulnerability, coping and growth from infancy to adolescence.* New Haven, CT: Yale University Press.

Neill, A. S. (1977). *Summerhill: A radical approach to child rearing.* New York: Pocket Books.

Nelsen, J. (1987). *Positive discipline.* New York: Ballantine Books.

Okun, M., Zautra, A. J., & Robinson, S. E. (1988). Hardiness and health among women with rheumatoid arthritis. *Personality and Individual Differences, 9,* 101–107.

Paivio, A. (1975). Perceptual comparison through the mind's eye. *Memory and Cognition, 3,* 635–647.

Patterson, G. R. (1982). *Coercive family process.* Eugene, OR: Castalia Press.

Pellowski, A. (1987). *The family story-telling handbook.* New York: Macmillan.

Perkins, K. A., Dubbert, P. M., Martin, J. L., Faulstich, M. C., & Harris, J. K. (1986). Cardiovascular reactivity to psychological stress in aerobically trained versus untrained mild hypertensives and normotensives. *Health Psychology, 5,* 407–421.

Piaget, J. (1960). *The child's conception of the world.* London: Routledge.

Piaget, J. (1965). *The moral judgment of the child.* New York: Free Press. (Original work published 1932)

Plomin, R. (1989). Environment and genes: Determinants of behavior. *American Psychologist, 44,* 105–111.

Prerost, F. J. (1989). Intervening during a crisis of life transitions: Promoting a sense of humor as a stress moderator. *Counseling Psychology Quarterly, 2,* 474–480.

Quigley, L. F. (1959). *The blind man and the elephant: An old tale from the land of India.* New York: Charles Scribner's Sons.

Rapp, D. (1991). *Is this your child?* New York: Morrow.

Reynolds, S. B. (1984). Biofeedback, relaxation training and music: Homeostasis for coping with stress. *Biofeedback and Self-Regulation, 9,* 169–179.

Robson, L. (1983). *Beloved fairy tales.* London: Christensen Press.

Rogers, C. R. (1942). *Counseling and psychotherapy.* Boston: Houghton Mifflin.

Roth, D. L., & Holmes, D. S. (1985). Influence of physical fitness in deterring the impact of stressful events on physical and psychological health. *Psychosomatic Medicine, 47,* 164–173.

Rotter, J. B. (1966). Generalized expectancies for internal versus external control of reinforcement. *Psychological Monographs, 80* (Whole no. 609).

Rutter, M. (1979). Maternal deprivation 1972–1978: New findings, new concepts, new approaches. *Child Development, 50,* 283–305.

Sapon-Shevin, M. (1986). Teaching cooperation. In G. Cartledge & J. Milburn (Eds.), *Teaching social skills to children: Innovative approaches* (2d ed.). Needham Heights, MA: Allyn and Bacon.

Sarbin, T. R. (1986). The narrative as a root metaphor for psychology. In T. R. Sarbin (Ed.), *Narrative psychology: The storied nature of human conduct.* New York: Praeger.

Satir, V. (1972). *Peoplemaking.* Palo Alto, CA: Science and Behavior Books.

Scheff, T. J. (1975). *Labeling madness.* Englewood Cliffs, NJ: Prentice-Hall.

Schunk, D. H. (1984). Self-efficacy perspective on achievement behavior. *Educational Psychologist, 19,* 48–58.

Selman, R. L. (1980). *The growth of interpersonal understanding.* New York: Academic Press.

Selman, R. L., & Jasquatte, D. (1978). Stability and oscillation in interpersonal awareness: A clinical-developmental analysis. In C. B. Keasy (Ed.), The XXV Nebraska Symposium on Motivation. Lincoln: The University of Nebraska Press.

Selye, H. (1956). *The stress of life.* New York: McGraw-Hill.

Sharmat, M. (1977). *I don't care.* New York: Macmillan.

Shatz, C. U. (1983). Social cognition. In P. H. Mussen (Ed.) *Handbook of child psychology: Vol. 3. Cognitive development.* New York: Wiley.

Smith, C. N. (1990). *From wonder to wisdom: Using stories to help children grow.* New York: Plume.

Smith, L. (1976). *Improving your child's behavior chemistry.* Englewood Cliffs, NJ: Prentice-Hall.

Spivack, G., Platt, J. J., & Shure, M. B. (1976). *The problem-solving approach to adjustment.* San Francisco: Jossey-Bass.

Spivack, G., & Shure, M. B. (1974). *Social adjustment of young children.* San Francisco: Jossey-Bass.

Spring, B., Chiodo, J., & Brown, D. J. (1987). Carbohydrates, tryptophan, and behavior: A methodological review. *Psychological Bulletin, 102,* 234–256.

Sternberg, R. J. (1985). Who's intelligent? *Psychology Today, 3,* 30–39.

Stroebel, C. (1983). *QR: The quieting reflex.* New York: Berkley Books.

Stroebel, E., & Stroebel, C. (1984). The quieting reflex: A psychophysiologic approach for helping children deal with healthy and unhealthy stress. In J. Humphrey (Ed.), *Stress in Childhood.* New York: AMS Press.

Taylor, S. E. (1991). *Health psychology.* New York: McGraw-Hill.

Thomas, A., & Chess, S. (1977). *Temperament and development.* New York: Brunner/Mazel.

Trower, D. (1980). Situational analysis of the components and processes of behavior of socially skilled and unskilled patients. *Journal of Consulting and Clinical Psychology, 3,* 327–339.

Tucker, D. M. (1981). Lateral brain function, emotion and conceptualization. *Psychological Bulletin, 89,* 19–46.

Viorst, J. (1972). *Alexander and the terrible, horrible, no good, very bad day.* New York: Macmillan.

Vitz, P. C. (1990). The use of stories in moral development. *American Psychologist, 45,* 709–720.

Warner, S. L. (1991). Humor: A coping response for student nurses. *Archives of Psychiatric Nursing, 5,* 10–16.

Waters, M. P. (1990). The silent lobby. In L. Alexander et al. (Eds.), *The big book of peace* (pp. 69–82). New York: Dutton Children's Books.

Waters, V. (1982). Therapies for children: Rational-emotive therapy. In C. P. Reynolds & T. B. Gutkin (Eds.), *Handbook of school psychology*. New York: Wiley.

Weinberg, R. S., Gould, D., & Jackson, A. (1979). Expectations and performance. *Journal of Sports Psychology, 1*, 320–332.

Werner, E. E. (1984). Resilient children. *Young Children*. Nov., 68–72.

Werner, E. E., & Smith, R. S. (1982). *Vulnerable, but invincible: A longitudinal study of resilient children and youth*. New York: McGraw-Hill.

Williams, T. H., & Handford, E. G. (1986). Television and other leisure activities. In T. H. Williams (Ed.), *The impact of television: A natural experiment in three communities*. Orlando, FL: Academic Press.

Wolpe, J. (1958). *Psychotherapy by reciprocal inhibition*. Stanford, CA: Stanford University Press.

Wurtman, R. J., & Wurtman, J. (1989). Carbohydrates and depression. *Scientific American*, Jan., 68–75.

Yolen, J. (1981). *Tough magic: Fantasy, faerie and folklore in the literature of childhood*. New York: Philomel Books.

Zolotow, C. (1968). *My friend John*. New York: Harper & Row.

Zolotow, C. (1971). *A father like that*. New York: Harper & Row.

Appendix 1

Suggested Readings

Attention Deficit Disorder

Barkley, R. *Hyperactive Children*. New York: Guilford Press, 1991.
Ingersoll, B. *Your Hyperactive Child: A Parent's Guide to Coping with Attention Deficit Disorder*. New York: Doubleday, 1988.
Parker, H. C. *The ADD Hyperactivity Workbook for Parents, Teachers, and Kids*. Plantation, FL: Impact Publications, 1989.
Silver, L. *The Misunderstood Child*. New York: McGraw-Hill, 1984.
Wender, P. *The Hyperactive Child, Adolescent and Adult*. New York: Oxford University Press, 1987.

Learning Disabilities

McWhirter, J. *The Learning Disabled Child: A School and Family Concern*. Lanham, MD: University Press of America, 1988.
Osman, B. *Learning Disabilities: A Family Affair*. New York: Random House, 1979.

Gifted and Talented

Dunn, R., K. Dunn, & D. Treffinger. *Bringing Out the Giftedness in Your Child*. New York: Wiley, 1992.

For various publications contact the following organizations:

American Association for Gifted Children
15 Gramercy Park South
New York, NY 10003
(212) 473-4266

National Association for Gifted Children
5100 North Edgewood Dr.
St. Paul, MN 55112
(612) 784-3475

United States Department of Education
Division of the Gifted
Education Building
Washington, DC 20208-5461

Allergies

Rapp, D. *Is This Your Child?* New York: Morrow, 1991.

Parenting

Dodson, F. *How to Parent.* New York: Signet, 1971.
Faber, A. & E. Mazlish. *How to Talk So Kids Will Listen and Listen So Kids Will Talk.* New York: Avon Books, 1980.
Ginott, H. *Between Parent and Child.* New York: Avon Books, 1969.
Ginott, H. *Between Parent and Teenager.* New York: Avon Books, 1971.
Glenn, H. S. & J. Nelsen. *Raising a Self-Reliant Child in a Self-Indulgent World.* Rocklin, CA: Prima Publishing and Communication, 1980.
Gordon, T. *PET in Action.* New York: Wyden, 1976.
Hayes, E. *Why Good Parents Have Bad Kids.* New York: Doubleday, 1989.

Miller, S. M. *The School Book*. New York: St. Martin's Press, 1991.

Nelsen, J. *Positive Discipline*. New York: Ballantine Books, 1987.

Windell, J. *Discipline: A Sourcebook of 50 Failsafe Techniques for Parents*. New York: Macmillan, 1991.

Normal Development

Schroeder, B. A. *Human Growth and Development*. New York: West, 1992.

Appendix 2

Sample Behavioral Contract

For the period ___June 2, 1993___ , to ___June 16, 1993___ , the following agreement is in effect:

Parental expectation stated in objective terms:

Consequences

1. Katie will make sure her bed is made by 10 A.M. each day.

   Fifty cents will be given to Katie for each day bed is made by 10 A.M. If bed is not made by 10 A.M., Katie forfeits the 50 cents. Her sister will be given the opportunity to earn the 50 cents by making her bed.

2. Katie will pick up all dirty clothes from the floor in her room and keep her desk neat and orderly.

   Fifty cents will be given to Katie for each day her room is neat and orderly.

3. Katie will refrain from verbally abusive behavior when she does not get her way.

   Katie will have a half hour of phone privileges each day there is an absence of verbally abusive behavior.

**Child's expectation of parents
and other adults:**

Consequences

1. Mr. and Mrs. Tofu agree not to continually nag Katie about doing extra reading.

Katie agrees to read the Week in Review section of the *New York Times* Sunday paper.

2. Mr. and Mrs. Tofu agree to keep getting Katie to soccer practice and games.

Katie agrees to help out with dinner, dishes, and preparation.

3. Mr. and Mrs. Tofu agree to stop bugging Katie when she is in a bad mood. They agree to allow Katie time to defuse before speaking to them.

Katie agrees to discuss the problem with her parents within 24 hours of the bad mood. She further agrees to tell her parents in a polite way that she needs time to herself before blowing up.

Parent's Signature _____

Child's Signature _____

Appendix 3

Stories with Resilient Themes

3.1. Accepting Oneself

Preschool

Frandsen, Karen. *Michael's New Haircut*. Chicago: Children's, 1986.

Self-conscious about his new haircut, Michael leaves his hat on all day. When the hat finally does come off, his friends do not even notice he has had a haircut.

Ginsburg, Mirra. *The Chick and the Duckling*. New York: Macmillan, 1972.

A little chick imitates the behaviors of a duckling until the chick realizes he cannot swim like the duckling and must go his separate way.

This list of books was compiled by Tall Tails (Cheryl Cufari), 55 Bedford Drive, Whitesboro, NY 13492.

Kasza, Keiko. *Pig's Picnic*. New York: Putnam, 1988.

A pig is not recognized by his special friends when they go on a picnic because of all the dressing up he does before going.

Leaf, Munro. *The Story of Ferdinand*. New York: Viking, 1936.

A little bull is happiest smelling flowers rather than fighting in the bullring.

Lionni, Leo. *The Biggest House in the World*. New York: Pantheon, 1968.

A snail father advises his son to keep his own shell house after he tells a story of the misfortunes that befall a snail that grows a large, spectacular house.

Peet, Bill. *The Spooky Tail of Prewitt Peacock*. Boston: Houghton Mifflin, 1973.

Prewitt is anxious to produce a bounty of tail feathers. When he does, they grow out of control. After much ridicule, he gathers respect when he uses his tail to save the day.

Grades K–2

Brown, Marc. *Arthur's Nose*. New York: Atlantic Monthly Press, 1976.

Arthur tries to change the look of his nose until he learns to be happy with his own look.

Brown, Marc. *Arthur's Eyes*. New York: Atlantic Monthly Press, 1979.

Although his friends tease him about needing glasses, Arthur learns to wear them proudly.

Freeman, Don. *Dandelion*. New York: Viking, 1964.

After dressing up for a party, a lion is not recognized by his friends and therefore not allowed admittance.

Koda-Callan, Elizabeth. *The Magic Locket*. New York: Workman, 1988.

A little girl has a hard time doing things right until her aunt gives her a "magic locket." Wearing it seems to bring her success when, in reality, developing a belief in herself is the true reason for it.

Sharmat, Marjorie. *What Are We Going to Do About Andrew?* New York: Macmillan, 1988.

Andrew can change himself into a hippopotamus, and his family learns to adjust to his new power.

Sheehan, Patty. *Kylie's Song*. Santa Barbara, CA: Advocacy Press, 1988.

Kylie the Koala can sing—a most unusual talent for such an animal. This brings scorn from her friends until one day she is named the best singer. Her friends suddenly change their attitude and gain understanding.

Grades 2–4

Blume, Judy. *Freckle Juice*. New York: Dell, 1971.

Andrew·wants to have freckles so badly that he buys a secret recipe in order to produce them. After much agony over the concoction, he finally learns that he is fine just the way he is.

dePaola, Tomie. *The Legend of the Indian Paintbrush*. New York: Putnam, 1988.

Little Gopher will never be a brave Indian warrior because he is so small. He uses his gift of painting instead to record his people's history and in the end leaves the legacy of the Indian paintbrush flower.

Estes, Eleanor. *The Hundred Dresses*. San Diego: Harcourt Brace Jovanovich, 1974.

> To feel important in the eyes of her classmates, a little girl tells them she has a large wardrobe when in reality the dresses are only drawings.

McDermott, Gerald. *The Stonecutter*. New York: Viking, 1975.

> Although he tries living his life as a variety of powerful forces, both human and natural, the stonecutter realizes he enjoys his original role best.

O'Shaughnessy, Ellen. *Somebody Called Me a Retard Today and My Heart Felt Sad*. New York: Walker, 1992.

> Written from the viewpoint of a mentally handicapped person, moving reflections are given about name-calling.

Palmer, Pat. *Liking Myself*. San Luis Obispo, CA: Impact Publishers, 1977.

> Introduces the concepts and meaning of feelings, self-esteem, and assertiveness.

Grades 4–6

Blume, Judy. *Are You There, God? It's Me, Margaret*. New York: Macmillan, 1982.

> Margaret approaches adolescence with many questions that she forwards in a humorous way to God for the answers. The resolutions actually occur when nature takes its course.

Kaufman, Gershen, and Lev Raphael. *Stick Up for Yourself! Every Kid's Guide to Personal Power and Positive Self-Esteem*. Minneapolis: Free Spirit, 1990.

> Discusses ways children can solve problems and make choices using positives approaches.

Little, Jean. *From Anna*. New York: Harper & Row, 1972.

Anna moves with her family from Germany to Canada prior to World War II. She earns a place of esteem in her family and new school by trying hard and doing her best.

Little, Jean. *Different Dragons*. New York: Viking, 1986.

Ben is not sure he wants to visit his aunt because he is afraid of so many things, including dogs. His aunt presents him with a Labrador retriever and proceeds to laugh at Ben's fears until she discovers one of her own.

Maynes, Steven. *Be a Perfect ＼Person in Just Three Days*. Boston: Houghton Mifflin, 1982.

A young boy decides he can be perfect in three days. All he has to do is follow the directions in a book.

Wallace, Bill. *Ferret in the Bedroom, Lizards in the Fridge*. New York: Holiday House, 1986.

Elizabeth's father is a zoologist; consequently, the family home serves as a menagerie for his work-related research. When Elizabeth runs for class president, she is convinced her low popularity is due to the animals. Only after her father grants her request to remove the creatures does she learn what is important to her and the qualities of true friendship.

Grades 6–9

Byars, Betsy. *The Pinballs*. New York: Harper Collins, 1987.

Three lonely foster children learn to care about themselves and each other.

Byars, Betsy. *Bingo Brown and the Language of Love*. New York: Viking, 1989.

Bingo realizes he must undergo some trials and tribulations before growing up.

Paterson, Katherine. *The Great Gilly Hopkins*. New York: Harper-Collins, 1978.

> An 11-year-old foster child tries to cope with her needs and fears. Only after she learns to accept her own situation does she open up to those trying to help her.

Rostkowski, Margaret. *After the Dancing Days*. New York: Harper & Row, 1986.

> A young girl befriends a disfigured soldier after World War I and provides him the fortitude to regain his self-respect.

Voight, Cynthia. *Izzy, Willy Nilly*. New York: Fawcett, 1987.

> A beautiful girl loses a leg as the aftermath of a car accident involving alcohol and learns to adjust to her life thereafter.

Wojciechowska, Maia. *Shadow of a Bull*. New York: Atheneum, 1964.

> The son of a famous bullfighter decides that he wants a different career and must tell his father of this decision.

3.2. Challenge/Survival

Preschool

Graham, Margaret. *Benjy's Boat Trip*. New York: HarperCollins, 1977.

> When his family goes on a vacation and leaves him behind, Benjy, a dog, is determined to find them.

Martin, Bill, and John Archambault. *Ghost-Eye Tree*. New York: Holt, 1985.

> A brother and sister are sent out to fetch a pail of milk on a spooky night.

Martin, Charles. *Island Rescue*. New York: Greenwillow, 1985.

When a group of children go on a picnic, a girl breaks her leg and has to be rescued.

Parnall, Peter. *Stuffer*. New York: Macmillan, 1992.

Stuffer, a horse, is raised by a girl who lavishes him with love. When she grows up, he is taken to another farm only to find himself mistreated. He survives this, however, and is adopted again by a little girl who restores his sense of being loved.

Purdy, Carol. *Iva Dunnit and the Big Wind*. New York: Dial, 1988.

Battling the big wind of a tornado, Iva nearly loses her fight until her children come to the rescue.

Scheller, Melanie. *My Grandfather's Hat*. New York: Macmillan, 1992.

A little boy has many good times with his grandfather. These memories, as well as his grandfather's special hat, which his grandmother presents to him, provide the strength he needs to accept his grandfather's death.

Grades K–2

Aliki. *We Are Best Friends*. New York: Greenwillow, 1982.

Two friends are separated when one moves away, and each must learn how to make new friends.

Aliki. *The Two of Them*. New York: Greenwillow, 1984.

A child and her grandfather share many fun times and special moments until his death, a loss with which she must learn to cope.

Burningham, John. *Grandpa*. New York: Crown, 1985.

A little girl and her grandfather share very special moments.

Christiansen, Candace. *Calico and Tin Horns*. New York: Dial, 1992.

Hannah's parents think that she is too young to help during the Revolutionary War, but she proves otherwise.

Sharmat, Marjorie. *Big, Fat, Enormous Lie*. New York: Four Winds, 1984.

A little girl tells a lie and lives with the guilt until she finally confesses.

Tejima. *Fox's Dream*. New York: Philomel Books, 1987.

A lonely fox wandering through the winter forest reflects on his long-lost family, his hunger, and the coming of spring. In the midst of sadness a vixen appears and brings hope of companionship to the fox.

Grades 2–4

Brenner, Barbara. *Wagon Wheels*. New York: HarperCollins, 1984.

After the Civil War a black family endures hardships traveling to Kansas to settle on the frontier under the Homestead Act.

Jakes, John. *Susanna of the Alamo: A True Story*. San Diego: Harcourt Brace Jovanovich, 1986.

One of the few survivors in the Battle of the Alamo, Susanna Dickinson was the one to inform Sam Houston of the outcome.

Ness, Evaline. *Sam Bangs, and Mooshine*. New York: Holt, 1966.

A small girl learns a near-tragic lesson in distinguishing fact from fantasy.

Rockwell, Thomas. *How to Eat Fried Worms*. New York: Watts, 1973.

Billy bets his friends he can eat worms and has to go through with it.

Stevens, Carla. *Anna, Grandpa and the Big Storm*. Boston: Houghton Mifflin, 1982.

A family lives through the 1888 blizzard that hits New York City.

Zelinsky, Paul O. (Reteller). *Hansel and Gretel*. New York: Putnam, 1985.

The Grimm fairy tale about a brother and sister who find their way back to their cottage after being held captive by a witch.

Grades 4–6

Byars, Betsy. *Trouble River*. New York: Viking, 1969.

Dewey has placed much effort into building a raft. When his family's frontier cabin is threatened, he uses the raft to transport himself and his grandmother to safety.

Byars, Betsy. *The 18th Emergency*. New York: Puffin, 1981.

When the toughest boy in town swears to kill him, 12-year-old Mouse finds little help from friends and must prepare alone.

Conrad, Pam. *Prairie Songs*. New York: HarperCollins, 1985.

Louise and her frontier family have survived on the prairie; now they share their survival skills with others.

George, Jean. *My Side of the Mountain*. New York: Dutton, 1988.

A boy leaves home and establishes a new one in the hollow of a tree in the Catskill Mountains. There he learns how to live by using the resources nature provides for food and clothing.

Paulsen, Gary. *The River*. New York: Doubleday, 1991.

Brian, a teenage boy, is commissioned by a magazine publisher to simulate a survival experience. Although originally contrived for writing purposes, the situation becomes a life-threatening episode. (This is a sequel to Paulsen's *Hatchet*, for Grades 6–9.)

Wallace, Bill. *Danger on Panther Peak*. New York: Holiday House, 1985.

When his grandfather is injured in an accident, Tom leaves the family ranch to summon help despite the fact that a panther has been noticed in the area. Tom indeed spots the wild animal and defends himself and his horse in a heroic encounter.

Grades 6–9

Conrad, Pam. *What I Did for Roman*. New York: Harper & Row, 1987.

While her mother is on her honeymoon, Darcie works in the restaurant of the city zoo. There she meets Roman, a handsome, intriguing zoo worker. As the summer progresses, Darcie learns about the father she never knew, as well as more about Roman. As Roman reveals his inner thoughts about his destiny, which ultimately ends with his committing suicide, Darcie strengthens her will to live and the relationship with her mother.

Holman, Felice. *Slake's Limbo*. New York: Macmillan, 1974.

Hounded by fears and misfortunes, Aremis Slake flees into New York City's subway tunnels to escape. He eventually emerges much stronger as a result of his experience.

Lord, Christa. *Shadow of the Wall*. New York: Greenwillow, 1989.

Living in the Warsaw ghetto during World War II, Misha is the only one who can sneak outside the wall to gather food for his two sisters and ill mother.

Mazer, Harry. *Snow Bound*. New York: Delacorte Press, 1973.

Tony decides to take his mother's car and run away. After he picks up a hitchhiker, his car crashes during a severe snowstorm, and the two are stranded. They learn to cooperate and improvise in order to survive.

Paulsen, Gary. *Hatchet*. New York: Macmillan, 1987.

Brian has only his hatchet to help him survive in the Canadian wilderness after a plane crash.

Paulsen, Gary. *Voyage of the Frog*. New York: Orchard Books, 1989.

David sails out on the water only to have a storm occur and destroy his boat. He must survive many days until help arrives.

3.3. Commitment

Preschool

Campbell, Alison, and Julia Barton. *Are You Asleep, Rabbit?* New York: Puffin Books, 1990.

One winter night Donald brings his pet rabbit indoors to sleep. Donald provides all the nurturing care necessary to make the rabbit happy and content before settling down to sleep himself.

Carle, Eric. *The Very Busy Spider*. New York: Philomel Books, 1984.

A spider persists in completing his web even though other farm animals try to divert him.

Freeman, Don. *Corduroy*. New York: Viking, 1968.

A little girl takes home a stuffed bear from the store and takes excellent care of him.

Kraus, Ruth. *The Carrot Seed*. New York: HarperCollins, 1989.

A little boy exhibits faith that the carrot seed he plants will grow and produce.

Piper, Walter. *The Little Engine That Could*. New York: Putnam, 1988.

A small, weak engine believes in himself well enough to pull a broken-down train into town so its cargo may be delivered on time.

Williams, Vera. *A Chair for My Mother*. New York: Greenwillow, 1982.

After a fire destroys all of their furniture, a grandmother, daughter, and granddaughter save all of their coins to buy an armchair.

Grades K–2

Coville, Bruce and Katherine Coville. *The Foolish Giant*. New York: Lippincott, 1978.

Although Harry is not a very intelligent giant, he loves the people in his village. They ask him to leave when he pushes his helpful but clumsy ways too far only to beg him to return when a wizard threatens them with his magic spells.

dePaola, Tomie. *The Art Lesson*. New York: Putnam, 1989.

A fictitious account of a renowned author-illustrator's interests and perseverance as an artist in his primary school years.

Isadora, Rachael. *Ben's Trumpet*. New York: Morrow, 1991.

Ben wants to be a trumpeter. One day a musician discovers his talent and helps him with his dream.

Lionni, Leo. *Matthew's Dream*. New York: Knopf, 1991.

A visit to an art museum inspires a little mouse to become an artist.

Palocco, Patricia. *Chicken Sunday*. New York: Philomel Books, 1992.

A little girl befriends two girls and their grandmother. The grandmother does many wonderful things for the children, and the children in turn work hard to earn money to buy her a special gift.

Steig, William. *Brave Irene*. New York: Farrar, Straus & Giroux, 1986.

A little girl overcomes great obstacles in order to deliver to a princess in time for the dance that evening a gown her mother has made.

Grades 2–4

Anderson, David. *What You Can See, You Can Be!* Marina del Rey, CA: DeVorss, 1988.

This book emphasizes the value of forming mental images of one's goals and of keeping the images in one's thoughts in order to increase the chances of achieving one's goals.

Booth, Barbara. *Mandy*. New York: Lothrop Lee and Shepard, 1991.

Mandy, who is deaf, and her grandmother take a walk together. Later Grandmother realizes her precious locket is missing. Although a severe storm has begun. Mandy goes out into the night determined to find the necklace.

Donegan-Johnson, Ann. *The Story of Harriet Tubman*. La Jolla, CA: Value Communications, 1979.

The life and work of Harriet Tubman, including the exhaustive efforts she devoted to the slaves in their escape out of the South to freedom via the Underground Railroad, is detailed.

Golenbock, Peter. *Teammates*. San Diego: Harcourt Brace Jovanovich, 1990.

This book describes the perseverance exhibited by Jackie Robinson during the 1940s that enabled him to enter major league baseball despite tremendous racial prejudice.

Jasmine, Cario. *Our Brother Has Down's Syndrome*. Buffalo: Firefly Books, 1985.

Siblings compassionately describe the behavior of their mentally handicapped brother and the special care he requires from the family.

Peet, Bill. *Chester the Worldly Pig*. Boston: Houghton Mifflin, 1965.

Chester wants to be more than a pig. After many failed attempts, his fame is acquired when he becomes an exhibit in a sideshow because of the unique design the spots on his body make.

Grades 4–6

Aiello, Barbara. *Friends for Life*. Frederick, MD: Twenty-First Century Books, 1988.

The fifth-grade video club's sponsor reveals she has AIDS. A variety of reactions are expressed by club members, but in the end they remain loyal and supportive to her.

Gardiner, John. *Stone Fox*. New York: Thomas Y. Crowell, 1980.

Willy will do anything to earn money to pay the taxes owed on his grandfather's farm, including entering a highly competitive dogsled race.

McGraw, Eloise. *Moccasin Trail*. New York: Puffin, 1986.

Jim Keath has lived with the Crow Indians for six years when he is called to help his family. He has to prove his loyalty to his birth family in order to be one of them again.

Meltzer, Milton. *Mary McLeod Bethune: Voice of Black Hope*. New York: Viking, 1987.

Showing great strength and commitment throughout her life, Mary McLeod Bethune devoted herself to helping those in need.

North, Sterling. *The Wolfling*. New York: Scholastic, 1980.

A young boy raises a wolf pup to maturity.

O'Brien, Robert. *Mrs. Frisby and the Rats of NIMH*. New York: Macmillan, 1971.

Mrs. Frisby asks the Rats of NIMH to help with the dangerous action of moving her ill son from the path of the field plow.

Grades 6–9

Avi. *Wolf Rider*. New York: Bradbury Press, 1986.

Andy musters all of his ingenuity and courage in order to uncover the person who is threatening a college library worker.

Gies, Miep. *Anne Frank Remembered*. New York: Random House, 1987.

The author relates the story of how she helped hide Anne Frank and her family during the Nazi occupation of Holland.

Hudson, Jan. *Sweetgrass*. New York: Putnam, 1989.

A 15-year-old Blackfoot Plains Indian girl wants to prove to her father that she is able to handle responsibility. She has her chance when members of her family and tribe contract smallpox.

Lowry, Lois. *Number the Stars*. Boston: Houghton Mifflin, 1989.

Danish Christians devise a plan and risk their own safety in order to help Jewish friends escape to Sweden during World War II.

Morpurgo, Michael. *Waiting for Anya*. New York: Viking, 1990.

Jo and his older friend Benjamin help Jewish children escape German soldiers and endanger their own lives while leading them to safety from Vichy, France, into Spain during World War II.

Rawls, Wilson. *Where the Red Fern Grows*. New York: Doubleday, 1961.

A young boy earns money to pay for two dogs he so much wanted. After finally obtaining the dogs, he raises his pets to hunt for raccoons in a money-making endeavor he undertakes to help out his family.

3.4. Conflict Management

Preschool

Carle, Eric. *The Grouchy Ladybug*. New York: Thomas Y. Crowell, 1977.

A grouchy ladybug wants to fight many animals of varying sizes. They are willing, but she insists they are not big enough—until she meets a whale that tests her. She ends up back home eating happily.

Hazen, Barbara. *Gorilla Did It*. New York: Macmillan, 1988.

An imaginary gorilla is blamed for a little boy's messy room.

Lakin, Patricia. *Don't Touch My Room*. Boston: Little, Brown, 1985.

Aaron's "perfect room" is turned upside down by a baby brother. The brother remains a trial until he is old enough to become a companion.

Rey, H. A. *Curious George*. Boston: Houghton Mifflin, 1973.

George, the monkey, is very curious, a trait that leads him into all kinds of troublesome situations until he learns to finally put it to constructive use.

Robertus, Polly M. *The Dog Who Had Kittens*. New York: Holiday House, 1988.

Baxter, the basset hound, is being displaced by Eloise, the cat, who is about to deliver kittens. When Eloise leaves her newborn kittens, Baxter is the only one nearby when they cry out for comfort, and he finds a new sense of purpose.

Seuss, Dr. *The Cat in the Hat*. New York: Random House, 1957.

A brother and sister are left alone one rainy afternoon only to have their house turned upside down when the Cat in the Hat arrives to perk up a rather dreary day.

Grades K–2

Blaine, Marge. *The Terrible Thing That Happened at Our House*. New York: Macmillan, 1980.

A family must learn to cope and accept responsibility when their mother goes back to work outside the home.

Cherry, Lynne. *Great Kapok Tree: A Tale of the Amazon Rain Forest*. San Diego: Harcourt Brace Jovanovich, 1990.

Many animals living in the Brazilian rain forest try to convince a man's ax of the importance of leaving the trees uncut.

Jones, Rebecca. *Matthew and Tilly*. New York: Dutton, 1991.

Two neighborhood friends argue over a broken crayon but realize their friendship outweighs this conflict.

Sharmat, Marjorie. *Sometimes Mama and Papa Fight*. New York: Harper, 1980.

Two youngsters react to their parents' quarreling.

Stinson, Kathy. *Mom and Dad Don't Live Together Anymore*. Buffalo: Firefly Books, 1984.

A little girl tries to gain an understanding of what her parents' separation means and what will happen to her as a result.

Viorst, Judith. *I'll Fix Anthony*. New York: HarperCollins, 1988.

Anthony harasses his little brother, who does much thinking about what he could do for revenge.

Grades 2–4

Brown, Ruth. *The World That Jack Built*. New York: Dutton, 1991.

A cumulative text that reveals the damaging effect Jack's building project may have on his surroundings.

Cameron, Ann. *The Stories Julian Tells*. New York: Knopf, 1989.

A little boy relates stories about his everyday growing-up experiences, many of which also include his brother Huey.

Catling, Patrick. *The Chocolate Touch*. New York: Morrow, 1979.

A boy's wish comes true: everything he touches turns to chocolate. However, as time passes, this "gift" begins to interfere with his everyday life.

Dahl, Roald. *The Magic Finger*. New York: Harper & Row, 1966.

A family that enjoys hunting is surprised when they are turned into birds and become the hunted.

Lawlor, Laurie. *How to Survive Third Grade*. Niles, IL: Albert Whitman, 1988.

Ernest, an unpopular third grader, is an easy target for bullying. His self-confidence is bolstered, however, when he meets a friend and experiences success for the first time in his life.

MacLachlan, Patricia. *Seven Kisses in a Row*. New York: Harper-Collins, 1983.

Aunt Evelyn and Uncle Elliot have much to learn about child rearing when they come to Emma and Zach's house to babysit for a week. The two children are ready and willing to teach them.

Grades 4–6

Bauer, Marion. *On My Honor*. New York: Clarion Books, 1986.

Joel dares Tony, a nonswimmer, to race to the river sandbar. A strong current pulls Tony under, and he drowns. Joel must live with the guilt and aftermath of being present and somewhat responsible for his friend's death.

Giff, Patricia Reilly. *Rat Teeth*. New York: Dell Publishing, 1984.

After his parents separate, Cliffie finds himself adjusting to a new neighborhood and a new school and shuttling back and forth between his parents' homes. Because of his protruding teeth he is an easy target for taunting, which makes settling in difficult. He discovers that new niches may eventually be found when one is patient and persistent.

Konigsburg, E. L. *From the Mixed-Up Files of Mrs. Basil E. Frankweiler*. New York: Dell, 1977.

The story of the escapades of Claudia and her brother James at the Metropolitan Museum of Art, where they stay when they decide to run away from home.

Kudlinski, Kathleen. *Hero Over There: A Story of World War I*. New York: Viking, 1990.

> While his father and brother fight in World War I, a young boy is responsible for looking after his ill mother and sister.

Mayerson, Evelyn. *The Cat Who Escaped from Steerage*. New York: Scribner, 1990.

> Chanah is emigrating with his family to America from Poland. They must deal with the fact that a cousin who is deaf and cannot speak may be sent back to Poland when they reach Ellis Island. The family also meets many survival challenges on the boat as they travel to their new home.

Robinson, Barbara. *The Best Christmas Pageant Ever*. New York: Harper & Row, 1988.

> The Herdman children want to be a part of the annual church Christmas pageant, and the regular members must do their best to cope with their unruly presence.

Grades 6–9

Avi. *Blue Heron*. New York: Bradbury Press, 1992.

> Maggie looks forward to her visit during the month of August with her father, stepmother, and their new baby. When she arrives, she realizes that the marriage is unraveling, and she must cope with the consequences.

Collier, James Lincoln, and Christopher Collier. *The Bloody Country*. New York: Four Winds Press, 1976.

> During the time of the Revolutionary War, the Buck family, hoping for prosperity, move from Connecticut to a more fertile area in Pennsylvania. However, the native Pennamites begin to resent the newcomers and take militant action against them. Ben Buck has a difficult time understanding this threat to the family mill that has ground the grain for the area for a long time.

The tension builds until many attempt a dangerous journey back to Connecticut. Those that remain exhibit their determination and spirit to hold on to what has been accomplished by their hard work.

Conrad, Pam. *Holding Me Here*. New York: Harper & Row, 1986.

After Robin's parents divorce, she and her mother take in a boarder named Mary. Robin discovers Mary's diary, which reveals her past and present problems. In her efforts to help Mary, a tense situation develops and Robin's own confusion about her parents' divorce surfaces.

Leeder, Carolyn. *Shades of Gray*. New York: Macmillan, 1984.

After being orphaned as a result of the Civil War, Will Page is sent to live with his aunt and uncle, a man who refused to fight and whom Will and others consider a coward. As the story unfolds, Will learns the meaning of courage through his uncle's actions and comes to an understanding about war and people.

Siegel, Beatrice. *The Year They Walked*. New York: Macmillan, 1992.

This book examines the life of Rosa Parks by focusing on her role in the Montgomery bus boycott.

Wisler, G. Clifton. *Red Cap*. New York: Dutton, 1991.

A Yankee drummer boy is captured during the Civil War and sent to the Andersonville prison camp, where he must learn to cope with his imprisonment.

3.5.   Control

Preschool

Bingham, Mindy. *My Way Sally*. Santa Barbara, CA: Advocacy Press, 1988.

A foxhound decides to apply her leadership skills in such a way that the changes she creates allow everyone participating in games to win.

Cole, Joanna. *Bully Trouble*. New York: Random House, 1989.

A little boy figures out an acceptable way to outsmart the neighborhood bully.

Peet, Bill. *Pamela Camel*. Boston: Houghton Mifflin, 1984.

A dejected circus camel places her own life in danger in order to prevent a train crash.

Polette, Keith. *The Winter Duckling*. Saint Louis: Milliken, 1980.

One little duckling decides to stay north for the winter to experience snow but fails to prepare for his own survival.

Sendak, Maurice. *Where the Wild Things Are*. New York: Harper-Trophy, 1983.

Max leaves his warm home to enter the world of wild things, where he leads and controls their wild rumpus.

Stolz, Mary. *Storm in the Night*. New York: Harper & Row, 1988.

A boy weathers out a thunderstorm when his grandfather tells him a story.

Grades K–2

dePaola, Tomie. *Michael Bird Boy*. New York: Prentice-Hall, 1987.

When a black cloud pollutes the air around his house, Michael investigates the source.

Hoffman, Mary. *Amazing Grace*. New York: Dial, 1991.

Grace proves she can handle the lead in the school play even though her classmates challenge her attempt.

Simon, Norma. *I Was So Mad!* Chicago: Childrens, 1974.

Children catalog things that make them mad and learn that adults get angry, too.

Sondheimer, I. *The Boy Who Could Make His Mother Stop Yelling*. Fayetville, NY: Rainbow Press, 1982.

An emotionally frustrated mother learns from her son a way to make life a little happier.

Udry, Janice. *Let's Be Enemies*. New York: Harper, 1961.

John is tired of James's bossiness and decides to tell him so.

Wilhelm, Hans. *Tyrone the Horrible*. New York: Scholastic, 1988.

Boland extends dinosaur friendship to Tyrone and is thwarted until he discovers a way to outsmart Tyrone.

Grades 2–4

Hazen, Barbara. *Alone at Home*. New York: Macmillan, 1992.

When Amy's babysitter becomes ill, her parents agree to allow her to stay home by herself after school. She realizes this is harder than it originally seemed. Using sound judgment as situations arise, Amy manages to stay in control until her parents arrive home.

Madden, Don. *The Wartville Wizard*. New York: Macmillan, 1986.

An old man fights a town of litterbugs by sending each piece of trash back to the person who dropped it.

Palmer, Pat. *The Mouse, the Monster and Me*. San Luis Obispo, CA: Impact Publishers, 1977.

This story offers children strategies to develop a sense of personal rights and responsibilities.

Viorst, Judith. *If I Were in Charge of the World and Other Worries*. New York: Macmillan, 1984.

Humorous insights on the concerns children have about their world and beyond are given in poetry form.

Young, Ed. *Lon Po Po*. New York: Philomel Books, 1989.

Three Chinese children must form a plan to keep the big, bad wolf from eating them.

Zemach, Margot. *It Could Always Be Worse*. New York: Farrar, Straus & Giroux, 1976.

A poor man goes to his rabbi for advice when he can no longer tolerate the noise and confusion in his home.

Grades 4–6

Dahl, Roald. *George's Marvelous Medicine*. New York: Knopf, 1982.

George is afraid his grandmother is a witch and concocts some medicine to take care of her.

DeFelice, Cynthia. *The Strange Night Writing of Jessamine Colter*. New York: Macmillan, 1988.

Jessie, a calligrapher, serves as the town historian, and 16-year-old Callie becomes her apprentice. Jessie also experiences "feelings" that reveal the future before it happens. As the story unfolds, Jessie's strength is passed on to Callie, the daughter of an alcoholic mother, and Callie learns she must follow her goals and dreams to completion.

McClung, Robert M., and Hugh Glass. *Mountain Man*. New York: Morrow Junior Books, 1990.

A frontiersman, mauled by a grizzly and left for dead by his companions, must use all he knows about the wilderness in order to find his way to someone who might help him.

Miles, Betty. *The Real Me*. Marietta, GA: Camelot, 1976.

Barbara takes a stand in order to play a "boy's" sport and assume her brother's paper route.

Schwartz, Linda. *What Would You Do? A Kid's Guide to Tricky and Sticky Situations*. Santa Barbara, CA: Learning Weeks, 1991.

A guide for children outlining appropriate behavior for a wide variety of situations.

Spinelli, Jerry. *Maniac Magee*. Boston: Little, Brown, 1990.

After his parents die, Jeffrey Magee becomes a legend in the town by attempting feats that leave people in awe.

Grades 6–9

Auel, Jean. *Clan of the Cave Bear*. New York: Bantam, 1981.

A remarkable girl living in prehistoric times shows superior intelligence and development compared to the other members of her tribe.

Gaines, Ernest. *The Autobiography of Miss Jane Pittman*. New York: Dial, 1971.

The story of a black woman who took strong measures to fight prejudice during her lifetime.

LeGuin, Ursula. *The Tombs of Atuan*. New York: Macmillan, 1971.

Artha gains control of the ancient powers of the earth when she becomes a high priestess. (This is Book Two of the Earthsea Trilogy.)

McKinley, Robin. *The Hero and the Crown*. New York: Greenwillow, 1984.

Arien uses her ingenuity to overcome obstacles that stand between her and the crown that will prove her rightful heritage to her father's kingdom.

Paterson, Katherine. *Lyddie*. New York: Dutton, 1991.

Living in poverty and despair in Vermont, Lyddie is determined to win her independence by becoming a mill worker in Massachusetts.

Rodriguez, Consuelo. *Cesar Chavez*. Broomall, PA: Chelsea House, 1991.

A biography of the Mexican-American who led migrant farm workers in their fight for better working conditions.

3.6. Decision Making

Preschool

Brenner, Barbara. *Rosa and Marco and the Three Wishes*. New York: Bradbury Press, 1992.

While out fishing, Rosa and Marco catch a magical fish that grants them three wishes. When an argument ensues over using the wishes, they end up being wasted.

Cole, Joanna. *Bony-Legs*. New York: Four Winds, 1993.

While out on a walk, Sasha encounters a witch and must decide how to escape her grasp.

Keats, Ezra. *A Letter to Amy*. New York: Harper, 1968.

A boy faces a dilemma when he wishes to invite a girl to an all-boy party.

Lionni, Leo. *Fish Is Fish*. New York: Pantheon, 1970.

A fish learns from a frog how to take steps to be happy just being himself.

Lord, John, and Janet Burroway. *The Giant Jam Sandwich*. Boston: Houghton Mifflin, 1987.

An imaginary village deals with a wasp invasion by creating a giant, sticky jam sandwich.

Slobodkina, Esphyr. *Caps for Sale*. New York: HarperCollins, 1949.

A cap seller must find a way to regain his caps when monkeys steal them while he is napping.

Zolotow, Charlotte. *Mr. Rabbit and the Lovely Present*. New York: Harper & Row, 1962.

A little girl and Mr. Rabbit decide on the perfect gift for her mother.

Grades K–2

Burton, Virginia. *Mike Mulligan and His Steam Shovel*. Boston: Houghton Mifflin, 1947.

When modern machines replace his steam shovel, Mike finds a way to prove his piece of equipment is still useful.

Carrick, Donald. *Harald and the Giant Knight*. Boston: Houghton Mifflin, 1982.

Harald plans strategies to get even with knights who destroyed his family's farm.

Steig, William. *Dr. DeSoto*. New York: Farrar, Straus & Giroux, 1982.

Dr. DeSoto, a mouse dentist who does not normally treat animals who are threatening to mice, must make a big decision when a fox comes to him with a toothache.

Viorst, Judith. *Alexander Who Used to Be Rich Last Sunday*. New York: Atheneum, 1978.

Alexander describes all the various ways he spends his money.

Ward, Lynne. *The Biggest Bear*. Boston: Houghton Mifflin, 1952.

Johnny Orchard must decide how he is going to rid his house of the overgrown pet bear he has raised from a cub.

Wood, Audrey. *Heckedy Peg*. San Diego: Harcourt Brace Jovanovich, 1987.

When Heckedy Peg turns each of seven children into a particular food, their mother must decide the identity of each in order to save them from being eaten.

Grades 2–4

Cameron, Ann. *Most Beautiful Place in the World*. New York: Knopf, 1988.

Guatemalan boy must make right choices in his life in order to overcome his impoverished life-style.

Dalgliessch, Alice. *The Bears on Hemlock Mountain*. New York: Charles Scribner's Sons, 1952.

Upon encountering a bear when doing an errand for his mother, Johnny must use his ingenuity to remain safe.

Hest, Amy. *The Ring in the Window Seat*. New York: Scholastic, 1990.

Stella saves her money for a ring. Before buying it, however, she decides to put her earnings to use for a more important purpose.

Locker, Thomas. *The Boy Who Held Back the Sea*. New York: Dial, 1987.

When he notices water coming through the dike, a Dutch boy saves his village by making the decision to hold his finger in the hole until help arrives.

Galdone, Paul (Reteller and illustrator). *The Three Wishes*. New York: McGraw-Hill, 1961.

A poor man and his wife earn three magical wishes and waste them when they argue over how they should be spent.

White, E. B. *Charlotte's Web*. New York: HarperCollins, 1952.

A little girl and a spider named Charlotte use their ingenuity to save their friend Wilbur, a pig, from going to the slaughterhouse.

Grades 4–6

Babbitt, Natalie. *Knee-Knock Rise*. New York: Farrar, Straus & Giroux, 1975.

Egan investigates a strange moan he hears in the village he is visiting. When he discovers its source, he must decide if he will tell the townspeople and ruin a native superstition.

Babbitt, Natalie. *Tuck Everlasting*. New York: Farrar, Straus & Giroux, 1975.

The Tuck family drink from a magical spring and have life everlasting. A human comes upon this secret and must decide whether or not to have the same experience.

Berleth, Richard. *Samuel's Choice*. Morton Grove, IL: A. Whitman, 1990.

A 14-year-old slave faces a difficult choice when the American Revolution reaches his front door and he is the only one who can help.

Lunn, Janet. *The Root Cellar*. New York: Penguin, 1981.

Rose lives with relatives in an old house in Canada. She discovers a root cellar and is suddenly transported back to Civil War times. She must use her courage and strength to help save one of the friends she meets there.

Naylor, Phyllis. *Shiloh*. New York: Macmillan, 1991.

Knowing an abused dog lives on the property adjacent to his, Marty Preston takes measures to kidnap and protect the dog from such treatment despite his parents' wishes.

Walsh, Jill Paton. *The Green Book*. New York: Farrar, Straus & Giroux, 1982.

When a group of Britons leave the dying earth, children have to make good choices to safeguard a new colony.

Grades 6–9

Avi. *The True Confessions of Charlotte Doyle*. New York: Orchard Books, 1990.

Charlotte must use quick thinking when she is accused of murder aboard a ship transporting her home in 1832.

Conford, Ellen. *Genie with the Light Blue Hair*. New York: Bantam Books, 1989.

The decisions Jean makes with the genie she finds in a lamp do not turn out to be as wonderful as she thinks they should be.

Crew, Linda. *Children of the River*. New York: Delacorte, 1989.

Having escaped the fearful Khmer Rouge army, Sundara is torn between remaining faithful to her own people of Cambodia and assuming the culture of her new friends at the Oregon high school she now attends.

DeFelice, Cynthia. *Weasel*. New York: Macmillan, 1990.

In the Ohio Territory in 1839, Nathan struggles with the decision to kill a villain named Weasel despite his father's efforts to point out the futility of this act.

Henry, O. *The Gift of the Magi*. New York: Simon & Schuster, 1988.

A newly married man and woman each make a decision about sacrificing something precious to make the other happy.

Miklowitz, Gloria D. *Anything to Win*. New York: Delacorte, 1989.

A football player begins to wonder if his decision to take steroids is really the right way to fulfill his dream of stardom.

3.7. Exercise/Nutrition

Preschool

Berenstain, Stan, and Janice Berenstain. *The Berenstain Bears and Too Much Junk Food*. New York: Random House, 1985.

Mama Bear tries to convince her family they need to eat more nutritiously.

Carle, Eric. *The Very Hungry Caterpillar*. New York: Philomel Books, 1979.

A little caterpillar eats his way through many nutritious and some not so nutritious foods before he turns into a butterfly. This also serves as a counting book.

Ehlert, Lois. *Growing Vegetable Soup*. New York: Harcourt Brace Jovanovich, 1987.

A boy and his father cultivate a garden and then use the produce to make vegetable soup.

Schade, Charlene. *Move with Me One, Two, Three*. San Diego: Exer Fun Publishers, 1988.

Blends concepts of movement, numbers, and animals with music. Such concepts are reinforced while children are exercising.

Seuss, Dr. *Green Eggs and Ham*. New York: Random House, 1960.

Horrible-looking green eggs cannot possibly taste good, or can they?

Sharmat, Mitchell. *Gregory the Terrible Eater*. New York: Four Winds, 1980.

Gregory, a little goat, is a terrible eater because he shuns the coats and shoes his parents encourage him to eat and prefers nutritious fruits and vegetables.

Grades K–2

Aliki. *Keep Your Mouth Closed, Dear*. New York: Dial, 1966.

Each time he opens his mouth, an alligator devours whatever happens to be in his way regardless of its nutritional value.

Ehlert, Lois. *Eating the Alphabet*. New York: Harcourt Brace Jovanovich, 1989.

A display of nutritious fruits and vegetables illustrates letters of the alphabet.

Hoban, Lillian. *Bread and Jam for Frances*. New York: Harper, 1965.

Frances loves bread and jam but thinks it a bit much after eating it for six meals in two days.

Moncure, Jane. *The Healthkin Food Train*. Mankato, MN: Child World, 1982.

Healthy foods are discussed.

Munsch, Robert. *Something Good*. Buffalo: Firefly Books, 1990.

Three children and their father disagree as to what would be good to place in the shopping cart.

Rhodes, Janis. *Nutrition Mission*. Carthage, IL: Good Apple, 1982.

The usefulness of eating wisely is discussed.

Grades 2–4

Austin, Trina K. *All Aboard the S.S. Nutrient*. Laguna Beach, CA: Trinas Press, 1986.

Discusses the importance of nutrition to the body's health.

Cole, Joanna. *The Magic School Bus Inside the Human Body*. New York: Scholastic, 1988.

Ms. Frizzle takes her entire class on a magical school bus ride through the human body, and the children gain an understanding of how the body works when it is healthy.

Hamm, Anita M. *Lisa in Sugarland: A Child's Book on Nutrition to Be Digested Before Eating*. Milwaukee, OR: Samara Publishing, 1978.

Discusses the importance of nutrition to the body's health.

Sinykin, Sheri. *Come Out, Come Out Wherever You Are*. Center City, MN: Hazelden, 1990.

Alexander needs to lose weight and learns to express his feelings while adopting good eating habits.

Smith, Robert. *Jelly Belly*. New York: Yearling, 1981.

Ned cannot stop eating although he keeps growing wider. This treats the phenomenon of the self-image that centers around an overweight problem in a humorous way.

Grades 4–6

Adams, Marylou. *Brighten Up at Breakfast: Helpful Tips for Heavenly Bodies*. Freeland, WA: Starbright, 1981.

Outlines good eating habits that keep the body healthy.

American Health Foundation Staff. *Great Meals, Great Snacks, Great Kids*. New York: Scholastic, 1990.

Provides information on meal planning for nutritious eating.

Berry, Joy. *Every Kid's Guide to Nutrition and Health Care*. Chicago: Childrens, 1987.

Outlines ideas that maintain good nutrition and health.

Jacobson, Michael, and Laura Hill. *Kitchen Fun for Kids: Healthy Recipes and Nutrition Facts for 7–12 Year Old Cooks*. New York: Holt, 1991.

Provides recipes for nutritious eating.

Jacobson, Michael F. *Safe Food: Eating Wisely in a Risky World*. Venice, CA: Living Planet Press, 1991.

Planning food that is nutritious and good for the body is the focus.

Singer, Marcia. *Eating for a Fresh Start*. Los Angeles: Play House, 1990.

Features meal planning and recipes for a vegetarian diet that enhances physical, mental, and emotional health.

Grades 6–9

Arnold, Caroline. *Too Fat? Too Thin? Do You Have a Choice?* New York: Morrow, 1984.

Discusses the nature of body structure and methods for controlling weight.

Kolodny, Nancy. *When Food's a Foe: How to Confront and Conquer Eating Disorders*. Boston: Little, Brown, 1987.

Eating disorders and overcoming them are discussed.

Neff, Fred. *Keeping Fit Handbook for Physical Conditioning and Better Health*. Minneapolis: Lerner, 1977.

Working out and exercising for good physical conditioning is discussed.

Ruckman, Ivy. *The Hunger Scream*. New York: Walker, 1983.

A girl who suffers from anorexia struggles to deal with the problem.

Salter, Charles. *Looking Good, Eating Right: A Sensible Guide to Proper Nutrition and Weight Loss for Teens*. Brookfield, CT: Millbrook Press, 1991.

Proper nutrition practices during the teenage years are discussed.

Tatchell, J. and K. Fraser. *Food, Fitness and Health*. Tulsa: EDC, 1987.

Proper care of the body for wellness is discussed.

3.8. Getting Along

Preschool

Cohen, Miriam. *Best Friends*. New York: Aladdin, 1991.

Two friends decide to work together to save some hatching chickens despite their previous quarreling.

Cosgrove, Stephen. *Fanny*. Los Angeles: Price Stern Sloan, 1987.

Fanny, a cat with only three legs, spreads friendship and concern for other animals in the farmyard, and they soon realize how nice it is to have her around.

Gertz, Susanna. *Frog, Duck and Rabbit*. New York: Four Winds Press, 1992.

Three animal friends make a prizewinning costume for a parade only after they realize that working together produces better results than name-calling.

Marshall, James. *George and Martha*. Boston: Houghton Mifflin, 1972.

A series of five short stories about two friends, George and Martha, and the episodes that challenge yet confirm their friendship. (Other stories centering around these two characters are also available.)

Sharmat, Marjorie. *The 329th Friend*. New York: Four Winds, 1992.

Emery Raccoon thinks he is boring, so he decides to throw a party for 328 friends. When no one pays attention to him even then, he discovers he can be his own best friend.

Viorst, Judith. *Rosie and Michael*. New York: Macmillan, 1988.

In spite of the tricks they play on one another, Rosie and Michael remain friends.

Grades K–2

Aardema, Verna. *Why Mosquitoes Buzz in People's Ears*. New York: Dial, 1976.

A baby owl is killed due to a misunderstanding among jungle animals.

Cohen, Miriam. *See You Tomorrow, Charles*. New York: Greenwillow, 1983.

Charles is blind but attends public school. He does his best and even saves the day when he and two friends end up in trouble during recess.

Lionni, Leo. *Frederick*. New York: Knopf, 1967.

Four field mice prepare for winter. Three gather food, but Frederick stores up beauty instead. When winter arrives, the mice realize that by working together they have everything they need to survive.

Lionni, Leo. *Swimmy*. New York: Knopf, 1989.

A little fish exhibits courage and initiative when he helps a school of small fish work together to overcome the threat of the large fish in the sea.

Lobel, Arnold. *Frog and Toad Are Friends*. New York: HarperCollins, 1970.

Several episodes that concentrate on the adventures of two loyal friends.

Steig, William. *Amos and Boris*. New York: Farrar, Straus & Giroux, 1971.

A mouse lost at sea is saved from drowning by a whale and later on is able to reciprocate the lifesaving act.

Grades 2–4

Dolphin, Laurie. *Georgia to Georgia: Making Friends in the U.S.S.R.* New York: Morrow, 1991.

A boy from Atlanta, Georgia, travels to the then–Soviet Republic of Georgia and learns about the richness of the culture there.

Everett, Louis. *Amigo Means Friend*. Mahwah, NJ: Troll, 1988.

Jose and George speak different languages, but that does not deter their friendship.

Howe, James. *Pinky and Rex*. New York: Avon, 1991.

Two friends support each other in many adventures while remaining their own separate selves. (Several other books are available centering around these two characters.)

Jukes, Mavis. *Like Jake and Me*. New York: Knopf, 1984.

Alex feels he and his stepfather, Jake, do not have much in common until he discovers one of Jake's weaknesses. Alex helps him and realizes they can be close.

Rylant, Cynthia. *Henry and Mudge: The First Book of Their Adventure*. New York: Macmillan, 1987.

A boy and his dog have many adventures while creating a warm, loving, loyal relationship. (This is the first of several stories involving these two characters.)

Wilner-Pardo, Gina. *Natalie Spitzer's Turtles*. Morton Grove, IL: Albert Whitman, 1992.

When a new girl joins the class at the beginning of the school year, Jess thinks she is losing her friend Molly. They find a way to work out the relationship and even make new friends.

Grades 4–6

Blume, Judy. *Just as Long as We're Together*. New York: Dell, 1987.

When a new girl moves into the neighborhood, she threatens Rachel and Stephanie's best-friend relationship until they learn that friendship can include a third party.

LeShan, Eda. *When Kids Drive Kids Crazy*. New York: Dial, 1990.

Discusses the development of lasting relationships and how to cope with those friendships that do not work out.

Lisle, Janet. *Afternoon of the Elves*. New York: Orchard, 1989.

Hillary works in a miniature village magically built by elves as she tries to learn more about and accept the strange life style of Sara, in whose yard the elves have settled.

MacLaughlin, Patricia. *Sarah Plain and Tall*. New York: Harper-Collins, 1987.

Sarah comes to stay with a motherless family. As the story unfolds, a loving relationship builds.

Scholes, Katherine. *Peace Begins with You*. Boston: Little, Brown, 1990.

Suggests ways children can protect peace in the world as well as the environment.

Speare, Elizabeth. *Sign of the Beaver*. Boston: Houghton Mifflin, 1983.

A young boy, protecting a newly built cabin while his father fetches the rest of the family, establishes a friendship with an Indian boy. Each is ultimately able to teach the other about his beliefs, and thus each begins to understand the ways of the other's people.

Grades 6–9

Lucas, Eileen. *Peace on the Playground: Nonviolent Ways of Problem-Solving*. New York: Watts, 1991.

Introduces strategies to solve conflicts peacefully.

McDonnell, Christine. *Friends First*. New York: Viking, 1990.

An eighth-grade girl faces evolving relationships, complex changes, and feelings arising from her first step into adulthood.

Mazer, Norma. *After the Rain*. New York: Avon, 1987.

A girl and her grandfather develop a loving relationship when they learn he is dying.

Mazzenga, Isabel Burk. *Compromise or Confrontations: Dealing with the Adults in Your Life*. New York: Watts, 1989.

Developing communication skills in order to effectively discuss issues with adults is the focus of this book.

Voigt, Cynthia. *Homecoming*. New York: Fawcett, 1981.

When Dicey's mother abandons the family, the children must work together in order to remain a family and avoid foster homes.

Voigt, Cynthia. *Solitary Blue*. New York: Fawcett, 1983.

Jeff has difficulty understanding his father's lack of outward emotion toward him. He is sure his mother would love him more if only she would allow him to live with her.

3.9.   Higher-Order Philosophy

Younger Readers (Ages 3–7)

Baylor, Byrd. *One Small Blue Bead*. New York: Scribner, 1992.

A prehistoric boy makes it possible for an old man to go in search of other men that might live on the earth. This story also illustrates the extension of self to the generations that follow.

Brown, Margaret Wise. *David's Little Indian*. Homewood, AL: Watermark, 1956.

David meets a Native American in the woods. They become friends and find excitement and fulfillment in each day thereafter.

Cooney, Barbara. *Miss Rumphius*. New York: Viking, 1982.

Miss Rumphius feels a sense of responsibility to do something during her lifetime to make the earth more beautiful.

Cosgrove, Stephen. *The Dream Team*. Los Angeles: Price Stern Sloan, 1974.

A caterpillar learns what it is to become a butterfly only when the time is right in the course of this life cycle.

Luenn, Nancy. *Mother Earth*. New York: Atheneum, 1992.

A powerful description of the gifts the earth gives, how all living creatures are a part of the planet, and how people can give something back to it.

Silverstein, Shel. *The Giving Tree*. New York: Harper & Row, 1964.

A young boy grows to manhood and old age experiencing the love and generosity a tree has provided.

VanAllsburg, Chris. *Just a Dream*. Boston: Houghton Mifflin, 1990.

A boy learns through a dream his role in preserving the earth through recycling and conservation.

Williams, Margery. *The Velveteen Rabbit: Or How to Become Real*. New York: Avon, 1975.

A stuffed rabbit becomes real due to the love of a little boy.

Older Readers (Ages 8 and Up)

Hamilton, Virginia. *In The Beginning Creation Stories from Around the World*. San Diego: Harcourt Brace Jovanovich, 1988.

Myths from around the world are retold to illustrate various beliefs on the creation of the world.

Jeffers, Susan. *Brother Eagle, Sister Sky*. New York: Dial, 1991.

A Suquamish Indian chief describes his people's respect for the earth and their fear for its destruction.

Saint Exupery, Antoine de. *The Little Prince*. San Diego: Harcourt Brace Jovanovich, 1971.

A pilot whose plane crashes in the Sahara Desert is taught the meaning of life by a boy from outer space.

Silverstein, Shel. *The Missing Piece*. New York: Harper & Row, 1978.

A figure that is incomplete sets out to find its perfectly fitting missing piece while enjoying its encounters along the way.

Wilde, Oscar. *The Selfish Giant*. New York: Simon & Schuster, 1986.

A once-selfish giant is duly rewarded by the visit of a very special child when he allows children to enjoy the pleasures of his garden.

3.10. Positive Perspective

Preschool

Blake, Robert J. *The Perfect Spot*. New York: Philomel Books, 1992.

A little boy and his dad look for the perfect spot to paint. The boy keeps suggesting places but the father negates each one until they both agree on a perfect spot in which to spend time together.

Carnes, Jeanette. *I Need a Lunch Box*. New York: HarperCollins, 1988.

A little boy watches with envy as his sister readies her new lunch box for the first day of school. He dreams about a new lunch box and all the good food he would carry in it. Just when he has given up hope of having such an item, his father surprises him.

Hutchins, Pat. *You'll Soon Grow into Them, Titch*. New York: Puffin, 1985.

Tables turn at last for Titch, who has been inheriting an older siblings' outgrown clothes.

Kraus, Robert. *Leo the Late Bloomer*. New York: Simon & Schuster, 1971.

A little tiger has difficulty reading and writing until in his own time he blooms.

Mathers, Petra. *Sophie and Lou*. New York: HarperCollins, 1991.

A lady mouse overcomes her shyness when she learns to dance.

Oxenbury, Helen. *I Can*. New York: Random House, 1986.

A positive perspective illustrating all the things small children are able to do, such as sitting, jumping, and walking.

Grades K–2

Aseltine, Lorraine. *First Grade Can Wait*. Morton Grove, IL: A. Whitman, 1988.

Not every child is ready to leave kindergarten, and this story provides the positive side of that concept.

Bunting, Eve. *The Wednesday Surprise*. New York: Tichnor and Field, 1989.

A little girl and her grandmother plan a surprise for the girl's father: her grandmother reading for the first time.

Grossman, Bill. *Donna O'Neeschuck Was Chased by Some Cows*. New York: HarperCollins, 1988.

> Donna O'Neeschuck is being chased not only by cows but by many other creatures. She eventually discovers that this is happening because of the incredible head pats she has distributed to each.

Nelson, Vakunda. *Always Gramma*. New York: Putnam, 1988.

> When her grandmother develops Alzheimer's disease, a little girl learns to deal with the change.

Peet, Bill. *Buford, the Little Bighorn*. Boston: Houghton Mifflin, 1967.

> When Buford notices his horns are growing out of proportion, he decides to rid himself of them. In so doing, he encounters and overcomes some important challenges.

Wilhelm, Hans. *I'll Always Love You*. New York: Crown, 1985.

> A child's sadness at the death of his beloved dog is eased by the thought that he always said "I love you" to the dog at the end of each day.

Grades 2–4

Adler, David. *A Picture Book of Helen Keller*. New York: Holiday, 1990.

> A concise biographical account of the little girl who was blind and deaf but left a lifetime of accomplishments.

Brown, Marcia. *Stone Soup*. New York: Scribner, 1979.

> Although suspicious of French soldiers at first, an entire village enjoys a soup they are led to believe is made from stones but whose main ingredients they are tricked into contributing from their own stores of hidden food.

Martin, Bill, Jr. *Knots on a Counting Rope*. New York: Holt, 1987.

Although an Indian boy does not always do things perfectly, he keeps trying, knowing his grandfather's love surrounds him.

Ransome, Arthur. *The Fool of the World and the Flying Ship*. New York: Farrar, Straus & Giroux, 1968.

A young boy who has no status in his family eventually outwits those much more powerful than he to win a princess's hand in marriage.

Rylant, Cynthia. *Miss Maggie*. New York: Dutton, 1983.

A young boy and an elderly recluse share a special relationship.

San Souci, Robert. *The Talking Eggs*. New York: Dial, 1989.

A girl earns riches by being patient and following directions.

Grades 4–6

Brittan, Bill. *Professor Popkin's Prodigious Polish*. New York: Harper-Collins, 1991.

A young boy sells to the townspeople a special polish that produces magical but disastrous results, but he follows through in order to resolve the situations that arise, thereby restoring order to the village.

Burnett, Frances H. *The Secret Garden*. New York: Dell, 1987.

Mary lives with her uncle and discovers the beauty of a garden behind a gate. She uses this site as a ploy to encourage Colin, her cousin, to want to continue living even though he is an invalid.

Cleary, Beverly. *Strider*. New York: Morrow, 1991.

Leigh Botts tells how he comes to terms with his parents' divorce, acquires partial custody of an abandoned dog, and joins the track team.

Levitin, Sonia. *Silver Days*. New York: Macmillan, 1989.

After escaping Nazi Germany and coming to the United States, members of the Platt family work together to meet their everyday needs as well as adjust to a new home.

Pfeffer, Susan. *Kid Power*. New York: Watts, 1977.

A spunky young girl organizes an employment agency for herself and her friends when her mother loses her job.

Shura, Mary Francis. *Polly Panic*. New York: Putnam, 1990.

Junior high begins with one traumatic experience after another for Polly Rhodes. She perseveres, however, and realizes that many wonderful experiences and friendships also await her.

Grades 6–9

Aaseng, Nathan. *From Rags to Riches: People Who Started Businesses from Scratch*. Minneapolis: Lerner, 1990.

Details success stories of people, including J. C. Penney and Steven Jobs, founder of Apple Computers, who took a risk in order to begin a business.

Banish, Roslyn. *A Forever Family*. New York: HarperCollins, 1992.

Jennifer Wong describes her life as an adopted daughter after spending four years in foster care.

Brittan, Bill. *The Wish Giver: Three Tales of Coven Tree*. New York: HarperCollins, 1983.

Four people are given wishes during a town carnival, each using a wish in a special way with unsuspected results.

Eareckson, Joni. *Joni*. Grand Rapids: Zondervan, 1976.

The autobiographical account of a young girl who becomes a paraplegic due to a swimming accident. After rehabilitation, she discovers she can be a successful painter by holding a brush in her teeth.

Seuss, Dr. *Oh the Places You'll Go.* New York: Random House, 1990.

A narrative, written in rhyme, centering around the goal-oriented accomplishments one will experience during a lifetime. It also includes the message that it is perfectly fine not to succeed at everything attempted in one's life.

Yolen, Jane. *Devil's Arithmetic.* New York: Viking, 1988.

Questioning her Jewish heritage, Hannah's belief is confirmed when she is transported back to the time of the Holocaust. She lives among relatives who eventually are taken to concentration camps, and she is powerless to prevent this from happening.

3.11.   Stress Management

Preschool

Blegvad, Lenore. *Anna Banana and Me.* New York: Atheneum, 1985.

A little boy learns how to confront scary situations after taking lessons from spunky Anna Banana.

Bourgeois, Paulette. *Franklin in the Dark.* New York: Scholastic, 1987.

A little turtle is afraid to put his head into his shell because it is dark. When he asks other animals about his problem, he realizes that all living things are afraid of something.

Cosgrove, Stephen. *Buttermilk.* Los Angeles: Price Stern Sloan, 1986.

A rabbit learns that scary things at night are really only part of his surroundings during the day.

Keats, Ezra Jack. *Peter's Chair*. New York: Harper & Row, 1987.

Peter's belongings are all painted pink in preparation for their use by his new baby sister. After "running away," he realizes his parents love him and decides to join in with the new baby's welcome.

Viorst, Judith. *The Good-Bye Book*. New York: Macmillan, 1988.

A child whose parents are going out for the evening comes up with a variety of excuses in order to keep them home.

Waber, Bernard. *Ira Sleeps Over*. Boston: Houghton Mifflin, 1972.

Invited to sleep over at a friend's house, Ira worries about his friend's reaction to his bringing his teddy bear for moral support.

Grades K–2

Adler, Katie. *For Sale: One Sister—Cheap*. Chicago: Childrens, 1986.

A child discusses the frustrations of having a little sister.

Cohen, Miriam. *Liar, Liar Pants on Fire*. New York: Dell, 1987.

Alex has a hard time adjusting to his new first-grade class and resorts to telling wild stories to impress the other children.

Cohen, Miriam. *First Grade Takes a Test*. New York: Yearling, 1990.

When a test is administered to discover who in the first-grade class is gifted, various students humorously express their interpretation of the test and the situation.

Steig, William. *Spinky Sulks*. New York: Farrar, Straus & Giroux, 1988.

Spinky is angry at his family. Although they try desperately to cheer him up, he realizes he must resolve his feelings in his own way in order to once again believe in their love.

Vigna, Judith. *I Wish Daddy Didn't Drink So Much*. Morton Grove, IL: A. Whitman, 1988.

A little girl expresses her reaction to her father's drinking problem.

Vigna, Judith. *My Big Sister Takes Drugs*. Morton Grove, IL: A. Whitman, 1990.

A girl tells about her sister's drug problem.

Grades 2–4

Cleary, Beverly. *Muggie Maggie*. New York: Morrow, 1990.

Maggie is fearful of learning cursive writing and uses all kinds of excuses not to do it. When the inevitable happens, she discovers that many new experiences are now opening up for her.

Fassler, David, Michele Lash, and Sally B. Ives. *Changing Families: A Guide for Kids and Grown-ups*. Burlington, VT: Waterfront Books, 1985.

Offers children advice on how to cope with issues that may cause stress in a family, such as divorce and financial problems.

Giff, Patricia Reilly. *Matthew Jackson Meets the Wall*. New York: Delacorte, 1990.

When Matthew moves from New York City to Ohio, he encounters new anxieties, including the disappearance of his cat and a very tough next-door neighbor.

Hazen, Barbara. *Tight Times*. New York: Viking, 1979.

A family struggles together trying to work out financial difficulties.

Kenny, Kevin, and Helen Krull. *Sometimes My Mom Drinks Too Much*. Austin, TX: Raintree, 1980.

> Conveys through the eyes of a child a sense of what children see and feel when a parent has an alcohol problem.

Martin, Rafe. *Foolish Rabbit's Big Mistake*. New York: Putnam, 1985.

> A rabbit is afraid the earth is breaking up and in turn scares other animals. Not until the lion analyzes what really happened do they learn they can handle the situation.

Grades 4–6

Aiello, Barbara, and Jeffrey Shulman. *Secrets Aren't Always for Keeps*. Frederick, MD: Twenty-First Century Books, 1988.

> After hiding her learning disabilities from her Australian pen pal, Jennifer is very apprehensive when the friend decides to come for a visit.

DeClements, Barthe. *Five Finger Discount*. New York: Delacorte, 1989.

> Jerry must live with the secret of his father's prison sentence while trying to make friends after moving to a new home.

Fox, Paula. *One-Eyed Cat*. New York: Bradbury Press, 1984.

> A boy who is not supposed to touch the rifle in the bedroom closet takes it out in order to shoot it just once. He shoots a cat and, not knowing if he has hurt it, lives with the guilt and must decide his next step after disobeying.

Little, Jean. *Mama's Going to Buy You a Mockingbird*. New York: Viking, 1984.

> Jeremy copes with his father's death by focusing on making new friends, trying new activities, and giving support to his mother and sister.

Pfeffer, Susan. *What Do You Do When Your Mouth Won't Open?* New York: Delacorte, 1981.

Reesa is thrilled that her essay has won a contest until she realizes she has to read it in front of five hundred people.

Seixas, Judith. *Living with a Parent Who Takes Drugs*. New York: Greenwillow, 1989.

Offers suggestions to children on how to cope with parents they suspect of taking drugs, as well as signs and symptoms of drug abuse.

Grades 6–9

Cameron, Eleanor. *The Private Worlds of Julia Redfern*. New York: Dutton, 1988.

In trying to deal with the death of a friend, Julia uses her interest in acting as her method of coping.

Conford, Ellen. *If This Is Love, I'll Take Spaghetti*. New York: Scholastic, 1983.

The humorous side of love problems are written about in story form.

Fleming, Alice. *What We Worry? How to Hang In When Your Problems Stress You Out*. New York: Macmillan, 1992.

Provides advice on how to cope with stress and how to develop a positive approach to worry.

Maloney, Michael, and Rachel Kranz. *Straight Talk About Anxiety and Depression*. New York: Facts on File, 1991.

Discusses the various kinds of stress a teenager might experience and ways of coping with stress.

Paterson, Katherine. *Bridge to Terabithia*. New York: Thomas Y. Crowell, 1977.

Jess and Leslie begin as competitors only to become best friends. Their friendship leads to the establishment of a secret kingdom that also claims Leslie's life. After tremendous adjustment, Jess learns to live on in order to capture his own dreams, and he draws on the strength his friendship with Leslie provided.

Zindel, Paul. *A Begonia for Miss Applebaum*. New York: Harper & Row, 1989.

Two high school boys learn that a favorite teacher is dying. In coping with this knowledge, they learn to celebrate life.

Index

349

Made in United States
Orlando, FL
20 April 2022

17036878R00225